Also by Brian V Peck:

Walking on the Moon

The Mythical World of 'Middle England'.
Does it Really Exist?

NOTES FROM
A SMALL PLANET

VOLUME 1

In

INDIA – THAILAND – VIETNAM – CAMBODIA –

AUSTRALIA (BIG OZ) & NEW ZEALAND

by

Brian V. Peck

authorHOUSE®

AuthorHouse™ UK Ltd.
1663 Liberty Drive
Bloomington, IN 47403 USA
www.authorhouse.co.uk
Phone: 0800.197.4150

This book is a work of non-fiction. Unless otherwise noted, the author and the publisher make no explicit guarantees as to the accuracy of the information contained in this book and in some cases, names of people and places have been altered to protect their privacy.

Published by AuthorHouse   05/01/2014

ISBN: 978-1-4389-0211-1 (sc)
ISBN: 978-1-4817-9994-2 (e)

For Esther

For Kerry, Kieran and Riley

with love.
from, Brian.
June 2023

Acknowledgements

Again I would like thank Ross Thomson of Authorhouse for accepting me as an author and publishing me. Also David Clifford the Operation Manager of the Firstgroup in Bath for letting me have several weeks off to research this project in Vietnam and Cambodia, on top of my annual leave. And everyone I was lucky enough to meet and talk too all over Southern Asia, even John from Castlemaine near Melbourne (sic) and lovely young Sarah, from Sweden. Noting that I am responsible for all the historical facts and any errors, if any that may be printed in this project. Also, I would like to thank Paul Kingdom (B.A. Visual Communications) and Chris Watkins in helping me redesign the new cover in 2013.

CONTENTS

"Regardless of how successful an artist may be in creating beauty, truth is always a goal". Oliver James 2007.

INTRODUCTION

On the 26th April 2005 the Guardian newspaper printed a very beautiful picture of a 'giant spiral Galaxy' very similar to the Milky way Galaxy, so we were informed by most Cosmologist '3 million light years from earth'. This specific Galaxy itself is 160,000 light years across, so when we look at a picture like this; some of us should be able to understand how insignificant this very small Planet really is in the big scheme of things. The available evidence seems to suggest that our Galaxy is nothing special within the context of the Universe, as a whole. In fact our little Planet we call earth is so insignificant that we are nothing more than a grain of sand on any beach in the world. All the hard scientific empirical evidence backs up this premise from 'The Birth of Time' by John Gribbin, to Martin Rees in the Our Cosmic Habitat and the rest of this whole community - Rees may go to church but it seems that this is because his 'class' does…not that he necessarily believes in a divine maker (BBC Radio 4). Voltaire was not a Christian but may have believed in an all powerful & benevolent deity and seemed to think that a belief in God was useful for the lower levels of humanity…but for sure said that if God did not exist we would have to invent him (Selected Writings Voltaire – Everyman edition p, xxii). In fact if we could bring the great Voltaire back from the dead he would be amazed that there may be water on other planets in the Universe and probably life forms with a lot more intellect than most Popes and the religious community; who once had Giordano Bruno burnt at the stake for questioning Catholic orthodox. Even the present British Monarchy seems to believe that she was ordained by God, in some strange 'natural order' of things.

Life itself may have started about three and half billion years ago - which for at least the first billion years of life, only existed in female form, (Steve Jones + Carl Zimmer)… some of these strange life forms may have been the first readers of the Daily Mail in little Britain…. so I have been told by the living stromatolites on the West coast of Australia (see below). Who we should really be praying to - because without these incredible life forms we would not be here because they helped to raise the oxygen level in the atmosphere so that people like Voltaire, Bill Bryson and my little self could write amusing books, for you all too read.

What I find so fantastic about most animals on earth is that it does not really matter where you go they will probably act in the same way. I noted this historical fact when observing Pigeons in Trafalgar Square in London and Pigeons in St Marks Square in Venice and Hanover square in London very recently and even Sydney. The males like most of us were after sex with the opposite sex (in little Britain we may have to get written permission for this natural act some time in the future, as 'yes can actually mean no' a contradiction in terms or am I going mad, like about 23% of the population - sic) in the usual display manner, dancing around in circles, with head bowed - the only difference in this case is that in London the Mayor is trying to kill them out - but in Venice if you a gullible tourist you should buy some food (1 Euro a packet) for them and keep them healthy and have your photograph taken them with them on your head. In this case perhaps the makers of shampoo are in cohorts with the Pigeons, what a cynical old git you are Brian! And just think that at least in Venice you are surrounded by water for rinsing it off. But how did that first man stand on water to put a post in to the bay to start this incredible surreal city…. that's what I was thinking while spending a few nights and days there in July 2005. They must have used a boat you twit surely no one can stand on water can they…well perhaps in fairy stories, they can. Or Christian fundamentals who literally believe in the word of the Bible, as if it's the truth the whole truth and nothing but the truth, and as we all know we walked with Dinosaurs last century… yes that may be correct; the Tory party (sic) was around last century, were they not? In 1650 Archbishop James Ussher was so certain that the bible 'and other historical sources' told the truth that he concluded that the earth was created on the '23 October 4004BC' (Quoted in Short History of Nearly Everything by Bill Bryson). I walked on the Moon in 1968 a year before Neil Armstrong; it is in my first book so it must be true, mustn't Archbishop? The ironic fact is that Catholic priests are now so low on the ground in most of Europe including Ireland that Priests from Poland are now being flown over on Easy Jet to England and Scotland 'to give communion' apparently sense 2004 there has been a huge demand for their services (The Guardian 15th March 2006). The Polish Plumber (sic) is now dead, long live the Polish Priests. Alice in Wonderland stuff don't you think?

This may also apply to any derivatives of any Religion I did consider this very recently when visiting the Cardiff Millennium stadium on the 2nd of July 2006 to observer 10,000 Jehovah's Witness, or should that have been biggest window cleaning gathering in the world (sic)… enjoying themselves at their convention. I went on the train from Bristol Parkway to Cardiff Central and sat right across from a beautiful woman, with her Mother - who was a spitting image of Sven-Goran Ericksson's live in lover called Nancy…..now popping up on a regular basis on 'Loose Ends' on BBC Radio 4. I was thinking through out the journey that she may have been fleeing from Little Britain after we had been thrown out of the World cup the day before in Germany. I did meet her outside the Stadium, by accident, about 11:00 am after I had my first look at the convention and her name was Ruth not Nancy after all, what a shame. And sadly she was married but at least she did not have a name tag on like most people there proudly informing everyone that there is 'Deliverance at Hand' if you believe in this tosh. I must admit that everyone there looked very smart in there Sunday best and did not look stupid but from the few that I spoke to most were certainly doing working class jobs mostly on a self-employed basis (Neil from Scotland, Denise from Bristol) so that when they are free they can proselytize their beliefs to the rest of us around the globe…..according to lovely Denise; Nigeria is now one of the most successfully places in the world for this process. The main tool that the lectures/Elders or what ever they were called - were using was the bible (Tim had one who I was sitting next to me and shown me what passages were being used) often quoting passages from this bag of lies (my view, but not Rod Little – so it seems!) and it seemed very selective to me often glossing over what was a known fact then that slaves were a legitimate source of exploitation (i.e.: Aristotle), at the time with many of the congregation taking notes, as is wage slaves now in this epoch. In the afternoon session I heard a mantra of this belief being repeated that I had heard 10 years before - when I lived in the West Midlands and thought to myself at the time that this is pure bunkum of the highest order. Basically sometime in the future when all the evils of the world have been done away with, (including smoking hopefully) - I presume when Bush and Blair are dead, for example. We are going to be ruled by God and his helpers 144,000 who are somewhere in space/time heaven or perhaps Glenn Hoddle's backyard; I am not to sure where they are waiting for this magic moment, to arrive....so there folks. Aren't reason, logic and rational thought wonderful? When Billy Connolly toured Australia in the mid-nineties he really took the piss out of this movement in his over the top wonderful crude and surrealist way. A real new hero of mine, as is Richard Dawkins who I first read at about the same time Connolly was on tour in Big Oz. On reading the God Delusion one of the many themes seems to be that at least some people who are better educated can see through all religious nonsense/blind faith, which I presume means people, like me.

However because Homo sapiens have larger brains then the Pigeons and most other animals we seem to think that we are more intelligent (see above for the evidence)...especially those terrible 'Guardian reading classes' who helped to suggest that all races are equal (sic), what a terrible crime. Don't you think so Dr Frank Ellis of Leeds University? A big mistake as very few animals to my knowledge kill other animals for fun and profit, we do. Or should I say the 'upper class' do for land and commodities and get the 'working class' to do the actually killing…bastards (Fahrenheit 9/11) for them. What I am saying is that humans in these specific life forms don't act like those pigeons but because of the incredible diversity of Cultures and languages throughout the Planet we may act in a different way to others some where else on the earth. This may be the way: we eat our food, make love or the religion we practise and belief in. Individualism is a very powerful weapon of Philosophy used in the West with many hidden agendas of the ruling class, but hardly anywhere else. Which may drive us mad according to Oliver James, in his recent book Affluenza if it is mixed with 'selfish Capitalism' and we speak English, apparently the Danes have not caught the infliction. But if we seriously thought about what we believe in; it is nothing more than accident of birth. So in little Britain we may belief that God exits in some sort of hierarchy - ordaining the Monarchy, the Aristocracy the middleclass and the 'working class' in that order - I don't. Where in most countries in Asia most do not have Monarchies, some may believe in God/Allah but hundreds of millions probably don't have any religious beliefs what-so-ever. The paradox to the British tradition of Monarchy and the tradition of Royalty in Hindu beliefs (or at least some) is that Rama was 'remarkably democratic – a King has no right to rule if he doesn't satisfy his subjects – Rama used to move around his capital after dark, disguised, to find out what the people thought of his rule' (Mark

Tully – India in Slow Motion p, 14).The chance of seeing Brenda (sic) doing this in London I would have thought would be very remote indeed. The chance of seeing a real Alien from the Andromeda galaxy would be more likely, I would have thought?

Rice may be on the diet three times a day, in the Far East, for some people… I met a young man in Croatia several years ago who had this diet every day, from South Korea and some members of the Nyangatom drink blood as part of their daily diet, as is the procedure of injecting 'frog poison' into your blood stream - in the Matis tribe of Brazil, which helps you to become a man, in their culture. Also making money the main action of most people now, but this is also an accident of this specific epoch and nothing else. A very good example of what I mean is that most Muslims in the world do not drink alcohol but in little Britain it is only against the law to give this specific drug to anyone under five. In the USA it is against the law to sell or give alcohol to anyone under twenty-one (Jeremy Vine Show BBC Radio 2).

So, therefore did we really have anything else on our minds, but sex and food 10,000 years ago, very unlikely I would have thought, what about you men and women of the world? In fact in today's in the Sunday Observer (10 February 2008) there is a little unknown fact about all women according to new research. At least 44% of women fancy their best friend's partner and 33% would do something about if they had a chance…well I never. And to my knowledge at this time we could not jump on a Boeing 747 and fly around the globe, in 24 hours, a camel or horse but nothing else.

My journey will be by plane for the long bits, but how does a dinosaur take off and land, its beyond me and for at least some of the time I will be thinking of food and sex, in that order. But also hopefully exploring the world in a satirical way like I did in my first two books about little Britain - while at the same time trying to be sensitive about people's beliefs, especially the cultural and spiritual ones, that we all believe in. I am afraid that I don't like Ernest Hemmingway have any religious beliefs whatsoever. And am also very cynical about how ruling minorities have used Religion as a form of social control for the majority while at the same time doing the complete opposite of what they are telling the masses, they should be doing, for thousands of years. If Religion is a 'moral code' that is okay by me but to pretend that you will end up heaven if you are a good person and hell if you are not to me is just rubbish of the highest order. All I can say after doing some of the 'worse jobs in history' and making love to several Aphrodite's' (sic) I know what I believe in. Heaven and Hell is on this very small planet and no where else. So there folks! Lady Thatcher (ex-British Prime Minster) who lives on a Planet called 'all Mad Cows are free' for most of the time (may have been born there), may tell you all something else, while drinking a gin and tonics, and dreaming of her young men she so fancied when in that exalted position in the Government (Spitting Image - British TV satirical programme). She may even be drinking privatised water with her whiskey (sic – the 1st country in the world to do it) - which is now a commodity like virtually everything else on her idealised Planet and to my knowledge it drops free from the sky, everywhere on this little Planet. Which is a good metaphor for some of the most despised tourists in the world according to a survey carried out by Expedia the on line travel service, who conducted 'a survey of tourists boards around the world that rated British tourists as the most obnoxious' – with the Chinese catching up fast.

Originally this project was going to an in-depth look at the major Cultures around the globe, with a satirical slant. But after having a very good think and rethink I thought that I am not Charles Darwin, who travelled around the earth on the Beagle between 1831 -1836 and basically changed millions of minds of how we evolved on this very small planet. I have also not got the financial resources of Ewan McGregor and Charley Boorman who drove around the globe on two BMW motorbikes, in the book of their travels the 'F' word is virtually on every couple of pages…what would your grannies thought of you? I don't know if they got their idea from Che Guevara when he and his best friend drove around apart of South America on a bike - but at least I was born in the Falkland Islands, South Atlantic and once owned a very rickety old motorbike, which never got out of the Medway Towns (Kent) in the mid 1960's and unlike Che; I am much older (at the time he was on his bike) with formed opinions and thoughts very similar to him.

In essence this little world is wonderful if you are rich and powerful but terrible if you are like the majority: poor and powerless. The basic structural nature of the epoch is what most people don't understand, which makes it very easy for the mass media; mainly owned by the rich and powerful to tell lies and propaganda on a daily basis with other agencies of socialisation and social control, to do the same per se. Or as C Wright Mills so correctly asserted many years ago: 'to be aware of the idea of Social Structure and to use it with sensibility is to be capable of tracing such linkages among a great variety of milieux. To be able to do that is to posses the Sociological Imagination' (Quoted in Human Societies, A Reader – Editor Anthony Giddens p, 7 1992). In fact if anyone thinks we are all living in a Pluralists democracy in the Western world, think again. 'Democracy for the Few' as Michael Parenti informed us in the 1988 but nothing else. Arundhati Roy a brilliant straight talking Indian lady, who now lives in Delhi, suggests: 'for all the endless empty chatter about democracy' the world is not only run by a few large multinationals companies, for profit - but three of the most secretive organisation in the world, making their decisions in secret. These are the World Bank, the World trade Organisation and the International Monetary Fund (Roy 2005 p 43 + 44). I would also agree what she says on the next page (44) that it is very unlikely that a world run by 'greedy bankers and CEOs' which nobody elected can last for ever and like me she is also a huge fan of Noam Chomsky. In the updated version of The Reasons of State (2003) she has written a brilliant little piece at the beginning of the book from Delhi and as she notes about social control now carried out mostly through free market dogma agencies - but just in case they see through the bullshit, like a few of us. So as she asserts: 'for this reason, they must be guarded against reality, reared in a control climate, in an altered reality, like broiler chickens or pigs in a pen' Chomsky 2003 - Forward viii – ix). In little Britain the

Ruling Elite are so terrified of this phenomenon that we are now one of the most spied upon people on the Planet.

Hence, like Bill Bryson and millions of others these days I will get in an aircraft, a train (very similar to Paul Theroux in 1979 and what an author to compete with), a car and other means that I have not thought of and enjoy my travels going around a very small Planet in a very big Universe and report my findings to anyone who wants to read them…including MI5 or MI6 who probably has a file on me and a 'green stamp' that looks like a 'Christmas tree' (sic). I was also thinking that after reading Plato's 'Republic' for at least the sixth time that if I was very lucky on my travels and should encounter a 'earth quake', a chasm opened up in front of me and I found a 'bronze horse' with a corpse inside who has a 'gold ring' on him. I could make myself invisible jump on a cyborg fly (half real insect, half robot) created by the nasty spies in the USA travel the globe for nothing. Make love to Catherine Zeta Jones without Michael knowing about it and travel back all for nothing. (Source: Plato's Republic and the Guardian 15th March 2006). What a thought, making love to Mrs Douglas for nothing - surely I am dreaming, ain't I? Especially when I have just saw a British TV documentary (April 2005 – Channel 5) about such a famous person now - who was born at the bottom of the heap in Swansea but seems to want to distance herself from even the pianists who accompanied her on the piano for over six years…when a struggling young rising star.

Chapter One

- The Aventure Begins In India -
Part One

Its 7pm on the 16th August 2006 and I am at London Airport terminal three waiting for my flight to New Delhi after being dropped off by Tom. My daughter's current boyfriend and she has decided to wait with me, while booking into the system (which was a complete nightmare and took hours...I could have had a three course dinner with 2 bottles of wine, while queuing) and I am thinking of a very funny film called Topkapi (1964 movie - Peter Ustinov won an Oscar in it) that I saw several months ago about a robbery in Istanbul as I will be flying over this wonderful city or there about; it seems very relevant to my thoughts. The reason being is that for the next few months I will be an innocent abroad - well not really, as I have done quite a bit of travelling - but at least I should always be aware like the movie that tourist are thought of by the indigenous people of most countries as simpletons who can be ripped-off very easy. The ironic paradox to this quandary is that most people in the first world think themselves in the main to be so superior to the locals. Just like the Pigeons in Trafalgar square and St Marks square who informed me that we always look down on stupid tourists and then shit on them...just like the 'upper class' and the 'petit bourgeois' around the globe, do...old boy! In fact throughout most of the world a different form of modus operandi operate where people barter for bargains when buying commodities what ever they may be - but not any more in the Western world, as the 'upper class' and their cohorts have decided that it's only them as a group who can barter with supplies; while the masses must pay the price that they dictate. The paradox being is that the gambling phenomenon is how the Capitalism works through out the globe - now even in one party State's....like China the USA and little Britain... or at least drifting into one and read Chomsky for further evidence of this proposition, in the USA. However very rarely does the retail price ever drop after supply and demand has equalised and if it ever does it is on a very small scale. The reason is that market fundamentalism is on the march like no other time in history where in places like India according to Chomsky, which is virtually 'governed by a proto-fascist party that is handing the country's recourses to foreign multinationals while preaching an ultra-nationalist line for domestic purposes, and had just been implicated in a horrendous massacre of Muslims in Gujarat' (Chomsky 2003 p, 133 + 134).Arundhati Roy puts it this way: "In a country like India the 'structural adjustment' end of the corporate globalization project is ripping through people's lives. 'Development' project, massive privatization and labour 'reform' are pushing people off their lands and out of their jobs, resulting in a kind of barbaric dispossession that has few parallels in history" (Roy 2005 p, 39). And if Vandana Shiva is correct 'suicides among poor farmers are an epidemic' (quoted in Pilger - 2002 p, 119). It seems for sure that in the last 10 years '100,000 farmers have committed suicide' (Channel 4 - 30th April 2007) according to Krishnan Guru-Murthy.

The flight it self was very comfortable and the food, was not so bad, and the air hostess gorgeous as I flew on Virgin Atlantic where at least you can stretch your legs without kicking the next seat in front of you and the possibility of knocking the coffee out of the persons hand; who may be trying to have a drink in front of you. I was also sitting alone so had time to read and think. In fact while reading the Lonely Planet, about India I got so frightened that I nearly jumped out of the aircraft; unfortunately I did not have a parachute with me so I could return home. Hence, I could not do it and if I did - I may even have landed on a nuclear bomb in Israel, Pakistan or India, which may have been worse, I think. Or may even have landed on a toxic waste dump in India, exported from little Britain if I was very unlucky. Ironically according to Arundhati Roy at least some of the toxic waste from the World Trade Centre 'is being dumped in Gujarat and then taken to Ludhiana and places like that to be recycled' (2004 - p, 132). I had glanced through it several days before and was warned by a young Indian man in Ryslip while shopping with Susannah (my darling daughter) that probably the USA and India was 'two of the most dangerous places in the world'...for tourists. Sadly today (3rd January 2007) while writing this up, on my computer - I read in the

Guardian newspaper that two British men have been killed in India over the last few months: Stephen Bennett in Roha and perhaps in very unusual circumstance (who may have been mistaken for a drug dealer – Sunday Observer 21st 10 2007), for example did the local police make up a fictional story, about his death (BBC Radio 4: 5th January 2007) and Mike Blakey in Dharamsala, but if we consider that according to the foreign office about 600,000 UK people visit India every year and nothing dreadful happens to them, apart from most getting a dose of Delhi belly ...it's not a bad record. However these are a few of the things that can happen to you according to Lonely Planet while visiting India. A commission shark attack, being badgered by touts, being told there is a riot when there is not one, the double booking of rooms, when it is not necessary, railway ticket needs a stamp, no it does not, for a fee, shoeshine scams, dodgy travel agents, exporting of precious gems, which are probably worthless. But the worst two seems that you may have your drink drugged to rob you on a train, or a bus - or worse still a restaurant may poison you so the crooked doctor can claim off your travel insurance. Now you see why I wanted to jump out of the plane, don't you? Where paradoxically according to Michael Wood the Story of India is very old indeed, perhaps as long as 70,000 years ago when man first walked out of Africa, millions of years before India were in fact a very large Island - and Harappa may have been one of the first urban areas in the world. Generations later the Sanskrit was invented and the Brahmans became the major priest class (BBC TV series) and still reciting the same texts as their founding fathers.

On arriving at Delhi international at 11:30 am, which was very efficient, compared with London. I was met by Sunny, Raj's brother-in-law (a friend who owns the newsagents close to where I live in Bristol) on a very hot day - who had given me a new mobile for him, which he was very pleased to receive. He also organized the taxi to take me to the Hotel Metro Tower ('deluxe' so it said) which was a very good thing as in the Western world you are never met with such enthusiasm to extract as much dosh as they can get from your wallet in such a chaotic way. From the first moment you enter the taxi arena outside of the airport - it seems to me that in India you are literally on another Planet or perhaps another Galaxy or in the surreal world of 'The life of Pi' (Yann Martel 2002 a book that won the Man Booker prize) and the 'culture shock' hits your senses with a massive blow to your cortex. It may even have been the place where someone thought up the 'chaos theory' or at least got the idea while visiting. Even Sanjeev Bhaskar a very successful Indian actor living in Britain recently suggested the 'chaos of India' in an excellent TV documentary about Mumbai. The horn starts to blast and the speed increases exponentially in direct competition with other traffic and did not stop until we were safely in a rather expensive hotel compared with what it said in the Lonely Planet (re –above)…about 1200 rupees a night, so I stayed one night. After a rest and a shower I ventured out into a very poor suburb of Delhi not far from the airport meeting several urban cows on the way and seeing the locals selling everything under the Sun, or repairing the 'invisible hand' (sic) which you may be able to see in this part of the world. In the Western world some men do say that there are many two legged cows on the streets; but so far I have never met a four legged one, in London, but you do in India. Noting that in London on the day before I set out for India I was visiting Covent Garden, seeing all the sites, etc for something to do. Like jugulars, some singing including an opera singer, who was very good and was, amazed how easy some of these tricksters manipulated the masses. But the biggest kick for me was when I over heard two assistants in Boots talking about some of their customers and one said to the other 'was she a wap' which apparently meant 'with a pulse'…when I asked one of them what it stood for, so I presume many haven't, what a bloody cheek.

It is not an exaggeration to suggest that at least in some urban areas of India like certain parts of Delhi, Mumbai, etc that Friedrich Engel's would be at home observing the same conditions as he was when researching The Conditions of the Working classes in England taken mainly from research in Manchester in the mid 19th century. The reasons for this state of affairs are historical and very complex: because of the caste system which is still very relevant today, its ethnic diversity and in recent time 'Hindu nationalism' and ruthless globalisation. But we should never forget - the British ruling class in there heydays were a ruthless bunch of thugs who treated anyone who apposed their rule with outrageous cruelty like they did in Delhi and other parts of India when the locals rejected their authority (Chomsky 2003, p182 + p183 and Mark Curtis 2003). Tocqueville was just as critical about Manchester as Engel's was, as he wrote 'from this foul drain the greatest stream of human industry flows out to fertilize the whole world. From this filthy sewer pure gold flows' (quoted in Nisbet 1967 p, 29). And to think that the last viceroy of India Lord Mountbatten and his wife had 5000 servants in Delhi when lording it over the Indian Nation, in the 1940's.

The thought of buying a meal on the streets on my first day was beyond me but I did buy a chai and sat down and observed the world around me. Thinking to myself that this is going to be hard work, which it was although I have Indian friends including Roy, from Kerala the State that Arundhati Roy was born in, (which has more educated people then any other State, but also they had the first police women in 1938) - who I shared a house with for three years, in Bristol – however I should state categorical from the start that I was only a month in India and you would need to live many times to see everything....which is part of the Hindu believe system or if you are not good in one life you may come back as something worse.....but surely not another persona like, Mrs Thatcher or Sir Dennis, would I?

As my Pears cyclopaedia 2002-2003 informs me: 'the two great doctrines of Hinduism are Karma and transmigration. The universal desire to be reunited with the absolute (atman or Brahman) can be satisfied by following the path of knowledge. Life is a cycle of lives (samsara) in which man's destiny is determined by his deeds (Karma) from which he may seek release (moksa) through ascetic practices or the discipline of Yoga (q.v.). Failure to achieve release means reincarnation – migration to a higher or lower form of life after death – until the ultimate goal of absorption in the absolute is reached' (Ideas and beliefs J25).

Not everyone in India is of this belief system as there are least 12% believing in the Islamic faith, 2.3% Christians, 1.9% Sikhs and several other smaller sects, etc…but the vast majority do believe in some form of Hinduism, which is very complex to grasp if you are from the more simple beliefs in the Western world. Even the wonderful beautiful very well dressed staff in the Raddisson hotel where I wondered into for a small meal and a drink of alcohol may believe in something…I don't. This upper class hotel, or very posh as my old Mother would say, cost a fortunate, about 10,000 rupees a night to stay in and even had a swimming pool and guards to keep the lower classes out, so it seemed to me. While eating I got talking to a highly intelligent young man (18) called Sean born in India. The reason he was there was that his best mate of 16 had just died suddenly and he was going back to the Punjab for his funeral instead of going back to the UK where he had been at school at Mill fields. One of the most expensive private schools in little Britain where according to Sean it cost 30, 000 pounds (sterling) a year to stay there - he also told me that many of the kids at the school are on drugs. Can this be possible the upper classes getting high on drugs, surely not? What would Brenda (sic) and Tony Blair say young people - I presume have another puff on me or snort or whatever you do with illegal substances or employ Keith Richards as a tutor. The ironic twist to being in India where at least one third of the population live on one dollar a day and absolute poverty is the norm for many - but according to the Guardian (August 2006) in the UK most women would rather buy a new pair shoes than have a meal…. slightly pathetic I thought. Considering that millions in little Britain live in relative poverty and if you are single and unemployed you are supposed to survive on less than 60 pounds per week, I think we should ask the unelected head of State how you should live on this, don't you? Well she may be worth billions (Sunday Times rich list about 12 years ago), so may understand this scandal, don't you think?

The next morning I got a mechanical rickshaw, a three wheeled contraption that operates something like a motor bike (some drives don't even wear shoes) to take me next to the area close to the New Delhi railway station which again was a new experience, for me. Well when did you see a whole family on a scooter, cycle, cows eating rubbish on the streets and a camel pulling a cart, in the Western world? After paying the driver I walk down the 'Main Bazar' in old Delhi another truly amazing street selling and repairing everything from nuclear bombs, to cycles - Brian stop exaggerating to changing money. This time I book into the Hotel Star Paradise, slightly over the top title, I think. A clean simple accommodation with a TV in my room, air-cooling, a shower, back up generator so it says, a very important facility in India, friendly staff and advertised in Lonely Planet, but that's all and only 400 rupees a day. I unpacked and venture out down the Main Bazar being very careful not to be knocked down by cycles, scooters rickshaws and cars not normally seen in London and the constant attention of everyone wanting to sell you the Moon. Well it is made of cheese so the Archbishop of Canterbury told me, recently at a dinner party.

After some time I sit down for a cup of chai and a chat to Rabi who was from Uttar Pradesh and spoke good English and was a self-employed rickshaw driver. Being such a friendly young man of 28, I took him for lunch at a nearby restaurant…he thought I looked about 40, yes Rabi and I am also six foot tall and a multi-millionaire author, just like J.K. Rowling worth 545 million pounds, in the bank! He informed that he eared about 1000 rupees a day which he had done for 7/8 years and would like to get married but it was a very expensive modus vivendi, in India. Which must be very frustrating for most young men, as nearly all Indian women are very beautiful? After lunch he took me for a coffee at another café and on the way bought one cigarette which apparently is what Gordon Brown wants for the working class in little Britain to do sometime in the future and to think that he once wrote a book called Where there's Greed. So Tony Blair told me from Cliff Richard's luxury mansion in the Caribbean. Who was having another rest after 'he flew to India to promote peace and flog arms for BAE systems' (Mark Thomas 2006 p, 120)? The last time I saw Rabi was when he took me to a very expense carpet cum jewellery store for a look that had guards on the door. The sort of place Charles may have taken Diana, when alive but every thing was far too expensive for me, including the fantastic rubies, but were they real? I should also note that according to the BBC World Service (13 February 2008) that by 2010 at least 1 million men in India may die of smoking related diseases. So perhaps it is a God send that my new friend Rabi can only afford too buy one cigarette at a time?

Back at the hotel I have a rest without BBC Radio 4, what will I do without it for 5 months, and then decide to go to the nearby Railway station to research the ticket procedure, for my journey to Agra the next day. Ouch the first thing in Lonely Planet is correct; I get harassed in a very ruthless way by three young men who are determined to get me across the road to buy a ticket at the entrance to New Delhi station. Which was apparently some sort of commission scam/con as it was nothing to do with a Government department, although that was what it said above the door. Not wanting too much stress I relent and go across and get fed a pack of lies. Just like the ludicrous idea that the 1000 richest people in little Britain are worth a total of '360 billion pounds'…but sadly this may be true. Where according to the Daily Mail (21st June 2007 – front page) the 'wealth divide' is now so enormous in little Britain that it 'could lead to rioting' sometime in the future.

Returning to my hotel I stop in the Everest Bakery cafe, for a cup of tea and met Reika a very bright young Japanese lady and Sadub an American and very friendly, from New Mexico dressed in Sikh garb. Could this be true I ask myself a man who speaks with a USA accent a turban on his head and very big beard? It seemed that Sadub was a yoga teacher on his way to Amritsar to teach yoga, so he informed me and not a con man on the make. As Reika had been to the railway station to get a ticket and Sudub also wanted a train ticket and new the right place to go we all went together to get ours. This time it was reasonable easy in that tourist at this station got preferential treatment in an upstairs large room, although for some strange reason you must show your passport. The main business of the evening over we venture back down the Main Bazar to a restaurant/café called the kitchen cafe where we had a very enjoyable dinner, on top of the hotel, with a very pleasant view of Delhi discussing the meaning of life...which for Sudub and I could mean would Reika sleep with one of us, tonight? She did not, but had been in Australia for a year and was going to travel around India like me on buses and trains. On the email system, since returning to little Britain she has informed me that she had a wonderful time in India, but got ill many times and was even robbed while asleep.

The next morning I get up very early as the train to Agra was going at 6am and met two very stuck-up Americans called Bryon and Trish on the platform waiting for the train. She was studying Law and he was a student in Delhi. I had a first class ticket, number 39 as no other was available, I had been told the night before, and so had a very pleasant seat all to myself, in an air-condition carriage. Across from me were another stuck-up American female and her French boyfriend from Paris. Seemed 'upper class' but very unlikely that they had written two books like me...sorry not boasting; but some people do get up my nose! The two hour journey to Agra, formerly the capital of the Mogul Empire and in 1991, had less than a million people, was very pleasant as we were treated like royalty, with armed guards and lots of staff. We were given a rose; bottle of water, sweets a free newspaper the Hindustan Times and a wonderful breakfast of tea, cornflakes and something that may have been a vegetarian cooked meal. The countryside around Delhi is very flat and uninteresting with strange contraptions sticking up about ten meters to the sky, along the way, a little like strange phalluses, from another galaxy. I also read in the Times about the shocking child labour practices in India, with the stats to go with the article and the complete opposite where in Southern India, about the most successful Indian lady working for Coca Cola and making a fortunate from her good luck. According to 50 Facts that should change the World by Jessica Williams there may be as high as '44 million child labourers in India'.

On arrival I insist to the taxi driver father and son by the look of it that I wanted to go to the Shanti lodge and no where else, which can cause arguments because many taxi drivers get commission for taking you to where they will get the best deal and no where else. They also hassle you for further journeys that you may want to do after being dropped off. I booked into the Lodge in an air-condition room for 500 rupees at the top of the hotel. This gave you a magnificent view of the Taj Mahal, just across the way, from the Shanti lodge which is now a new wonder of the world – voted for by about 10 million people. A huge Mausoleum built by Shah Jehan in memory of his favourite wife who died in child birth, in 1629, after having 14 children and took 20,000 men, 20 years to build. I have a small rest and a cold shower (no hot water which is not unusual in the third world) and walk around to view this magnificent edifice, for the first time in my life. The locals get in for 20 rupees tourist were charged a whopping 750 rupees, which included a bottle of water, probably the most expensive water in the world. This being India we went through a strange ritual to get in as if we were entering an aircraft at Heathrow airport, and was not allowed to take a mobile phone into the wonderful grounds.

Made of marble this is a site to behold and to think about seriously it was built in the honour of a women. Hence, being a very cynical old git, about most things in life - I could not help but notice that all the women going around the site seemed very happy and no doubt thinking to them selves about the power that they have over men for being born female and nothing else. While writing up these notes, waiting for the photo of me - I am observing a Western family being given all the information about the place, from a tourist guide who had three young daughters all looking bored out of their tiny little minds, but Mum a very sexy mature women was lapping it all up. I often think of this phenomenon in a very similar way that the upper classes have over the masses, for just being born into their specific class. Sir Paul McCarthy a very rich pop star is having one of these built in his back garden in Hove in little Britain in the honour of Heather Mills too get rid of her. I was told that it may be cheaper than a divorce by a very rich tabloid journalist who phoned me from his mansion on Mars. For prosperity I have a photo taken, of me on the same seat that Diana the Princess of Wales had hers taken when she visited the place over ten years ago on her own, which must have been a Friday because that is the day the place is closed for VIP's only. Within this huge complex at the far corner there is a very modern toilet, which most tourists soon learn is very unusual in India. There is also a lovely little Museum where we are told that if poison was used in food the plates on show would change colour, or brake, if this process happened - a paranoid group of people so it would appear, very similar to the very rich in our epoch of Modernity, I would suggest. On my back to the hotel I have a cold drink in a near by café and got speaking to a chap from Vigo in Spain and his girlfriend from France who were both shocked at the level of poverty in India, today. Which is very ironic, if you think about seriously because according to Gordon Brown the days of Britain having to apologise for the British Empire is over – whose polices over generations may have caused '21 million' Indians to die (The Guardian 13th April 2007 - John Pilger, Mike Davis) and throughout the world millions more. In fact according to Chomsky (1993) regions like Bengal in India was very prosperous before the English Elite crimes of plunder started - even in some cases turning rice fields into poppy (p, 18) fields for export to China. Now like then Britain is still pushing the so-called 'free trade agenda' on the whole world, which helps the ruling elite and their cohorts (Curtis 2003 p, 220) and hardly anyone else. And according to Arundhati Roy 'the WTO has now forced India to import rice, wheat, sugar, milk, all these products which India has in abundance. The government's warehouse are overflowing with excess food grains, while people starve' (2004 - p, 77). And to think that in the First World War as many as 60,000 Indian men may have lost their lives fighting for the British Empire (BBC 2 -29th June 2007). How ironic don't you think?

In the evening, I have a macaroni dinner, with a glass of beer very close to the Shanti Lodge called the Yash café on the top floor, with several other tourists, which again was very pleasant as I could observe the world around me from a few floors up. What does strike you, although in theory we drive on the left hand side of the road here, the same as the UK - is that, there does not appear to be any rules on the road whatsoever, in urban Indian society - a bit like driving a trolley around a British supermarket, you could say. Especially when one minute you may see a peddle rickshaw with no lights and then the next minute two camels pulling a cart driving in no particle path on the road. I can also report that I had a wonderful sleep - the best since landing in India and a lovely breakfast the next morning on the top of the buildings restaurant, with some other Western tourist and Monkeys who just popped over for a chat about the meaning of life. Not the Protestant work ethic so they told me....well I never. But they did ask me why if we are so stupid, as Monkeys we don't smoke while some of you do. I could not answer the question, unfortunately to complicated for me...a simple homo sapien male, who's only needs in life are a little food a little alcohol and a little sex, in that order.

About ten o'clock I say goodbye to the very friendly staff at the Shanti Lodge and get a mechanical rickshaw to the bus station, where I meet Pete and Adam from Australia, going in the same direction as me, to Jaipur. They are father and so from Geelong near to Melbourne, I had never heard of the place but apparently it is a University town and very nice. The bus driver charges me a few rupees for putting my suit case on the bus, a first for me; for this procedure and we are off for the next six hours, on a pretty rickety old bus. I took to Pete and Adam straightaway as they were two intelligent people, hopefully a bit like me and in Pete's case quite well travelled and had been in India in 1997. The plan being for him and Adam this time to end up in France to walk the Camino trail about 700 miles as the crow fly's. After visiting his relatives in Germany, as his Mother was from German and his dad was Polish with a lot of dynamic tension between them in Australia - because only his Mother could speak English. I don't really know what they thought of this ex-colonial serf from the Falkland Islands, but one thing was for sure, they had never met a person from that neck-of-the- woods, before. The scenery was extraordinary because the sites are so different from most places in Europe that I have visited. People herding goats, the site of buffaloes, camels and so on doing various jobs on the land, in a way I had never seen before. After three hours on the road we stopped for a thirty minute toilet and refresher break and I had a samosa and a cup of chai and then we are off again for another three hours. Pete told me a good joke, while on the bus which went well with the scenery about two cows who were talking to one another and discussing mad cow disease with the other one, saying something like 'what are you on about Mary I am a Pig'. When coming into Jaipur (pop 2.32 million) a huge black bull comes cantering down the road and everyone lets it pass, giving deference to a Bull is rear indeed in the world, but it happens all the time in India and to the whole cow family. The good side to this state of affairs is as most people are vegetarians; in India I don't think I saw one McDonalds, in all of my travels, there. Pete and Adam being so well organised they had already booked ahead for accommodation, so he just rang them up and they sent a taxi, which I also took, weren't they kind? The reason for their actions were simple as when you come into a new city/town in India you are aware very quickly - that you have many friends who wants to take you to a hotel and mount Everest if you wanted to go there, for 100 rupees plus. The Pearl Palace hotel, owned by Mr Singh was a delight and much better then thing I had saw so far in Delhi or Agra and run in a perfect way by young Raj. Although they did not have a spare room Raj allowed me to rent a whole dorm for 300 rupees a night, down stairs. The shower however was a little worrying as the light switch was very close to where the water was flowing, so I did think - would I see tomorrow to myself while in it, on several occasions.

The rooftop restaurant has wrought-iron sculpted chairs and an extraordinary peacock canopy and was very relaxing with a good view of Jaipur, called the Pick city. Adam and I sat next to Rob and Zena from London, Pete was seeing how to cook in the Indian way in the kitchen. Adam and I had a beer and an Indian meal, for years I have really enjoyed Asian food, so I felt right at home. Rob was a practising Archaeologist, who smoked and Zena a teacher with a very good figure…well I am a man. Rob had discovered a new site in Devon and got very excited when explaining all about it and the dig to come. Will I find a spoon or fork in the draw today, sounds exciting doesn't, only joking Rob - as I love TV programmes about this whole process, as well. Pete joined us as the evening progressed and informed me that he had also been a water engineer and a teacher and son Adam was a computer programme, he also had another son called Daniel. Trudy his daughter was a buyer for a huge firm in Australia called Target and ironical she came to India on a regular basis to buy goods cheap. According to Pete she was given about 13 million Australian dollars to buy goods at whole sale prices and the return in theory was 100%. I don't really know what Pete thought of this process because I did not ask him, but as he seemed such a decent human being and into self sufficiency, at home. It seemed like a complete contradiction and structural problem of the system, to me and the main reason that Capitalism per se is so successful and the poor are poor and the rich are so filthy rich. According to the Guardian (3rd Sept 2007) some of the biggest retail business in Little Britain are exploiting the working class in India so disgracefully that some are just paid '13p per hour for a 48-hour week', for producing garments for their stores. Stop philosophizing Brian and get on with it. In fact according to the Sunday Times Rich List (2007) the top richest 50 people on the Planet are now worth a staggering 611 billion pounds, in comparison of what I have just written. You may also wonder why in Little Britain according to the Guardian (28 December 2007) when there is so much hunger in the world that 35 million pheasants are now reared for shooting every year mainly by the upper classes; not for eating but just fun. As they note 'most of those that are shot are not eaten, but burned or buried in mass graves'.

For some reason I did not get a very good sleep, so in the morning, after breakfast I felt a bit tired to explore the city. But as Pete and Adam were such good company we went out and explored. On a rickshaw straight to the City Palace a huge Pink complex of such diversity it would take a million words to explain every aspect of it, and it had a spotless toilet - passing a guard outside a bank with a gun which looked like double barrel shotgun. Hence, I would suggest in any city like Jiapur it is not an exaggeration to quote what the lonely Planet says on its back cover about this whole continent and that is, we should all 'discover the sensory overload that is India'…. because you will never forget it for the rest of your life; whatever you may truthfully think of the place.

Adam took a photo of me with a snake charmer we saw weapons of old and we had a chat with the current Royal Family. Well actual no we did not but apparently Prince Charles the next in line to the British throne is a big mate and plays polo with him, so we were told. One of his ancestors had 108 wives, so when the hell did he eat food or sleep if there were so many women to please… the mind boggles. Johanna I think we will have sex on the 13th of September next year is that okay, darling? But I wonder for how much longer can the caste system last, which is very similar to the British class system as Pete said to me on several occasions. When the locals watch TV what planet do they think they are on if all the people in the world are rich apart from them This is not true, but it is often what is portrayed on the idiot box, for everyone to see, rising expectations has always been a major threat to the ruling elite and probably one of the main underlying reason that they are trying to keep the majority down.

Within the complex we could also buy many goods, when a young man kept insisting that I buy a tea-shirt for 50 rupees - I said I would buy it if his family bought my daughter for a million - as he was a very attractive young lad, I am sure Susannah would have liked him. Pete was in the bartering mood and nearly bought a piece of cloth for his new girlfriend but kept changing his mind about which one would please her. I think a million bucks in your back pocket may have hit her 'hot spot' quicker Pete. Only a cup of wonderful Indian chai, which I bought, could calm us all down and a good think about the grand nature of the whole place. Leaving the City Palace we also looked around an amazing outdoor astronomy complex, which is probably unique in the world.

Looking through Lonely Planet on my return I notice that not to far away from the hotel I could have a massage, so off I went in a rickshaw to the Kerala Ayurveda Kendra or KAK for short, to see the wallah. Where I was asked several questions by Dr Mahendra Sharma B.A.M.S – 'why would a super fit 58 year old man, from another Galaxy want a massage, in the first place'? 'Good question Dr Sharma, one I have been told it is very stimulating and good for you and helps to relieve stress, which India has buckets galore, in the cities'. In fact it was the first time ever that I have had a full body massage with hot oils and it was incredible. Worth every penny so I gave the young man 100 rupees, as a tip. On my return I had a ride in a peddle rickshaw another first; as the man kept getting lost and having to ask directions, well Jaipur is a large place folks. Raving about the experience to Pete and Adam, on my return to the hotel - I think they thought I had got slightly loopy, as I said something like I have had something better then sex. If that assertion was over the top the dinner again was very good in the upstairs restaurant, as was the conversation. While at the Pearl Palace hotel I also met Norbert and Ruth from Holland who had driven, overland all the way to India in a Landover through Turkey, Iran, Pakistan, taking nearly four months. They informed me that in Iran most of the people they met were not very happy, who is in little Britain Norbert? And in theory you could not share a room if you were unmarried, as he was not married, I presume that he lied about his marital status. Again ironically even Prince Harry who has just been told that he can not stay in Afghanistan to fight the Taliban - because everyone now knows he is there - has just said in an interview that he is not to happy about living in Little England!

After breakfast next morning the three wise men again venture into the city for another look around, I gave some cash to some children who were begging and 3 bananas, doing a little good for mankind and hopefully gaining some good Karma, so the next time I will came back as a very sexy women and have lots of power over stupid men for doing nothing. For lunch we go the telesest hotel where there is the tallest restaurant in Jaipur which revolves the 360% every 45 minutes. I have a sandwich and a chi, Pete and Adam have a delicious Indian dish. The waiters look fantastic all dressed up in their finery and we are three scruffy Western backpackers, I wonder what they thought of us? On the way back to the hotel before leaving for Jodhpur we look around a very modern art gallery, selling paintings from all over India and they were very good. I don't know what Brian Sewell (sic) would have thought, but I know what I like.

The day before Adam had got the railway tickets for the three of us so about six pm we set off for the railway station and the second trip on a train for me, in India. This time I was not in first class but some where in the middle as the carriages behind were full of Indian people who were jammed in like sardines in a can. The train was very slow and as it was dark there was not a lot to see, apart from many neo-middle class Indians using their mobile phones, including an angel next to me in tight jeans and high heels - so I took out Mark Thomas's brilliant book called 'As Used on the Famous Nelson Mandela' and read. The utter scandal of the arms trade around the globe - where he informs us for example; about at the height of tension between Pakistan and India British ministers were in the thick of it, helping to flog arms to India. So that we could watch a nuclear war on CNN, wonderful stuff Mark. Keep it up. At the same time as this was going on Clare Short another one of Blair's ministers were in the process of trying to evacuate staff in the whole region just in case it went nuclear, according to Thomas. In other words 'half of the British cabinet have ended up as pimps for BAE systems' (Thomas 2006 p, 122) and to think that Blair says he is a Christian, absolutely pathetic! What perhaps really sticks in your gullet about this whole business if Mark Curtis is correct that normally the British arms trade actual sell arms to both sides; that may be in a conflict situation? Curtis asserts that in 1999 that '8.3 million' worth of arms were sold to India and '1.5 million to Pakistan' (Curtis 2003 p, 188). 'In 2000 nearly 700 export licences worth 64 million were approved to both countries' (ibid) by 2002 it had gone up again.

I also read in the International Times on this journey, two seats up from me that 'rich women are more likely to divorce, then the poor', when taking notes. I presume that this will only apply if there is not a nuclear war in the region. Pete bought me a very pleasant vegetarian cutlet and a cup of chai, very tasty. I also had a one of those

Albert Einstein moments that may or may not be true on the train. This is the basic hypothesis, why are India young men so friendly towards one another? The answer may be that because of the caste system and the arranged marriage system they do not have to compete for the opposite sex like we do. Why the hell am I writing a book that may never be read by more than 100 people when I could be doing something more constructive like eating fish and chips, or drinking a good bottle of red wine; which I am doing while writing this up.? In little Britain and the USA it would seem that many young men would rather join gangs and kill one another, perhaps they all should come to India on a sabbatical.

On arriving at Jodhpur at 1am or just after, there may well have been a nuclear war just down the road as thousands and thousands of people were sleeping on the railway platforms. I have never seen a site like it in my life and I was told the next day that a very important religious festival, on going for a month was happening just down the road and this was the reason for this phenomena. In fact it was quite a struggle to walk through the complete chaos that was Jodhpur railway station that night. Pete and Adam had organised a taxi so we very lucky and got transported towards the Cosy cottage, in the old part of the Blue city as it is called - but had to walk up a small hill to the accommodation for the last 50 meters or so. Pete for some reason got very upset and was not to happy with the digs that was at least 500 years old and the current owner Joshi's family had lived in the place for eight generations. I was housed in a very small tin hut that only cost 200 rupees for the night and had a terrible dream about the Falkland Islands where for some strange reason my friend Neil Watson, I once worked with him - sold me a horse, for 80 pounds - but when it won a race he would not pay me the winnings, very strange indeed. What did it mean; I have not got a clue, and was beyond me! As the night before in Jaipur I dreamt I was flying, something like Superman.

The next morning Pete had calmed down and we all had a very pleasant breakfast together with a Monkey. I had honey toast a banana lassie and a chai and also sat close to a very sexy French woman, laying on a swing contraption and her admirers, with an incredible view of the huge Meherangarh fort, just across the way. In this area of India you can go for a camel ride, but decided against it as I did not want to get stuck with some upper class British twit telling me stories of how wonderful the British private school system is, when it is not. Pete had done this in 1997 just down the road in Jaisalmer; for three nights out in the desert. The reason that this city is painted Blue is that it helps to keep the insect population at bay (Lonely Planet, - p, 204), but I did not see any evidence that this was true. The walk to the Meherangarth fort only took fifteen minutes and cost 400 rupees to get in. It also supplied a tape recorded with an Oxford accent explaining all the information about the fort. We walked for four hours and were overwhelmed with the share beauty, size and complexity of the place. Something that really amused me – was how it seems that opium has been used for a very long time in India as an ice breaker, in a drink, in meetings doing trade, etc and was never illegal in times gone by. The views were also magnificent as you could see across the valley where the current Royal family are now in residence. (P, 206 LP) Who may play polo wearing jodhpurs riding breeches tight below the knee with our next King?

The strength of character should never be forgotten about Indian culture, now and in the past. For example, very few people would ever throw themselves on a funeral pyre, which women did from this fort and through out India, for centuries. Even having to go through the procedure of buying a railway ticket can be very frustrating, not forgetting that hundreds of millions are surviving from day to day at substance level. On arriving back at the Cosy cottage I decide that I would like better accommodation in Jodhpur then I had last night. So I have my last cup of Chai with Pete and Adam and head off in a mechanical rickshaw to the fantastic Devi Bhawan owned by Rambha and Prithviraj members of the Raja, who have two children one girl ten and a boy of twelve at boarding school - but run by Rackish a Basil Fawlty on speed (sic), with twelve staff. On arrival at 18:00 I dive straight into the lovely swimming pool and get my self into a relaxed mode, in this little island of paradise in a sea of chaos. Meeting a very attractive Mum from Wales with her two sons, who were really enjoying themselves in the pool? She had worked for Save the Children about fifteen years ago in Katmandu Nepal and like the Indian culture. This was a private home of for Rambha and Prithviraj but nine years ago they decided to turn it into an up-market hotel. (p, 209 LP) Because it was so successful they were doing extra building work on the complex, with men and women working on the site, the women carrying stuff on their heads.

Dinner was as delicious a Thali special served by very smart staff as was the aesthetic nature of the place. Two young French women, sitting next to me were not too friendly, but who cares. I have noticed on several occasions that the French who travel abroad seem a bit snooty, well at least the ones I have met. And I thought the whole idea of the French revolution was to get rid of privilege, and snobbery. The British never did which was a shame, because according to my Mum our relatives actually guarded that old usurper Napoleon I (Bonaparte – 1769 -1821) when he was in exile in St Helena. However, if nothing else at least France is now a Republic and in the main the masses are better educated and certainly a lot more Political aware then in little Britain by a million miles. According to Mark Cutis just after the French Revolution; the ruling elite in little Britain were so afraid of this great event that they basically declared war on the working class, which I should say is still in full pelt in the 21st century 'with Tory mobs conniving with the magistrates, often looting and burning the house of radicals and dissenters' (Curtis 2003 p, 240). While in India it went on for over two hundred years where even killing people was often on the agenda like the Amritsar massacre where 'at least 379 innocent people' were shot after some riots in 1919 (the Observer book of Scandal p, 47).

I had a lovely sleep and an excellent breakfast, of Chi, fruit, an omelette, and a lassie - after another swim in there brilliant swimming pool. While having a swim a male peacock walked across the lawn by and he told me that he was John Prescott's grandfather out looking for his secretary. I told him he was in the wrong country. At breakfast again I had the two same French women as company, whose attitude changed dramatically when I told them I was a published author....it made my day.

My plan was to head south on the train so I was lucky that Rackish was able to get my ticket for me. As I was going to travel until the afternoon I decided to have a bludger (Australia slang) day just relaxing, thinking and taking notes, in the large lounge and chatting during the day to the beautiful lady owner about certain culture aspects of Indian society. She even gave me a handshake just before leaving, so I was highly honoured that a lady of such high birth should be interested in me. The rickshaw driver took me straight to the carriage that had been reserved for me, so leaving Jodhpur in a much happy state of mind then when I arrived. The first person I met on the sleeper train was a very intelligent man called Bhavin Popat who has a MBA and an Engineering degree. We had a good conversation about many issues including the difference between Western families and Indian families. The main difference appears to be that Indian family's pool their resources where in the Western world we are obsessed by Individualism and certainly in working class culture you are supposed to stand on your own two feet very quickly without a lot of financial help, from anyone. He even informed me that his old Dad puts his pension he gets from the Railways into the central pot. I also met a Mother and daughter from the USA who were not stuck-up this time, as they were Indian themselves and Jay (born in Mumbai and very bright) and his beautiful wife and seven month old daughter who live in Wembley, England; but are going home to show off their lovely little daughter to his family. I also met some very young backpackers that had been everywhere including the Andromeda Galaxy, I think.

CHAPTER TWO

- IN INDIA -
PART TWO

On reaching Mumbai (Bombay) after an eighteen hour journey and not being completely organising like Aussie Pete and Adam, on the recommendation of Jay, who probably thought this bloke was a bit of a twit - but I did not sleep well so very tired. I head off in the wrong direction I should have went and ended up at a very expensive hotel, which I declined. I turn around explore the beach with some very friendly children and head back to where I should have been in the first place, very close to the Leopold complex, three days later, through suburbs, slums and so on, by rickshaw and taxi…a joke, I think! The site of beggars without arms and people trying to sell you everything under the sun, on the street, including books can be a bit alarming to say the least. I book into the Volga 11 by the friendly staff for 800 rupees for two nights, very small but clean. If I had a pet cat, with me - there is no way I could have swung it, anywhere, far too tiny. After the booking in process is over and a shower, which can take some time because by the time you find your passport in your suitcase/backpack and cash the world may have turned again. I head down stairs to the Leopold restaurant and have some breakfast cum lunch. This was the first time that I had ever seen two processes in action that was very strange at first site. If you ordered a meal you pay after you have finished, like virtually every place in the world - but if you ordered a beer you pay before you get it and secondly tables were reserved for clients that did not exist. The reason being because this place is so popular especially with backpackers and tourists that all the tables get full very quick and as most are Westerns we do not like sitting with strangers. The management try to stop this happening by controlling the seating arrangements and pack more customers into the place. To make more money, Brian stopping being so stupid/cynical you idiot – when will you learn, nothing you see with your eyes is real. Haven't you read '1984' by George Orwell yet? The contradiction in this place being that it said on the wall that you had to be 21 to buy alcohol when many young back-packers where just out of their nappies and virtually all drinking the stuff.

After the excellent meal I head down the road to see if I can get some more dosh from somewhere, a hole in the wall, a bank or wherever. During this process I meet a young man called Babu, from Jaipur who also had two sisters begging on the street, so he told me - a shoe shine boy who said that I looked like a Bollywood star. The reason may have been that he wanted at least 400 rupees to buy the proper box and the tools to do the job, because without he was not allowed to practise his trade on the streets. I find a cash point at the nearest petrol station and then walk back up the street with Babu, let him clean my shoes, for cash and said that I would see him later in the evening after I have a rest and a think about his proposition. Sadly I did not see him again - so it did play on my conscious a little that perhaps I could have helped him, but was it a genuine case of hardship or a complete con, one is never too sure in the developing world (third world).

The rest in the Volga11 was really needed as was the evening meal in the Leopold restaurant of Korma and rice and chi, with no master plan at hand, after dinner I decide to stroll around to what in Mumbai is called the Gateway to India. Named after the British Royal family who landed in the year dot and said we need more of your commodities serfs, for peanuts, wake up or else we will send in the warships again. I just made this up, but in reality not far of the truth. In fact I had read in the Indian Times during the day that three years before in this exact same location 52 people had died here in a bomb explosion. I also read for the first time ever in the same paper that one of Britain's richest women, J.K Rowling of Harry Potter fame employs body guards. The way it was written was that she only employed one guard, but this seemed to me very unlikely if she was paying 150,000 pounds (sterling), for the privilege - so I guessed that it should have been explained in the plural and not in the singular format. On the same day in the same paper I also read that chai (tea) may be good for you, hopefully they are correct as I drink large quantities most days. Especially when on the computer writing up my adventures around the globe, which have all taken place - according to Bill Bryson in his latest brilliant book the

Thunderbolt Kid - he suggests that his friend Katz who he went walking with in the USA and wrote about in a Walk in the Woods; said that what he wrote about in that book was 'mostly fiction'…not in mine Bill.

On my return I return to the Leopold complex and order a beer and take out Noam Chomsky's Hegemony or Survival – America's Quest for Global Dominance to read, for the second time, paying in advance for the beer which was an outrageous 100 rupees. Just afterwards I get accused, by one of the waitress of not paying for my meal the night before, in the restaurant - as I was a sleep on the train, at the time this did not make sense. So I got quite upset with the management as I had evidence to prove it. I did think about it later and was wondering that perhaps reading Noam Chomsky in India may be against the law? If only Blair, Blunkett, and Prescott et al could read the great man, and understand what he is saying, we may have a better world. But in essence are they capable of reading the great man or anyone who has not got a wallet full of dosh, in his back-pocket…anyone for a Knighthood sir or is that a Lordship, one never knows with crooks like these running the 'froth on the coffee' in little Britain! My analogy of liberal democracy is the froth on top of the coffee and to borrow a metaphor of Noam Chomsky it is the 'deep structure' that really matters - but very rarely discussed by the mass media or most academics for that matter!

The next morning I get my first experience of Delhi belly, was it the Korma the night before or a meal on the train or the anti-malaria tablets? But had decided that I would go out to Elephant Island from the Gateway to India, anyway - before leaving I got talking to a very bright and beautiful young Indian lady from Puna, who had come to Mumbai for the day to walk with her boyfriend for a few hours. She was training to be a Doctor and seemed a bit concerned that I should be taken the tablets that I was for malaria, when according to her I should be taking something else, while also explaining the dowry system in India, to me. I told her that I had a daughter, as well and that she was allowed to live with her boyfriend, but she assured me that at least in theory this was not allowed in Indian Culture...but the body language seemed to me that she would have loved to aped most girls in the Western world. The boyfriend was an Officer in the Navy and after she qualified as a Doctor she wanted to do the same and when he walked up he seemed a very lovely young man. I hope that they have loads of children after they get married, in two years time. Perhaps I am one of the first Western person to notice a trend in this society, even if only in the abstract, because guess what according to the BBC world service programme. I some time listen to it in the very early morning, they interviewed one couple who lived together before getting married and a young women in Mumbai who had just moved in with her boyfriend (week ending 9th February 2007) after meeting him the day before, so she said. If you were not aware the British Fleet in 1662 'under the earl of Marlborough arrived off Bombay and demanded the cession of the Island from the Portuguese' (Ling 1980 p, 54) although Charles II in 1661 had already had got control of the place through his marriage to Catherine of Braganza.

The trip to Elephant Island, on a very old boat which took an hour, was exciting because I was sitting very close to a chap who was dressed as a pirate, was this going to be a remake of Treasure Island, I asked myself and the rest all looked very cosmopolitan. All looking forward to the adventure of exploring the world around us, in a rational and questioning way. With one exception a big black guy was also on the boat from Washington so he told me, and what really worried me - was this a recce for an invasion of India by the USA in 2010? This is a state secret so please don't tell anyone that you have read this or I will be in big trouble with the CIA and M16. This may not be as stupid as it sounds because if the great Alex Jones is correct, the USA is probably going to invade Iran and then smash China in to the ground. When we got to the Island, which looked exotic, I was expecting to see at least one Elephant, but not one - only very small monkeys, dogs and tourists. 'The Portuguese renamed it Elphanta because of a large stone elephant near the shore. The statue collapsed in 1814 and the British moved and resembled the remaining pieces at Victoria Gardens, where it stands today' (LP p, 719)...so there. In fact the trip was really to see the carved statues in the caves which were splendid. The statues were very old (probably 'created between AD 450 and 750') but I could not help but notice that the belts around the hips of the women looked like a modern belt that some young girls wear, now in little Britain to show off the main assets. The truth however according to the Lonely Planet is slightly more surreal if you are a cynical old git like me, and is related to Shiva which is actually male and not female and 'is the destroyer, but without whom creation couldn't occur'. But can take many forms including 'uniting both sexes in one body'….incredible, don't you think?

Looking across the bay there is a nuclear plant that apparently makes drugs and according to a guide who was chatting to another tourist Alexander the Great, got to this region of the planet, but surely it was not the tea that killed, him was it?. He was also questioning what the carvings in the caves were all about and did they really have anything to do with Indian culture whatsoever. Before leaving I have a cup of Chai and take some notes and speak to one of the mature female translators that travel on these trips just in case you need some help, with your own analysis of the trip

On the way back, I am still afraid that the Pirate may make his move, and rob us all so to divert my attention from these anxieties - I start chatting to Frank and Catherine a lovely couple from Dortmund in Germany and would you believe it they have cycled all the way from Germany on pushbikes and going to Australia hoping to return through Russia. Truly amazing that's all I can say, going to Exeter one way   from Bristol about 100 miles, the way I went, was enough for me - just before I set out on this incredible adventure, of my own.

Because of this adventure I decide that I will stay another day in Mumbai, so the next day I am very lucky that I meet Pinto from Kashmir who sleeps in his Taxi, every night and can speak good English, near my hotel. He has been in Mumbai a year pays three hundred rupees a day to hire the taxi and his wife and baby lives back home. For a small sum of money he has agreed to take me on a trip around Mumbai, for a few hours. The first stop is the largest outside laundry in the world. An a truly amazing site of hundreds of people washing clothes outside and according to Pinto they wash clothes for 5 star hotels, hospitals and so on. To me it seemed pretty horrific; but probably only a little worse then working in a call centre in little Britain, where uneducated middle aged women seem to run them. The next stop was the Gandhi museum where the great man lived between 1917-1934. This was a very unusual museum as it was his home at one time, with lots of books, knickknacks, etc and little models of what he had been doing - in a chronological order of his life. Including the year he got shot in 1948 the year that I was born. On the return journey, because it was a Sunday, without much traffic around - he took me for a good site seeing tour of this large cosmopolitan city and to the railway station to get my ticket to Goa.

In the afternoon I take a walk around the Colaba area visiting the David Sassoon library, something that would not have looked out of place in the nineteenth century, in fact it may have been 150 years old and the gardens were very relaxing, with pigeons for company. I also visited the Johangir Art Gallery where there were pictures of flying horses and Elephants and a copy of the Mona Lisa, having her hair done. Picasso would have been at home here. Downstairs they are selling all sorts of carvings, sculptures, antiques etc, since 1930 so I was told, and the detail was quite incredible on some of it. Upstairs I meet my great hero Jean- Jacques Rousseau; well not really, his remains are in the Pantheon in Paris. But as soon as I saw this piece of art I thought of him, called a 'Celebration of a thinker's day' in fact I would have called it 'man was born free but everywhere he is in chains' (an axiom of Rousseau's). The reason is that the statute of the man is sitting on a plinth, one hand under his chin tied up in cable with lights on. I would say your enlightenment would start once you have read him, not when the lights were switched on, on this statue that is if it was possible.

Something that I really enjoy when travelling is the eclectic mix of people from around the globe that you meet on your travels, some already mentioned. In the Leopold Complex, a café since 1871 was a very good place to meet others, where I met Isaac from Richmond in Yorkshire who was lucky enough to be a movie star for a day at the Bollywood studios in Mumbai. It seems that he played a London policeman with a Yorkshire man's accent, but was very excited that he had been in a film, called Run-Run. I wonder if wonderful beautiful Shilpa Shetty was in the movie with him, because if she was not when writing this she is in the Big Brother house in a very stupid reality Channel 4 show in little Britain. I have not been watching it because it is beneath me, nothing but low culture or more truthfully 'Prolefeed' for the masses to my mind. It seems that she is a big Bollywood star in India and appearing in this show has caused uproar because some of the low life on it has been abusing her with insulting language. The good point however is that at least 20,000 people have complained about the way she has been treated...so not everyone is racist in the United Kingdom. Gordon and Tony (sic) were confused that so much fuss has been made about this show, even in India. But let's face it, are these two on Planet earth, in the Milky Way galaxy - especially now that Gordon has discovered the philosophy of Gandhi; one of the few great men of the twentieth century, when most of his best friends are multi-millionaires! This is very ironic because according to the Sunday Observer on the 4th March 2007 in the Dharavi slum that I certainly went past in Mumbai and near my hotel you could actual pay to go and see some slums, which I thought was quite pathetic. Because part of India problems is 'poor infrastructure, weak government, searing inequality, corruption and crime – converge in Mumbai like nowhere else. Here, where 4 million pound penthouse look over filthy slums, India class divide is at its starkest' (P, 38 -39). Then go on to explain that there is hope because of India; obsession with small businessman and recycling.

I also met Nazimuddi a young Muslim man who was in the Indian navy and all dressed up in his uniform, who according to Krishnan Guru-Murthy are discriminated against in the labour market and when wanting to buy property in Hindu apartment blocks (Channel 4 30th April 2007). This was a serious well educated young man who seemed to think that being Indian was more important than his religious beliefs and was not impressed with young Indian women who dressed up in Western clothes, who drank alcohol and smoked. In this complex on most days you would see a few trying to be sophisticated Western's, smoking and drinking. An oxymoron I think, as many do you know that are in this mode and smoking is not good for you girls (see above).

Ben was from Camberley in Surry, real Tory country and a committed Christian to boot. He had completed a PPE from Essex University; his father had been in the Army for thirteen years and was now a priest in Camberley. Jesus save me from this tosh another contradiction, I think, as I don't belief in it, whatsoever and he may have not even existed, so I have read recently. Apparently Ben was born in Hong Kong and could speak some Chinese languages, clever lad. It seemed that he went to Kerala for a wedding in southern India and then he went to Kashmir where he was ripped-off and nearly killed. It happened to me in London a few years ago Ben. In essence we had a real good chin-wag about many issues from, Delhi belly to 'a few individuals can make a difference' which I disagree with completely - as it's mostly about the structural nature of any epoch that is important. What ever you call it is irrelevant! How it is organised is the very important point of the whole matter. Did you say you had a PPE degree Ben? Being a Tory he was constantly given me the old mantra that private enterprise works, without State subsidies I kept thinking to myself, but where, another Galaxy, or surely not Vietnam is it Ben? Another point he kept making was that it is not only the left that is altruistic to others but also Christians? I again can not see a lot of altruism in this world; now, in fact many people are so horrible they don't deserve to be alive. But I think young Ben was an exception to the rule....keep it up lad, that's all I can say.

The next evening I get Pinto to take me to the Railway station, for the train to Goa after resting on a spare bed for 3 hours of another Ben's in the Volga 11 during the day as my diarrhoea was not very pleasant. This Ben also seemed like a very compassionate young man, so there is more then one, good. Hoping that someday, I will meet Pinto again; so if I have made some dosh from writing - I could buy him a taxi or whatever, or persuade J. K. Rowling to part with a few thousand for him. Surely she could afford a new Nimbus 2000 for him (sic)? On the sleeper I met another Ben, Jennifer and Will all from little Britain. These young people had been nearly all over the world and where very stimulating to talk too; Ben on a gap year and the others just taking a year out after Graduating. Will's father had been in the Army for 35 years and left as a Colonel and he was going to meet his parents in Calcutta in a few weeks time and so well organised, so he told me…to do more travelling. Especially where his ancestors had been in there past, helping to prop up the British Empire, now according to John Pilger there are more than a million men under arms in the Indian Army, Air force and Navy 'consuming almost half the national budget' (Pilger 2007 p, 237). Jennifer seemed a very compassionate young woman and was the girlfriend of Ben. What I wrote in my notes at the time was that these young people seemed, to me very aware of other people's cultures in the countries that they had visited and you had to adapt to these Cultures, very quickly, especially like the skill/art of bartering, in most places in the globe. Apparently in Burma young Ben was asked if he would like to buy some, cigarettes, some drugs, a girl or finally a gun, all by the same man, I am pleased to inform you all, he declined the lot. I also talked to a very friendly middle class couple who had shared our little area on the train who had been to Mumbai for a day or two but did not like the place - as they were small business people from Madgaon. The wife was an out standing beauty even though she was now in her thirties; I am coming back as an Indian man that is for sure or a duck (sic) the next time around.

As no one had a master plan on reaching Goa we all got off at Madgaon negotiated a deal with a taxi driver to take us to the hotel all together. Which worked out much cheaper doing it as a collective group together - unfortunately the deal must have been too good because we had to walk up the beach to reach the hotel, we planned to stay in. Jennifer did not think it was up to her standards so we had a cold drink and got another taxi to the Star Beach Resort in Colva. My new young friends did not think that the place was worth 600 rupees a night so they re-negotiated a new deal for 440 rupees a night. I was pleased with the place as I could have a swim in their smashing pool, which always helps you to recover from a long journey and then a rest. In the evening I went out to dinner, at Anoshka's on my own in the small village for a fish meal with a pinacolada (Spanish origin), an excellent meal but the portion a little small for such a hungry soul, with an upset stomach, like me. And the Bollywood movie on in the corner was very confusing, showing on a very small TV, in the corner, it looked like girl meets boy and the hell we go through to win her over. For example, according to the movie, Walking the Line (biopic) about Johnny Cash's life story he nearly died trying to win over June Carter…but they were married for many years; so I presume the suffering he went through was well worth it.

The next morning at breakfast Ben informs me he is also writing a book, about his travels and planning to stay in the Goa area for at least a month, by renting an apartment. Will is off to the north of Goa and I am planning to go to Palolem in the south after reading in Lonely Planet that it was one of the most relaxing places in the whole State. Which was part of the Portuguese Empire until 1961 when the Indian Government said you have had this place for 400 years, it's about time we took it back, so there. Well I don't think Goa is in Europe is it, only George W Bush and Condoleezza Rice would not know where the place is?

I take a mechanical Rickshaw to Palolem a bit expensive for such a short journey but well worth the experience, no trains today so I was told, which may have been a lie and the bus queue looked very long - often wondering if we would make it because this guy thought he was Stirling Moss on a racing track. We make it to the Oceanic hotel, just and are booked in by beautiful Urmila, (who has a boyfriend and has worked for 4 years at the hotel) for five nights which is owned by an English couple, Les and Sheila - who are on holiday back in England at this time. After a shower and rest I venture down to the beach to see what all the fuss is about in Goa and walked all the way into the centre of town, along the beach, where the local fisherman still ply their trade. It is a very attractive area of India, as the population is very low here and the beaches are lovely with few dogs and a few cows wondering around searching for their swim wear. Am I on mind altering drugs or just an amusing little man, trying to be a bohemia artist?

At this time of year there are not a lot of tourists, in this part of India, so prices are probably more affordable to poor serfs like me. After a quick swim in the warm sea I walk into the Star Attraction a very pleasant restaurant cum café right on the beach and order a lassie, for peanuts, relax, take out my note pad and think to myself, aren't I a lucky bastard. I am told by one of the barmen at this café that one of the current jokes in Goa at this time of year (end of August 2006) is that 'there is more dogs in Goa than tourists' and the trouble is that they have no money and don't drink alcohol, how sad. I spend the rest of the day, relaxing taking notes and reading Catch 22 given to me by Paul Harris a few years ago and a must read before you die, for everyone who is a 'wap'.

After breakfast on my second day in Goa I still have diarrhoea and decide because the British drugs I bought with me, did not work I must do something positive about it and walk to Chaudi to cash a travel cheque and get some medicine that may work. This being India I walk into the local bank to get my travellers cheque cashed and they say we don't do it here, go next door but one, to the chemists. But I don't want a packet of condoms I want a cheque cashed, I thought to myself. I walk into the chemist who was very busy and waited to be served by the very friendly intelligent chemist and they were correct; I could cash my cheque and get some medicine. I take a mechanical Rickshaw back to the hotel have a rest and venture down to the nearest small beach for a swim. It was so quite I could have been on my own desert Island with sexy Sue Lawley for company. My only companions were a few dogs and an old fishing vessel not in use today. However I was very lucky today because out of the blue I see a huge bird, flying in across the horizon and guess what it was not a bird but Prince Charles with a pair of wings attached trying to save the Albatrosses. He said 'is this the Falkland Islands peasant', and I said 'no this is Goa, you are lost you anachronistic man from Highgrove, so get lost, before you lose your head in a

French style revolution, it is coming but I don't know when…probably when at least 50% of the population has a degree, but can't find a middle class job'! He flew off without saying another word.

The first impressions I had of South Goa was when I first went to Cyprus in the Royal Air Force in 1968, the smell the beauty and the very relaxed life style. This is very ironic because Stirling Moss had taken me to the Bhakti Kutir complex when I first came into Palolem run by a very laid back hippy couple from Germany. The price was a bit high and that's why I decided to go to the Oceanic hotel, just around the corner, which was a little cheaper. Although the first time I saw the place I thought to myself that this may be the Garden of Eden, and Adam wasn't in. The next morning I decide that I must visit them again as I am intending to write a book about this whole process and these people seemed like a good sort to gather information on the place. In fact the husband a lawyer was out of town, recovering from illness - but Ute was in with her three beautiful children, ages 12, 9 and 6. I also met Greg from New Zealand, who was a small businessman setting up a kayak business in Goa and Liz who was the teacher Ute had brought from the UK, to teach the children and her husband Jivan from Manchester but his family was original from Delhi. Ute had lived in Goa for eighteen years and in her youth was a real cracker…not bad even now. So to go with the cracker I have a pancake and a cup of chai and a good conversation that went well with my thoughts and words. Why did I join the Royal Air Force, at 18, marry the wrong woman and have three children - instead of becoming a hippy, smoking dope and bonking women, all at the same time. I think I took the wrong turning somehow, but hopefully not too late to make up for lost time, in the future. Greg had lived in the UK for ten years, working in the PR racket and was 38 and getting worried that he was not married and Liz had been an actress before becoming a teacher and Jivan had worked in the film business, working on 'Vanity Fair' at one stage of his career. Ute had a female duck that was slightly paranoid because she had seen her friends being eaten by the dogs, so kept close to humans for protection and Ute was studying reincarnation. I presume just in case she comes back as a female duck. All I know is that if she comes back as a female duck I want to come back as a male duck, 'duckspeak' for…quack, quack. For those who don't know already 'Ute' in Aussie slang means 'utility, Australian equivalent of a pick-up-truck'…she was nothing like one.

Something, very important I have forget to tell you all – with all this excitement about Ute, playing on my mind is that each morning at the Oceanic hotel I have been having a swim in their pool. You will not believe what I am about to tell you but it is the truth, the whole truth, and nothing but the truth. On the first morning after I booked in I met Freddy the Frog and guess what in a previous life he was Mrs Thatcher father. Truly amazing don't you think? The next morning I met not only Freddy but also Freedy the Frog and she was Mrs Thatcher's mother in a previous life. She was very upset because I told her everything that Freddy had told me the day before. In essence what he told me was that his daughter was a very beautiful little girl, when young, but unfortunately when she helped out in the shop. She used to stand on a chair and when weighing anything she pushed the scaled down just a little, with her fingers - so that daddy could make a little extra out of his customers. Mrs Thatcher's mother was horrified, how could she do that Brian, that is quite disgraceful…yes ma'am I agree completely. For those who don't know 'Margaret Hilda Roberts was born in Grantham on the 13th October 1925. She was brought up in a flat above her father's grocer's shop with an outside lavatory and without a bath or running water' and the rest is sadly now history (Jones et al 1991 p, 394).

During my stay in Palolem, in the evening I visited the Cuban café cum restaurant on at least two occasions for a drink and a read of Catch 22 and had three dinners in the Good Shepherd run by very friendly staff, on the first occasion I was listening in a conversation between two American girls and a English bloke, the girls were probably from Utah because they did not drink alcohol, in the Good Shepherd. They were all reading books as well so the conversation was rather disjoined and lacked any coherent logic that I could make out. This may have been because an old hippy couple sat just across from me was probably smoking dope, I think - so perhaps I was getting high with out even knowing it and I have not been to Mill field's school, in lovely Somerset!

The next two nights I was joined by John Dyke from Launceston in Tasmania, who was also travelling around India in a serious walking mode. We got on very well because we were of similar age, were both well read and he had heard of Noam Chomsky, my hero - he was a social worker in Launceston. One of the main themes of our conversation was how long would ruthless neo-Liberalism last for? No conclusion was reached but on the second night he gave me Arundhati Roy book called 'An Ordinary person guide to Empire', after I told him that I was going to buy 'The God of Small Things' by the same author, which I did a few days later on the beach in Goa, from a young man from Calcutta. The book turned out to be one of those brilliant critiques of the epoch that it is hard to put down. He was very impressed with 'The God of Small Things' but I found it hard to get to grips with it, the reason that I am now reading it, for the second time and surely men don't really do those naughty things in cinemas do they? Apparently it was thought of as obscene in the State of Kerala where wonderful Arundhati Roy was born and for this reason a criminal case was brought against her and may still be pending some day (David Barsamian 2004 – p, 9).

Most people who visit India either hate the place or really like it, I am still thinking about the whole experience even when writing this up several months later. The reason may be because of the culture shock and the unexpected phenomena may hit your senses with pure laugher or disgust and did I really see that – like a cow in a restaurant but not on the menu. I saw this experience twice in Palolem so it must be true; I was told by John that apparently this is a regular occurrence with this restaurant called the Little Italy. It seems that the cow comes up from the beach is given a bun and then goes back to her friends, in a better frame of mind, so Mrs Thatcher told me. I also saw a man in the Cuban with a skirt on and no shoes - is this taking cross- dressing a little too far? Even as something as simple as taking a bus ride on the local bus can seem strange the first time. This is because there is some times at least three people running it - the driver one taking the money and another one blowing the whistle when all the customers are on the bus.

A must for me while in Goa was to visit the Cotigao Wildlife Sanctuary on a scooter, so the next day (3rd September 2006) I head back to the Good Shepard, from the Oceanic hotel who told me they would hire me one out for the day for 250 rupees. I had not driven a motor bike for over 42 years so this was going to be a very pleasant experience, I was hoping and it was. Who am I today, Che Guevara, Steve McQueen or Ewan McGregor? Che, I think because we are both on the same mode of thinking about Capitalism, it's rotten to the core, read 'Gangster Capitalism' for the real evidence - or I could be Steve because I am the same height as him, when he was alive, of course. The freedom of the road feels different from driving a car, especially when in India because there is not a lot of traffic in Goa and you never know when you may meet a cow or a whole family on a scooter. The scenery is always changing and very pleasant in this area of the continent. The journey took me up the Margao road and into the park, paying a few rupees for the privilege; where at least in theory there were dangerous animals: Gaur, Samber, Leopards, spotted deer and snakes I only came across several Monkeys and nothing else although if I could have found two towers that was supposed to be in the park, several miles apart - I could have seen some more, so the Lonely Planet told me. In fact I even walked for a few miles, as the roads were not too good in several places, looking for these bloody towers only coming across an old man at his home and I think his daughter – who may have thought that I had just popped in from Mars. They were not too pleased to see me, so I had a drink of water an orange and pushed off down the track pretty sharpish, back to the scooter. The rumour I heard from the Monkeys was that they day before some West Midland tourists had visited the place dismantled the towers and had taken them back to little Britain, to reassemble them as dog kennels and rent them out to their cousins, who can not afford to buy a home anymore, there is now not one house in little Britain under 100, 000 pounds (Guardian 23rd April 2007). But would a Monkey ever tell the truth about British tourists from the West Midlands one of the natural homes of ruthless Thatcherism, I doubt, do you? In fact according to the recent documentary (September 2007) with the incredible Bruce Parry he was told by a Buddhist Monk that he will be coming back as a Monkey and then a chicken, so if you think that I have gone the way of Nietzsche, think again!

The ironic twist to this little part of my story is that when I came out of the park, on the scooter I got stopped by the local police for not wearing my helmet. He was going to charge me 400 rupees but decided that 100 were enough after I told him that no one wears helmets in Goa, so why pick on me? On the 4th of September 2006 I decided that I would move closer to the bus serves out of town and say goodbye to beautiful Urmila, so sexy she could have been a Bollywood star and moved into the Good Shepherd - which was also a hotel for one night, cashed a traveller's cheque with a friendly man called Benny. Feeling like a king after playing Steve McQueen for a day, or Che I decided that I could do anything - so I have a long swim out to a small Island in the Arabian Sea. A very relaxing experience, something like sex with out the big bang I always think, the lunch was not bad either served by lovely young Sahoo who was excellent at his job, in the Star Attraction, right on the beach. In the evening I go to the Cupid restaurant for a beef steak dinner, just across the road from Little Italy where I had seen the Cow experience. The meal was very pleasant, as was the person who run the place and told me that he was a genuine Goan person and not an outside usurper - coming into Goa just too cash in on the tourists trade, like many do. After dinner before going to bed I was watching the Ganesh festival, from my balcony going through the streets, of Palolem - I don't know what the hell was going on, but it was very noisy and was told the next morning that the young men dancing with red banners on their heads and setting off fireworks, and collecting money, were 'celebrating good luck'. I presume the dogs on the beach in Goa that had missed being castration probably thought the same thoughts 'ain't I lucky, I still have my balls' –they were the ones with smiles on their faces, that's how I know!

Having completely recovered from Delhi belly and time running out to return to that city, before I go on to the next step of my journey - I leave on a bus to Madgaon, saying goodbye to the very friendly staff in the Good Shepard. I would like to have travelled too Kerala, Chennai, Bhopal where thousands died a few years ago in a shocking accident etc...but time will not allow for this experience, this time around. According to Private Eye (1185) many people in Bhopal are still suffering from the after effects of this terrible tragedy mostly caused by abandoned chemicals leaking into the water supply.

On arriving in this little town of 94,400 I get a taxi to the sister Hotel of the one in Palolem with the same name, at Aquem - Alto. I have a cup of chai at the front of the complex and a think about plan A, do I get a plane bus or train, or a rickshaw to my next destination, if they exist in this part of the Universe? Or plan B which may a ride on a boar, camel, an Elephant or John Prescott's granddad, or whatever. I did investigate a train trip but apparently this was not possible tomorrow to Panjim. When I get back from the train station I pick up 'The God of Small Things' and start to read a very complex book by wonderful Arundhati Roy.

Getting lost in any book has been part of my life for the last 50 years and it was no different today, so by the time I realized that it was time for dinner it was dark outside. Hence, walking into town from the hotel was a little bit tricky, through the dense traffic - but as this is India a friendly local gave a ride on the back of his scooter, as another person did in Palolem a few days before, for the large sum of 20 rupees...85 to the pound, 2006. I had decided to have a drink of alcohol before dinner or with it - unfortunately I could not find a restaurant that served alcohol with your meal. However I was very lucky to find a small shop just off the main square selling beer. The owner N.L. Pevablui who runs it let me join him in shop for a good old chinwag (sic) about everything under the sun and of course some aspects of Indian Culture. He had been a bank manager for 26 years, his wife also worked in a bank and he had two lovely daughters. Being a very friendly Hindu gentleman at about the same age as me we got on very well, I think? What always fascinates me about the human race - is why do people belief what they do. Normally most Sociologists will inform us that it is the epoch/culture that you are born into and the socialisation process that we all go through to be human. Apart from many working class folk in little Britain, that do badly need some re-education, to be partly human… joke, in the past and present tense! Therefore in this case I kept trying to find out from Mr Pevablui what he thought of his religious beliefs concerning reincarnation, hopefully in a tactful manner. In other words what was he in a previous life a mouse, a fly another human being or whatever? He would not answer directly because only the absolute (God) – atman –Brahman knows, so there. An Indian Hindu lady and friend, working at Royal Mail in Bristol, a few years ago told me that she did not want to come back as anything, but go straight to God. We parted hopefully as friends… he probably thought to himself where does this twit come from, another galaxy? Then I had a lovely Asian dinner at the end of the lane and a slow walk back to the hotel, in the dark.

The next day after breakfast I get a bus to Panaji and a taxi to the Alfonso Guest house, for one night - just over the bridge from the bus station. After booking in I walk down a small lane to a small restaurant called Viva Panjim for a lassie and a light meal; where I met Robert from South London who was just about to have his lunch, as well. He needed it as the night before he nearly got killed on his bike. He also told me some very funny outrageous jokes, which I have forgotten. The Lonely Planet informs me that this was a place that 'most travellers bypass' but I didn't so I have a stroll around this small town of 98,915 people and was quite impressed with the area I walked through. This place felt different - in essence a much more modern canvas then some other urban areas of the big cities and smaller ones, for that matter and most people were well dressed. I also bought myself a bus ticket to Pune and in the evening I had a very pleasant dinner back in the Viva Panjim served by Jk who is a Hindu and the other waiter is called James and he is a catholic so he informed me. Both very smart and pleasant young men who told me that when they get bored with stupid tourists, like me - that they talk to the fish in the tank, for some respite, this did not happen but may be what is in their heads during the day and night - just a thought? Their boss lady was very attractive and spoke perfect English, especially on the mobile.

The next morning I have a cooked breakfast on the roof area of omelettes chai and rolls, which I needed as for some reason I did not sleep well although one of the cleanest hotels that I had stayed in so far. As the bus to Pune was not leaving until the evening I venture into town and take a bus to the Calangute beach to investigate the great smear that these young people who write for Lonely Planet, put out about the hippie generation. Basically the premise seems to be - were these people human or some sort of aliens, from another Galaxy? This is what they say: 'Calangute was the first beach to attract hippies travelling overland in the 60s, then the first to secure the rampant package and charter – tourist market in the 90s. Its India's answer to the Costa de Sol and, in high season at least, its centre is an over-hyped, over priced, over-crowed strip of mayhem' (LP p, 779).

Well that's telling you straight is it not? But it also says that out of season the prices come down. I was lucky in that I was there in the first week of September so prices did not seem dear to me, although all I had after visiting the beach was a spot of lunch in a pleasant café near the beach. After lighting from the old bus I walk down to the beach and see if I can see any hippies making love on the beach, in group formation. Sadly not one hippy to be seen, a few tourists but mostly indigenous Indians with their clothes on having their pictures taken against the backdrop of the lovely beach that was too rough to swim into day. In fact the sea was so rough that there was guides keeping the people away from the beach, I just laid down on my towel and observed the world about me when a dog came down to share my space with me and a lovely Indian family - who also wanted to sit under the tree, with me. The lunch was very pleasant with a beer as was the conversation I was listening in on behind me. Two Englishmen probably from London trying to fathom out the meaning of life and shall we stay here or go home, seemed to be the basic theme of it. 'Well this is heaven; but I miss the fish and chips and the din of London traffic, don't you Trevor. Same here George and I even miss my ex-girlfriend, she was not much too look at, but was a really good shag (sic)…if you say so old man'?

On my return to the Capital of Goa and lots of time on my hand I venture into the Panjim Inn, a splendid 300 year old building with four poster beds where they also sell paintings for a cup of chai and a read of the Indian Times from the 6th of September 2006, that I had bought the day before. An amusing piece I read and of course counter culture to Western ways was how in 1936 a law was passed in Delhi that stated that if you were caught kissing in public you would be fined 50 rupees and still relevant, so it seems. But I was very lucky because I was kissed by Shamina a very beautiful Indian lady who I met at University, in Bristol in 1996 and she actually gave me a very passionate kiss, in her lodgings, one night after an evening out with some other students on the same course and then said something like 'that's all you are getting Brian'…so there! Just across the way there was also an art gallery, so lots of high culture in this area of Panaji. Before leaving and paying a whopping 36 rupees for the tea - I left a copy of both of my little books on their book shelf, hoping that at least one tourist or a local would pick it up, read it and not use it for toilet paper, sometime in the future or when on Sue Lawely's desert Island (sic). I say this because just across the way from where I was reading the paper and having my chai, on the balcony was a very wealthy looking international businessman with his secretary dictating some very important work. This is how it may have gone: 'will you sleep with me tonight darling (she was gorgeous)…well I may do let's finish these treaties of pure tripe for the UK market and the Blair Government first shall we, darling? You know what a pimp those bastards are for BAE systems, so let's try our luck and sell them a new type of nuclear bomb, made of cow shit (we have lots of it); they deserve it, don't they? They have screwed us rotten enough in India, over the centuries, now it's our turn'.

At 7pm I was at the bus station waiting for the bus to go, but this being a developing country, what ever it says on the ticket may not be true. About 6 years ago while I was travelling in Southern Africa you waited till the bus was full and then it went. After many trips to relive myself, at the back of the bus - as there was no toilet on this bus it left about 45 minutes late and headed out of town on some of the roughest roads that I have ever been on. A bus journey at night is not really a very pleasant experience anywhere in the world, as is a plane trip, because simply it is nearly impossible to sleep, and on this bus it was completely impossible. This being night time you could not see anything either but what worried me the most was the thought of the bus driver running into a cow on the road and ending the true meaning of life for all of us...living and breeding, I think! The trip took all night with a few stops for the toilet and I thought to myself that I am far too old for this sort of journey again, so vowed to myself that this would be the last one, if I have my way.

After negotiating the next peace treaty with China, before it is bombed out of existence by the Yanks, I mean what will it cost to take me to the Sunder hotel with the taxi driver, which cost a staggering 750 rupees, a night, so not such a good deal, I have a very good rest and a shower and venture outside for a look around Pune. I was not very impressed with Puna as we shall see later, which was a shame because it is this city where Gandhi was interned for two years in 1942 and where his wife and secretary for 35 years also died. This is also the place where the Bhagwan Rajineesh's famous ashram is situated in the leafy northern suburbs. Basically it is where many Westerns, who are lost souls come to find the meaning of life and use all the facilities that they have at a price, which is not cheap according to the Lonely Planet (p, 749). In essence slightly ironic as a million Indians probably died when the British decided to dived India into two different States 60 years ago, don't you think?

I find the meaning of life in a very pleasant meal just around the corner from the hotel and just before dinner at 17:50 I saw on the BBC World (TV programme) what the King of Swaziland thinks is the meaning of life which is apparently is, having 13 wife's and just about to have the 14, this is quite ironic because he is only 38 and Swaziland is not a rich country. I don't think little Britain can complain too much, about this phenomenon - because we have a very rich monarch and millions of poor people, living in relative poverty, and after Brown's latest Budget (21st March 2007) a lot more, snap! The next morning I get a taxi to the National hotel two minutes from the train station and book in for 470 rupees. This is a very famous old colonial building a little bit worn around the edges, with very high ceilings.

For lunch I walk to the Satman restaurant where on my way I am pestered by quite a few very poor people begging and so on. As a humanist and a poor person in little Britain myself, for most of my life, it very hard not to get very angry about what you see in the huge cities in India, or anywhere in the world, for that matter, where most people have very little. Che Guevara got most of his left wing ideas from travelling through South America in the early fifties and who could blame him! After lunch I take a small walk through a little part of Pune, before retuning to my hotel I have a hair cut and a face massage to calm me down…it worked. I paid him handsomely. When I get back I meet lovely Kate and her boyfriend Max reading and relaxing close to where I am sleeping.

I introduce myself as another Voltaire, didn't really just another struggling author trying to make a career change. Kate was in the process of nearly finishing reading the 'Life of Pi' so she gave it to me a few hours later, when we met for dinner.

But a few hours before this happy occasion I had perhaps the most harrying moment of all my time in India. I went out about 4 pm thinking that perhaps I could buy a chai and a small dough cake for high tea, something that the very rich pay a fortunate to have in little Britain. But as I was approaching the small café just outside the Hotel I saw a lovely young girl begging very close to the café, but being completely ignored by the neo-middle class, of this city. In a meter of where they were cooking the dough I saw the owner or at least the person running the place given food to a bird. I could not believe that any one could be so insensitive - here was a living poor human being begging, but he also completely ignored this staving girl, which you could see in her eyes, her real need for food…she was unaware that I was looking at her. So I bought three dough cakes and had one for my self and gave her two and then left in complete disgust. Thinking about this for hours later I could not think that if these people were Hindus, but did not know for sure – however if they were; there is a massive contradiction at the heart of their whole belief system. You work it out! And perhaps the complexity of India should never really be guessed at as today (28th April 2007) in Bath I met a young Indian man from Puna working in a shop who was Muslim married to a Hindu girl and he told me that his and her parents did not mind this arrangement. Noting that although millions died of 'avoidable famines' under British rule they were very rarely reported but kept hidden 'by tight control of the media' (the Observer Book of Scandal p46).

According to the Herald Tribune (19th September 2006) about one third of the 1.1 billion people who live in India 'live on less than a dollar a day' and has had '7.7 billion dollar inward investment up to 31st March 2006' mostly American, I presume. Like virtually every society that has embraced Capitalism and India is no different and wouldn't Max Weber be amazed if he was alive today (sic), somehow the rich has got to legitimise their position in life and I would suggest as does Trevor Ling (at least subliminally) that Religion helps in this process. So if you are poor like this little girl and me for that matter - it is due to the natural order or in India the 'Law of Manu' (Ling 1980 p, 107). Not forgetting that the true reason that this little girl was completely ignored by the people on the street may be because of 'the widespread secularisation of life in India'…but to my way of thinking very unlikely. This quote is again from Ling and is probably true about little Britain - as he also notes about the pure hypocrisy of a small ruling elite who at least pretend that they believe in religion, when the vast majority do not.

Kate, Max and I walked up the road until we found a restaurant that we thought fitted our taste, but did not sell alcohol. The meal was very tasty and the conversation went on for some time. With all sorts of issues and topics being discussed - Max was from London and Kate was from Scotland, he was a design graduate and although a conservative was a little cynical about why people join political parties and go to meetings, in the first place. Apparently Kate's sisters both worked in Hong Kong and one is married to an Australian and Max has made a couple of short movies and wants to be part of the movie industry. On the way home we buy a bottle of beer each and return to the hotel for further talks on talks, perhaps what makes us all human. I think we left with the thought that Kate was going to buy my books, but would she understand them, that is what I was thinking as we parted.

The train was to leave at 07:50; I had bought the ticket the day before I went for lunch with the help of a young man who helped me through this trying business in India - queuing for at least 45 minutes, for the reward, I also gave him some dosh for his help. So I got up at 6am shaving, showering etc, just before the lights went out in a power cut. The train left on time, I was in C2 seat 35 and most people on the train was reading the Indian Times, Pune edition, but the Monkeys near the track were not, as we progressed towards Mumbai. At Mumbai this time I book into the Hotel City Palace, close to the railway station in a small room with a TV and air-conditioning. I even had some meals in my room, for the first time in my life while travelling. I did have a good walk around this part of the city and even popped into a bookshop where my number one hero Noam Chomsky's 'Failed States' was 'on the best selling list' and they were even selling Michael Moore's books. But what I noticed the most is that everything is up for sale here, you name it some one will supply it, especially near the hotel. I could even buy four James Bond movies on one DVD for about 100 rupees, in little Britain you can still pay 20 pounds (sterling) for a Sean Connery bond movie in Bath, to this day. I could even buy some very sexy DVD's as well so I was told. However DIY (sic) is certainly something that most Indian people would never do from what I could see, which may be a good thing as in little Britain, it is nearly an obsession, religion - especially with people like my brother et al.

It was at this time in Mumbai that I had the brilliant idea after walking up a street near the hotel and seeing a cow walking up the street in conversation with small business people (joke maybe, but she did tell me that her name was Margaret No 6) that this would be the ideal place for Mrs Thatcher to come back in her next life as a urban cow, Margaret No 7. She could eat rubbish and chat to her favourite people, small entrepreneurs. At the same time I was thinking that her son; sir Mark Thatcher could come back as an Indian hairdresser for ever, the first time he would have ever done anything useful, in his whole life; as Indian men are obsessed by there look of their hair…sorry friends, but it is true.

After more site seeing for another few hours I catch the 16:15 from Central TS to Delhi where I am in the same sleeper as Riza Haziri from wonderful Croatia. I soon learn from him that he cannot get too grips with Indian culture, its own modus operandi and despises the place completely. His favourite modus vivendi about India was 'oh my God…I don't believe it' meaning the site of so many poor people living a subsistence existence and so on. But I am glad to inform you that we got on very well as he was a mature man who had actually been a successful football coach in Melbourne, Australia. So to pass the time of day on such a long journey we played several games of chess, that I won…not boasting Riza and general chatted about the meaning of life , for example, most new belief systems in the world and especially in India, was a 'reaction' against another older faith/belief, where we had been travelling, etc. On arriving at New Delhi train station the next day we walk through all the hassle back to where I had stayed before in the Hotel Star Paradise, on the main bazaar. Where according the Cambodia Daily (7th December 2007 source Reuters) in New Delhi they are trying to bring in a new law of jaywalking because at least 900 people are killed each year trying to cross the road, it seems the police are having real trouble implementing the law as so many are very poor and can not afford the fines and some just don't understand the whole new idea.

The next few days I spent with Riza was interesting and delightful as was meeting Jo Scott in the Mo Mo Cave (café) a teacher from New Zealand who was teaching English in Korea. The only down side to the three days I spent with him was that he told me his sister and father had been killed in the civil war in the old Yugoslavia.

Riza and I visited the Red Fort a very impressive massive building nearly 500 years old, had several drinks in a bar on the Main Bazar. Visited the biggest Mosque in India, went to the National museum in the new part of this great city; where I started to get a very new strange disease, what I call 'musem-ites'. Some artefacts were 4000 years old, just about the time the British Tory party was being born, I think. Had dinner again in the Kitchen Café and another one in the Malhotra Restaurant where we got talking to a delightful young couple, from Brazil (Patricia was from Brazil he was from Germany) who complained that now a days if you are women you are very unlikely to get the smallest of treats for being a women...'even a bunch of flowers was beyond most men', so she said! Which I thought was quite ironic because this place was one of the dearest (50 rupees for one slice of Nan bread) restaurants that I had visited in a whole month in India. On my last night in India we went again to the Kitchen Café with a delightful young women called Angela, who was just about to start a chemistry PhD in Leeds in the UK, who we met in the local bar. She had also worked for Save the Children in Nepal and her middle class parents were from Glasgow. I had a Chicken sizzler, a lassie and the next morning I took terrible ill with diarrhoea and vomiting. Being with Riza, in the same hotel, was very lucky because I had to book out of my room at ten - but the flight to Thailand was not until the evening so he let me lay on his bed, when he was out getting a visa for Malaya, going in the next few days. When abroad it is probably easier to make friends then when at home because of the circumstances that we are in at the time, especially in places like India, it was with Riza but no doubt most people that I saw in Croatia certainly looked laid back when I was there a few years ago. So it was sad to say goodbye to Riza and get the taxi to the airport, but hopefully I will meet him again and have a meal and drink, with him and his family in Croatia and even beat him at chess, well you never know do we?

CHAPTER THREE

- SOUTHERN ASIA - THAILAND

It's just after 10:00am on the 16th September 2006 and I have just landed at Bangkok airport for the first time in my life, but still feeling ill. The first impressions that hit your senses is that these people who live here are very deferential to their Monarchy - as it says at the airport 'we love our King', I read this when waiting for at-least thirty minutes getting through the passport system. I cannot remember seeing this at Heathrow airport, or any airport in little Britain, for that matter about the British Monarchy. I get the 'meter taxi', for 300 Bart the cheapest version of getting from A to B and head into town towards Th Khao San road where I get dropped off. I book into the D & D Inn a very big upmarket back-packer accommodation, by a smiling young women and one of the best in Thailand, but not that cheap by Thai prices, for two nights.

After booking in I head straight to the swimming pool at the top of the hotel for a swim and to relax after the flight. According to my notes I wrote up at the time

I am completely overpowered by just about everything about Thailand, even though according to the BBC World service in 1997 there was an economic crash and according to Chomsky writing in 1993 was one of the poorest countries in the world at one time. This includes the shear beauty of all the women and how exotic they are - how relaxed every body seems to be and as we know from Lonely Planet they don't like 'conflict'. This is why we can be pretty sure that in a previous life Mrs Thatcher was never a Thai person. They do hassle you a little if you are a Western person but not much, the food is wonderful and cheap and so on and on. Not forgetting that this specific road has got to be one of the most amazing in the world, with Robbie Williams ringing in your ears everywhere. I think if I tried I could even buy some active brain cells that work and don't lie for Bush and Blair, well they do need some, don't you think! One site that did amuse me was t-shirts with 'No Money, No Honey' on which is taken from a book, and in essence about sums up how men have to pay for sex anywhere in the world, in many different forms. The site of not seeing at least three back-packers in every square meter is very rare indeed on this road. But any idea that they are all 'middle class' is about as true as there was WMD in Iraqi. Mr Blair may have believed it but no one else did and to think that this very rich man has now changed his religion, from protestant to catholic, again with not one shred of hard evidence that God exists. Before dinner I nip into the local chemist and by some medicine for my upset stomach from a gorgeous salesgirl. Is this good for an old man's heart, I ask myself as I head back to the D & D Inn for dinner with sexy young women everywhere you look. And the reason may be simple if Lonely Planet is correct because this may be the place that static civilisation started, over 10,000 years ago and as sex is a very powerful motivating force in society this may have been the reason that man got stuck in to impress these beautiful women. Jean-Jacques Rousseau did think that this was a terrible mistake, but he had never seen a Thai woman, had he…when he wrote the Discourse on Inequality in the 18th century?

On my first night I have a noodle meal with a glass of beer, it may seem strange from I have just wrote but this was probably the only meal I had in the whole time in Thailand that it was not as good as every other meal I had, over the month I was there. In the morning I get a wonderful free breakfast, part of the deal in the D & D Inn and sit next to a very friendly mature French couple called Danielle and Rene from southern France. They had also travelled in the UK and the USA, but having to go home in the next few days to play bridge, with their friends. This is what they told me, so I presume it was true, but if I leave paradise to play bridge it will have too be in my next life on another Galaxy, not in this one. The fish swimming around the D & D complex also seemed much more laid back and relaxed; so certainly not Western people in a previous life. They told me it was a very good life being a fish apart from when you ended up on a plate for dinner.

As I was feeling a little better I head down the road towards the Grand Palace complex costing about 300 Barts to get in. This place is certainly something very special indeed; it could even have be a Hollywood movie set without Tom Cruise or John Travolta anywhere in site. According to Lonely Planet Bangkok first appeared as a power centre in 1782 with 'Rama I' which was to become the 'Chakri dynasty' which 'continues as the ruling family of Thailand to this day' originally called Siam and in1939 changed to it's present name and not as homogenous as the ruling Elites would like us to think. I spent several hours wondering around this huge complex in shear awe of the splendour and the size of the whole place. The walk back was going to be via the big Buddha but I changed my mind and slowly wondered back to the Khao san area, where many people were wearing yellow tee-shirts and black trouser in honour of the King for being on the throne for 60 years on the streets. When I first saw this it did cause confusion in my mind as I thought they were all working in the tourist industry, but apparently this is not so. In fact in 2007 the King of Thailand was 80 years old, the same age as the British Queen.

Today I had dinner out in a lovely restaurant, while watching stupid little rich boys play English football, well is there really any logic for a kid to be paid 100,000 pounds a week to kick a bladder around a small piece of ground when about three billion people are living on two dollars a day, and many are going hungry. During the next day I just relax around the area have lunch on the street and a swim in the pool waiting for 6pm to come around and a chat with Lee and Jeremy from Sydney. I also listened in on some very amusing conversations when reading near the pool where a young lad with his mates - was telling them that he had been had chatted up by a gay guy, the night before, which he completely disapproved off. Saying something like 'how do you know that you are not gay'?

I had decided that I would spend a few days in Chaing Mai, because of Ben and Jennifer telling me how wonderful it was in India - so at about 17:30 I get a taxi to the Hualamphong train station for an overnight train up north. The help at the station was very impressive as all the staff wanted help silly tourists, like me; who did not know where to go and so on. On the sleeper train I meet several young back-packer Australians also going to Chang Mia and Shane from North Ireland, who did not drink or smoke…the first miracle of the journey, so far. Rachel, Megan, Emma and Natasha were all from Tasmania where I was to go further on in my big adventure. They were all very bright and intelligent young people and I enjoyed their company - Rachel even gave me an article by my hero Noam Chomsky which I had not read. So before I go to sleep when they are all in the bar; some where on the train I read it with awe, like any work of the great man. Being on a sleeper is slightly different in Thailand then India - because in India they do not make your bed where in Thailand they do. At 09:30 we arrive in Chaing Mai and we all go our separate ways; I get a rickshaw to the S K House which is a very nice little back-packers hotel/lodge, run by smiling happy people. What a difference a culture makes to how we feel. The rooms are very basic but it is only 300 Bart per night and there is a lovely little swimming pool for their guests. After having a swim in the pool I venture out in the rain and buy myself a cheap little camera. While having dinner in a small restaurant very near the S K House I am reading the Herald Tribune (19th September

2006 – Andy Xie) and according to them many Chinese people watch American movies which mostly emphasise that all Yanks are rich, so in theory because of this pure propaganda they all want to be rich, but there is no way that this is going to happen, which I thought was a bit rich. As John Tierney suggests in the same paper that 'Capitalism' has a 'heart', surely a contradiction here somewhere but at least he is correct - because he asks why do so many people 'hate' the bloody system, perhaps because it does create massive gulfs between the rich and poor - just a thought John!

The next morning after breakfast and a swim I am ready for a really big adventure, having booked it the day before. To my knowledge my latest hero Bill Bryson has never gone on such a trip. As I am about to have with five German lads two young women from Japan, Christopher and Tanya from Australia a lad from Mexico and wonderful sexy Aphrodite's mum from Hong Kong because she is fifty but does not look like it. We are picked up in two mini-vans and a guide called Abba and two drivers. After driving for at least an hour we go for one and half hour ride on an Elephant. I was with Rodriguez the Mexico lad who was at University in Australia; it was an incredible ride with the Elephants determinate that you feed them bananas before they will go anywhere, so not fools are they? Then we had lunch and a three hour trek up and down hills through rice fields, etc with Abba who was David Attenborough, Bill Oddie and Ray Mears (sic) all rolled into one. To round off the day we go on a bamboo raft for thirty minutes on a river. I was with Aphrodite's mum, who could not swim so very brave to do this, project. Hence, I had to have my legs around her body, on the raft that was travelling at quite a speed with a lad guiding the contraption. At times it did seem a bit dicey because of the speed we were going and how the driver was larking about. I had never done this before like the ride on the Elephant so it was a glorious day out. To top this I went out with Aphrodite's mum to an expensive restaurant, for dinner - the food was crap, the conversation difficult but being with a very attractive women made up for the food and the trouble trying to understand Chinese...pigeon English. On the way back to her hotel she was so overcome with my presence and sexuality she invited me in for a night of passion, I turned it down, no I didn't, well would you? This seems to the problem that the Thai flight attendants are now facing in a fictional account of their lives in a soap opera. In essence in real life do they get up to the same things as the new soap opera is suggesting, like fighting in the aisles and passionate stopovers that is being shown in Thailand at the moment (Guardian – 22 January 2008).

In the morning we visited a shopping complex. Aphrodite's mum did some shopping and got some wonderful pictures of her, looking incredible sexy. While in there I saw some shop assistants eating their lunch while working you would never see this in little Britain for all the tea in China. We also had a light lunch in the complex, with beautiful women everywhere and then went back to her hotel to pick up her luggage and on to the very small airport where she was going to Bangkok and then on to Hong Kong, the same day. I went home for a good rest and a swim; well I needed it after all that passion. This was my Rubicon day/night for me; because after you have made love to an Asian lady there is no going back. For my last day in Chaing Mai I decide to hire a scooter and have a good ride around the city including up the road past the Zoo to take some more pictures of the city from a distance. It was very enjoyable being Che Guevara for another day, I even met an old British man who lives in the city and cycles up this specific hill every day. Before taking the bike back I visit a glorious temple and a wonderful garden and have a cup of tea and a chat to an American who had been all over the world - but informed me that Thailand was the best country in the world, to live and that is why he is intending to stay here for the rest of his life. I think that the only thing that I noticed that can be a nuisance if you are not used to it - which is taking off your shoes even just to use the computer in the D&D Inn.

Again from my notes while eating dinner I had written 'that this place is shear paradise' especially if you are a Western man. I also wrote that there does not appear to be 'any nonsense about the dogma of Individualism' which is the essence of reaching Nirvana, ironically according to people like Karl Popper et al. I did notice several older men with quite young females, in some bars and restaurants - this is not to say that in some strange way they are doing anything illegal… but all Asian women seem to look young anyway, perhaps all the old ones are locked away some where, either in the cellar or the loft. The only complaint I heard while eating in Chaing Mai was from a young Dutch female back-packer who said that she was 'fed up being a walking ATM machine' to her friends. I presume when she was being pestered and hassled, which is a bit of a cheek as millions are a lot poorer then we are. However this was nothing compared with the 'Thailand's dangerous coup' according to the British Economist (23rd -29th September 2006) which I only heard about because my oldest son had texted me from England to be careful Dad. On the same night about an hour later a friend called Eden text me - to say that there had been a bomb scare in Royal Mail in Bristol. where I used to work. The end of the worlds is nigh, I was starting too think after this and reading in the Lonely Planet of the few small scams that can happen to you in Thailand.

The train from Chaing Mai to Bangkok was apparently derailed so I had to go on a bus travelling through the night, on my return journey - which I had done in India and was not impressed at all. Again not impressed but by about 4 o'clock in the morning we were back in Bangkok where I am lucky to book into a very cheap room next to the D & D Inn for about 200 Bart and the mandatory sleep for several hours, to get over it. When I got up I was expecting to see tanks on the street and so on but there was very little of the Military around our area of the city. This was a bloodless coup and according to the Economist since the '1930's' there has been '18 coups'. Not all bloodless so it seems but 'corruption flourished under a succession of Military-favoured prime ministers and was bad, too under the opposition Democrats in the late 1990's' (Economist September 23rd - 29th 2006 p, 11) - so very similar to most of the world then, including little Britain. Where so many rich crooks hang out that doesn't pay tax, where the indigenous 'wage slaves' do - that I am re-naming the place TCGB...meaning The Crooks of Gordon Brown?

For the rest of the day I visited the 'big Buddha' where there was a presence of troops but all smiling and very happy, from what I could see. Where I took several pictures and stood in awe at the size of the statute. The birds in the cage however did not look to happy too me. The catch being that you had to pay to have them released, I could not believe it, myself - to surreal by half for me; something like living in little Britain - but not the long walk back to the Th Khao San road and another rest. Before dinner I have another swim in the D & D pool, very naughty because I was not booked in here and a wonderful full oil massage by a very beautiful woman. No wonder that this place is so relaxed with an incredible friendly culture, very sexy women, wonderful food and most people not raising their voice. What more can any man want, an egoistical culture, Politicians, Lawyers and Western Priests who would not know the truth if you hit them in the face with a wet fish, fish and chips, piss poor weather and warm beer, no thanks?

The next part of this adventure was to take the sleeper train to Surat Thani unfortunately we were supposed to arrive at about 8am but was late so basically the bus that picked us up did not take us to the correct port. After some waiting around for a ferry that was going to take us to Ko Samui, which did not come or may not have existed; we had to get on another bus which took us to another port further down the cost. The ticket original was supposed to be an all inclusive train and ferry affair package - but because of the delays, cocks up etc it did not so we had to buy a ticket for the ferry. Considering it was only a few pounds it was hardly the end of the world. The trouble was that I don't think any of the passengers on our bus was aware because of these delays – which meant we ended up in Ao Thong Yang port instead of Na Thon on Ko Samui. When we arrived at Ao Thong Yang I could not get on a mini-bus with some other people from the ferry to the other side of the Island. So when one driver tried to rip me off, was going to charge me the same price as six other people in the same vehicle - I told him to get lost and walked up the road to a very small hotel, called the Baan Ta-luanoz guest house. This was probably the only time in a complete month in Thailand that I got stressed out because of this con-man, as I had to walk for at least two miles with my suitcase on wheels… to the hotel. Sometimes in life a cock up cum mistake can turn out to be a positive instead of a negative. This is what happened to me on this occasion. After my rest and a shower I venture down the road to a very posh/upmarket restaurant called Big John's, certainly one of the best that I have ever been in – in all my life on this little Planet, in the Milky Way Galaxy. Well how do we know that there is not an Island called Ko Samui and a Big John's somewhere in the Andromeda Galaxy, we don't do we? During the meal there was traditional Thai dancing and a wonderful show all free and part of making the customers happy and after the meal they even took me home, for nothing. If this was too happen in little Britain it would have been in a dream, or may be a nightmare.

In the morning I get a very cheap taxi across the Island to the Big Buddha area and book into the Shambala complex of separate bungalows for a good negotiated price for five nights which must have been out of season for that price. This place is owned and run by Jules and Jessica and would agree with Lonely Planet that this is a laid back place with a slight hippy feel about it. The warm beautiful sea is only two seconds from your door, which adds to this exotic destination. Because I had got so stressed out the day before I venture down the road for a massage from Nan - it was another wonderful experience from the 'Land of Smiles'. The next day I hire a complete snorkelling outfit from the people next door and go snorkelling for a few hours around the shore near by to the Shambala complex. Considering that the Island only a few miles from this one is supposed one of the best places on the Planet to dive and snorkel I was expecting that this may have just as good. Not so; I could hardly see anything at all, an ideal place too hide WMD but that's about all.

After dinner I meet my new Aphrodite for the second time in the Sky bar, I had met her for about thirty minutes in the afternoon before I had my massage, helping her with her English. Where the original Aphrodite had come out of the sea in Cyprus this one came out of the sea in Ko Samui. You could say that Richard Gere fell in love with Julia Roberts in Pretty Woman – I fell in love with Aphrodite (late thirties); because she was so loving towards me for helping her with her English lessons and other favours and her beauty. She is my Catherine Zeta Jones look alike and I am not worth millions like Michael Douglas. In fact from what I can see in Thailand like Southern Africa making love with the opposite sex is no big deal - like it is in the West, enjoying yourself is what life seems to be all about here, and so it should. Whatever the truth is about how women perceive men from quite a young age (all stupid apart from Dad, I would have thought) - I presume and how we can all be manipulated by our normal healthy needs and vice versa - for example: may I suggest middle class feminists in the Western World assimilate and try and understand Maslow's Law of Hierarchical needs and the structure of our epoch and now with the comodification of everything, especially over the last thirty years. In essence does anyone like being exploited...I know I don't! Or as Marx correctly wrote: 'political power, properly so called, is merely the organized power of one class for oppressing another.... The executive of the modern state is but a committee for managing the affairs of the whole bourgeoisie' (quoted in David McLellan Marx fb 1975).

The only downside that I could see about Ko Samui is that it is all about making money out of silly tourists and their love affair with 4 by 4's. This whole country is in love with these useful functional trucks, from what I observed while travelling around the country. But even Jules was complaining that some people were going 'bust' in Ko Samui because the 'Government has tightened up on Property laws'. However I would suggest who has not heard a small business people complaining about the State if they can rip them off, in one-way or the other – all over the world. This is what I was thinking about when having a very lovely dinner of Thai duck curry with pineapple and tomatoes, delicious in the Shambla restaurant. However once you have been to Chaing Mai which is very cheap, you do notice that Bangkok and Ko Samui is a lot more expensive in relative terms.

To impress my new Aphrodite I hire a scooter out for about fourteen days, well I can't afford a Private Jet like Douglas, can I? Then take her for a ride on an Elephant

- a ride right around the Island visiting the Hin Lat Falls and a number of beaches for a swim; relaxation and the tan to go with it. But I had to do more something real extraordinary, like flying to the Moon in a spacecraft made of wood. Don't be silly Brian start talking sense, so here goes. Aphrodite had told me that she would like to visit Phuket which is on the south east side of Thailand, for a holiday sometime in the future. The next day I try to make her dreams come true by driving her up to the ferry at Na Thon on the scooter. We get on the ferry and head towards Dan Sak which takes an hour and half. And then on to Surat Thani where 1500 years ago it was part of the Mahayana Buddhist Srivijaya Empire according to Lonely Planet. The road was wide and virtual traffic free most of the way but after travelling for at least two hours - I thought that perhaps I had bit of more than I could chew, in one day; so decided that Krabi (pop 29,300) would be a better choice for the first night. It is very simple to drive in Thailand for anyone from little Britain because they drive on the left. The only difference when driving along the main roads that we were on was that to come off on the left you actual make a right turn then go back up the road to turn off left, on the other side of the road - slightly confusing but true. We also had to come off the main road to get some fuel in a little town about an hour or so from our destination, as there were no petrol stations on this main road. I also passed five girls on two scooters chatting while driving along the road, not something you would ever see in little Britain or most places in the world, I would have thought. By the time we got near Krabi (a region as well) it was starting to get dark, but very beautiful and surreal scenery as you come into the area – just like Aphrodite. During the first part of this journey Aphrodite did say 'that I am scared Brian are you sure that you know what you are doing'. 'Don't worry sweetheart I do this sort of thing all the time, hire out a little scooter get a sexy Asian lady to share the ride and head off to somewhere I had never been before'. I was lying of course! Probably the craziest thing I have ever done in my whole life but it was worth it. The first night in Krabi was spent in a small hotel, after booking in and a rest we went to a wonderful restaurant, for dinner. On the way there I got a puncture which I only found out about after dinner, on the back wheel. So I had to push it the 100 yards back to the hotel, but very lucky for me between the restaurant and the hotel there was a repair garage that put a new tyre on in the morning. Well this is paradise, so everything is so easy, for men.

After this major surgery on the scooter, which was very cheap to repair - while having a smashing breakfast in the same restaurant we have a small drive around the town and find out what time the ferry goes to Ko Phi Phi Don in the afternoon. While waiting we have lunch and I send a few emails to friends around the globe, including Nancy Jennings; from the same place and watch a movie on the television. At the allotted time we drive down to the ferry terminal park the scooter up because you are not allowed to take any vehicles on to Ko Phi Phi Don and do the paper work which was a bit of a hassle, as the assumption seemed to be that we had landed from Mars and not Ko Samui. There is nothing in the literature that I could find that once we got on the old ferry the sea would get very rough, indeed and cost 350Bart one way, each. On the day that we went to utter paradise this happened too us - it was one of the most frightening experiences that I had ever had, poor Aphrodite was nearly sick. Water coming in everywhere and the little old boat rocking and rolling all over the place and to think that we were on our way according to Lonely Planet to 'one of the most beautiful islands in Thailand'…heaven - but I am a secular humanist so believe that heaven and hell is here and no where else, so was not eager to die before I am an old man, hopefully in one of my Aphrodite's arms.

There is no doubt about it these Islands including Phi Phi Don and Ph Phi Leh where the movie the 'Beach' was filmed is one of the most beautiful places on earth. This was my conclusion so we stayed two nights and forgot about going to Phuket altogether. On landing, as we had not booked in advance there is a lottery system for the accommodation, so everyone does some bartering until you get roughly what you need, a clean room with a shower, for a reasonable price. Once all the plans are agreed we get on a small motorbike with a side car and travel the half-mile to the digs. The room was small and spotless and next door I met Steve from Essex who had sadly broken up with his girlfriend, of three years before setting off on his travels. Hence, I presume the reason that he seemed a bit gloomy about travelling in the developing world; where according to Steve it is a very dangerous practise to-do. Like getting gassed on buses and robbed or being held up at gun-point in Bangkok.

Once wonderful sexy Aphrodite is made up and ready - it takes for-ever just like most women in the world, when putting their war paint on. Well I have had girlfriends from Africa as well as the UK, so know something about this whole process, who once said 'the world is a stage and we are mere actors up on it', surely not Shakespeare was it? Because if he did Women of the world are the true masters of the stage, in most walks of life, they never stop acting, do they men of the world? We venture around the corner to a very small restaurant cum bar run by Chris from Paris who with his beautiful Thai wife was nearly killed in the tsunami of Christmas 2004. The whole place was completely crushed and according to Chris 3000 people died in this area, at-least his pet squirrel survived. But now rising above the ashes like a Phoenix and where ever you look building work is progressing, Lonely Planet writers are aghast and these happenings. Dinner was lovely as was the sweet back at the hotel - after and the little walk we took through the town. The next morning after breakfast we go to the beach for a swim, snorkel and relax - on the way it started raining so before the swim we had to run for cover in one of the restaurants cum bars. When you are sharing your time with such beauty meaning the place as well Aphrodite you can start to float off to other places that don't exist as you are on such a high, as if I had joined the hippy movement, unfortunately for me I am about forty years too late. The lunch was not bad as well where I met another Englishman who was writing a travel book so I shared my experience with him; I think that he thought that he had met James Joyce in Pula - instead of an ex-colonial serf who only had six years formal education, on Phi Phi Don. After more fun and frolics we returned to the hotel for a rest and another dinner in Chris's lovely restaurant and some more gorgeous ice cream or should that be hot pudding. After breakfast on the third day we climbed the hill over looking the Island and the view was magnificent, where we took several pictures and just admired the whole place in all its glory. A walk over to the other beach on the North West side and a walk into town for the ferry back to Krabi. Going back was calm and very relaxing; picking up the scooter was dead easy without any hassle, this time. I had decided that I would like to visit the area around Ao Nang, so off we went on our little scooter towards our destination. Once we got into the little town I saw a sign for a hotel so took the dirt track down to an incredible little place called the Green View Village, not in the Lonely Planet for some reason because it should be. Aphrodite was so impressed that we booked into the complex for two nights for 600 Barts. Before dinner we had a look around the little town where I bought Aphrodite some clothes which made her happy. Then off to dinner at another wonderful restaurant, just down the road where before we ordered the meal the heavens opened, I did think that we should have built the Ark but after about an hour it stopped and we managed to move to a drier area of the restaurant. Thai food is wonderful, especially the fish dishes which are my favourite - after I have some photos taken of us for prosperity we go back to the Village for some more sweet or should that be some more hot pudding.

In the morning we have a very pleasant breakfast in the glorious Village restaurant sitting just above some Japanese Gold fish looking very relaxed and happy. And would you believe it they actual spoke to me during our English breakfast and they were not as happy as they seemed. Because apparently some of the female fish are very bitchy to one another especially in the mornings when putting there make up on – especially Sandra the dominate female who wanted to hog the only mirror in the bathroom from Nede and Ennovy, the two very sexy mature fish, her nearest rivals. Thank God I was born a male, that's all I can say. During the day we went to the local beach for a swim and some vitamin D, I tried to swim out to one of the small islands but decided that it was a little too far. However when the tide went out Aphrodite and I managed to walk to the other Island close by to investigate for whatever there may have been to see, not a lot but it was worth it. Lunch was just as good as the scenery and the beach around this part of the Krabi region. Something that I did notice when in Ao Nang you will often see three or four people on a scooter like India and young boys driving scooters - dinner in the evening was just as delicious as our lunch near the beach.

After breakfast the next day we head back down the road towards Surat Thani, according to Lonely Planet there was still lots of things to see, so sometime in the future I must return. Going back the weather was not as good as coming so several times we had to stop because once the heavens opens it rains like hell. For lunch we stop in a small local restaurant in Surat Thani for some more wonderful Thai food. I can't get enough of it, just like Aphrodite, I especially like the soups. The ferry only cost me 250 Barts for both us and the scooter to go to Ko Samui where to go to Phi Phi Don one way for one person was 350Bart, quite a contrast in prices, don't you think?

By the time we get back to the Big Buddha Beach area it is starting to get dark so I book into the Chez Ban-Ban complex for my final few days in Thailand - just down the road from the Shambala where I had stayed previously. Aphrodite and I are both so tired that we both drop into bed for a good rest.

According to Lonely Planet Ko Samui (pop 45,800 – part of the 'golden egg -laying goose') is the second most popularly resort next to Phuket in Thailand with a plethora of restaurants, excellent beaches resorts and so on. Certainly the beaches at Hat Chaweng and Hat Lamai are very popular where I took my lovely Thai dish, for a swim and relaxation. Near to the Big Buddha where I also took Aphrodite for a look around - there was even a BBC restaurant, not run by ex-staff from this august institution in London, I don't think! But you never know as some people like Jeremy Paxman (BBC News-night and Author) and the Radio 2 disc jockeys earn so much they have got to slash their spare dosh some where, have they not? And we pay them through a ruthless regressive tax, on the whole population of little England, where you can go to prison if you don't pay it, or can't afford to pay it or the 1000 pound fine…bastards.

As I noted before in this chapter, something I kept thinking about while in Thailand you do not see old women anywhere, the reason I am telling you this is that I asked Steve from New Zealand this question, who owns the Office bar and restaurant but he seemed very perplexed. I think that because there are so many beautiful young Thai women everywhere including Steve's wife/girlfriend, called Jit (a lovely tree so David

Bellamy told me) you completely forget that there is such a thing as old women; this also applies to pregnant women. While having dinner in Steve's bar one night I met Dan and Barbara from the USA who actually live in Ko Samui and seem to love it, apparently they were going to Phuket but because of the tsunami they got frightened about moving there and I don't think that Bush is going to invade the place, well not for a few years, we hope. I would have also got very frightened if I had high tea in a hotel in little Britain because it can cost you '60 pounds', today and now becoming very popular with the 'upper classes' there. I had high tea in the Chez Ban-Ban on several occasions for 150Bart and probably tasted twice as good, as the expensive hotels in little Britain.

Another down-side to little Britain apart from the weather and the need to understand how class works, especially the correct nouns to use if you are unlucky enough to meet the 'upper class' - is that we are afraid to be friendly to one another, and even touching another person apart from shaking hands is very unusual indeed. But in Thailand this seems to be the norm - people like to touch one another and be open to one another. On the last day I was with Aphrodite I took her for lunch on a scooter near the little airport where she treated me. And what I thought was very amusing was that she seemed to be talking about sex with the young girls in the restaurant as if we were discussing the weather in little Britain and it was nothing to be ashamed about. The idea of this happening in most places in the Western world would be like suggesting that Lord Sir Jeffery Archer's of the NGC 4314 Galaxy, or is that Western-Super-Mare CV was a real one and not a work of fiction like his books.

'On the Beach' restaurant just down the road from the Big Buddha beach was the loveliest restaurant I took my Thai dish to for a wonderful three course dinner on my last night in Ko Samui, next to the beach. A bit expensive but really worth every cent as there was even live music with a father and son duo, which seemed to love one of my adolescent heroes, called Elvis Presley, because nearly every second song was one of his. The last meal was wonderful, but the thought of leaving Aphrodite was something like the journalist that Michael Caine recently played in a Graham Greene's movie (from the book, which I read in Saigon), The Quiet American; set in Vietnam in the 1950 and 1960's. In essence very sad indeed but hopefully I will return and see her again. The last night was very relaxing and passionate and very sad in the morning when I waved goodbye to her from the open taxi, taking me to Na Thon. I wonder if I could buy Aphrodite from her dad 'for two pigs and a handful of shillings', just a thought and a joke - as this is what Errol Flynn did once in the South Pacific according to David Bret, sounds very good value too me.

When I got to Surat Thani I was going to go back to Bangkok on a train but some how got conned into taking a small mini bus for a cheaper price. With several other people including a big Brit from Clevedon who must be one of the most unpleasant English people I have ever met abroad. He was only an English teacher, in Bangkok with his wife but I think because he comes from Clevedon (near Bristol) that he thought he was a British Aristocrat - why the hell did we not have a French style revolution 200 years ago? Although I was sitting very close to him he never spoke once, while on the Bus, what did I say about the English a little while ago? During the journey I did speak to him once, out side of the bus but when we stopped for dinner at an incredible road side restaurant; he deliberately kept away from me while eating.

Although it is very hard to criticize Thailand in anyway because of their so friendly culture apart from there support for 'the Japanese in WWII to seize back Cambodia and Lao territory returned to French Indochina in 1907' (LP p, 38). However I did notice that when we were getting close to the Capital at 12:30 am, that even at that time of morning many Lorries were still on the road. You would not normally see this sort of active in the Western world. Also in southern Thailand there is a problem between different ethnic groups (More 4 News 25 July 2007) where even the State may be using 'brutal methods' to crush the insurgents and vice-versa. Also according to the Guardian (July 31st 2007) at least 1.5 million Burmese work in trades that many Thais don't want to do and sometimes in dubious circumstances for very low wages. Not are all are legal migrants, so it appears and some are sent back. Also according to the ABC Australia broadcasting service (8th December 2007) before the 2006 Army coup thousands of people may have been killed by the state for drug offences that may even not have happened., just because you could report people you did not like to the police. And according to Chomsky in the Vietnam War the CIA funded Thai troops to fight in Laos 'without the authorization of the congress' (Chomsky 2003).

For my finally two nights in Thailand I stayed in very cheap accommodation near to the D & D Inn on Th

Khao San road, where according to the Daily Mail's on sale in the shops - 'British taxes are soaring' and it's the 'middle class' who are hardest hit, poor sods. I feel so sorry for Daily Mail readers don't you? As I do wonder if the six million who read this tosh on a daily basis; have any active brain cells in their little heads. I was also watching Bono and friend on the Larry King show from the USA when having breakfast and was not impressed as he seemed very confused about how our epoch works. His intentions may be honourable as he has now been knighted for his efforts to get rid of third world debt, which will probably never happen in my lifetime, or even my grandchildren's for that matter - but when U2 is worth '469 million' (Sunday Times Rich List 2007) you do start to wonder are these pop stars promoting themselves or the cause? But would he do what Howard Slater has done; who to me sounded like a neo-saint - who I met on the last night in BKK at a local eating outlet on the street, near my digs. Having a few drinks with him after in a nearby bar. Apparently he had been travelling for over seventeen months with many months in India where he met Chandra and her son in Calcutta, who was living on the streets in makeshift accommodation. He told me that he actually lived on the streets with her & son and helped her out with food and so on, something I don't think Bono would dream of ever doing, do you?

I got ripped-off only for about the second time by a taxi driver on the way to the new incredible out of this world new Airport which is not so far out of the city as Taxi drivers like too tell you. What was truly amazing about the place that you where offered free food and drinks before the flight, something you very unlikely to see in little England in a million years of evolution.... so I took it. I also read a notice which said 'Long live the King' at the Airport - which is something else you may never ever hear in Britain, if Charles the 3rd loses his head in the Guillotine party on top of the Tor, that I am arranging, after my death. Well Voltaire did it, why can't I?

But before this happy event happens I am back in Bangkok (BKK) arriving from Battambang in Cambodia by bus in December 2007, never to be repeated again in my life-time because the road is still under construction - having been there and Vietnam researching the final part of this project. Again getting into Thailand from Cambodia took sometime at the passport control point at Poipet - because there was only two officers checking our passports. But for company I did have Richard and Caroline a lovely well educated English couple who are doing a world tour over a year, who I had met in Battambang. Richard who in real life is an accountant is a budding Bob Dylan, so he informed me, is there a contradiction here I ask myself and Caroline is into Man-management - something I thought all women were into! On arrival in BKK I book into the Chart guesthouse next door to the D&D Inn on the Th Khao San road. I had stayed in this place before - so were well aware that it was cheap and very basic. The next morning I pop up to the swimming pool in the D&D Inn for a swim against all the rules of the great game. Also as this was my third time on this road where most backpackers stay while visiting BKK; it did not seem as incredible as the first visit. In essence slightly dirty and a little bit sleazy and of course more expensive than other parts of the city, even a few

streets away. But at night it takes on a glamorous feel
of excitement with humour thrown in and what about
this for pure satire as seen on the back of my door in the
Chart guesthouse. An Aussie upset by what a Brit had said
unrepeatable in print about Aussies, wrote that POME
stands for 'Prisoner of Mother England' very true for the
many of us, living in relative poverty, in Little Britain. As
I was shattered travelling most of the day before I have
a relaxing day by the pool: thinking, reading, writing
notes and planning my last few days before flying back
to Britain on the 16th December 2007. In the evening I
decided to have a fully body oil massage at the Yannee,
one of the best experience you can have anywhere in the
world. Tonight I was also extremely lucky as I had very
exotic Chor which means a flower, who I had last year in
the same place, but this time with a new hair style which
made her look very sexy indeed, even with my glasses
off.

The next morning I am up early as I am getting a
mini-bus to the River Kwai, it was meant to leave at 7am
but eventually we left sometime after 8am from Th Khao
San road with Lewis Hamilton's tutor behind the wheel.
On several occasions I did think I am not going to see
my 60th birthday at this rate because of his very risky
driving practices which went on for over two hours. The
first stop was the war cemetery was where we nearly all
ended up in with this young man driving near the river;
it was kept immaculate by the gardeners. I took several
photos of the graves including A.H. Withnell who was
26 when he died and F.C. North who was 43 when he
died, both in 1943. Then on to the war museum and
bridge which was not the original one, a little of the

original is in the museum as I understand it. We had to pay about 50 Bart to get into the museum but well worth it with lots of historical evidence from this period of history as was the walk over the metal bridge. I took lots of photos including one of the original inside the museum, as it says on a plaque: 'The Old khwae River Bridge Built by the Prisoners of War and Japanese Army's Control' not very good grammar but who ever wrote this was not English, I presume. Also according the photos I took in the museum there was many nationals who built the bridge but in the movie it was suggested that it was mostly the British prisoners of war who built it, surely not another pack of lies from the English Ruling Class, again was it?

The only sad truth about this place now is that it is just another tourist trap for the unwary, where in the war it was a hell-hole for the people working on the bridge, but I did buy a T-shirt as evidence that I had been here. Recently I had heard an old man on Desert Island Discs (BBC Radio 4) who was actually here and his description of the place was horrendous. Man's cruelty to other people he can get power over seems to be an on going process for the time being and that is why this is not the end of history and if Francis Fukuyama and his cohorts think this way they need their heads tested for sanity. The movie called the Bridge on the River Kwai made in Sri Lanka in 1956/57 hardly touches on the suffering of the men building the bridge - but the conflict between Colonel Saito and Colonel Nicholson. In fact if anyone wants too understand the British class system get a social science degree and study this movie in depth, its well worth it. Alex Guinness won an Oscar for his role as

Colonel Nicholson who would not consent to manual work for the officer class.

The guides on this tour were excellent as there were many different groups all together doing different things. Some like me was on a one day trip; others were on a two day and so on. The next part of this day out was to actually go on a train for about 40 minutes after being taken down the road in a taxi with Lewis Hamilton's father driving this time. We made the train station just; I think and had a splendid journey through this part of Thailand which is very pretty with the river and hills in the background. After taken several pictures and enjoying the whole process we are taken for lunch on a boat tided up to the river bank. The meal was wonderful all part of the deal, I sat next to a French couple from Paris, not stuck up this time as they were normal working class people. Then on to Sai Yok Noi Waterfalls a natural small wonder - where I spent about two hours with Sam from north Lincolnshire. Who had spent six months travelling to: America, Latin America, Big Oz and the Far East. He had gone to Oxford as an undergraduate studying biochemistry, but afterwards went into accountancy, apparently living near to the great Richard Dawkins, when at Oxford. Sam was a very interesting young man because he was an expert on pig farming, which his family had been doing for some time, with other commodities in Lincolnshire. And sadly it would seem that pigs don't have sex anymore, but special seaman is bought into the farm for the females to be impregnated by hand, or whatever and after six months the young pigs are slaughtered for market. It would seem that if the meat is not up to standard as sanctioned by Marks & Spencer through the abattoir you are in trouble. I feel sorry for the pigs my self and just hoping that I don't come back as one of Sam's family in my next life, especially a male one!

On the way back to BKK in the min-bus I was sitting behind two delightful young women, called Kirsty & Ingrid and Hans next to me - who had also been to a Temple where some Monks keep animals including Tigers. It would seem that one Tiger got excited seeing sexy Kirsty and peed on her. I suggested to her that it was probably Errol Flynn in a previous life, as I remembered it from the chapter about Big Oz, he did a lot of bonking with very beautiful young women when alive in that form, lucky git.

On arriving back in Bangkok (BKK) I decide that my last few days in the city should be in better accommodation then the Chart guesthouse, so I moved next door into the D&D Inn again - booked in by some of the most pleasant young people that I have met in Thailand.

The next day I had what I call an hours walk through the urban jungle dodging traffic, conman and every other variable we all meet in any large city to the Dusit Palace Park; according to Lonely Planet a must see while visiting BKK. Especially the amazing Vimanmek Teak museum who 'in the early 20th century Rama V lived in this graceful 81-mansion and today it contains a treasure-trove of early Ratanakosin art objects and antiques' (LP p, 115). But before I got in to the park I had to pay 100 Bart for the privilege of seeing this magnificent teak building and a stroll in the gardens before I went into this complex. Strangely as it may seem we were not allowed to take anything like cameras or bags into the building itself, not to sure why but that was the rules, so we put them into a locker for 20Bart. At the time I did find the whole experience quite bizarre because before you could enter the building you were told to take off your shoes and then you had to wait for your correct language group to form, so in my case it was an English group. You were not allowed to go around the building on your own, only in a group. However the whole experience was well worth it apart from time to time you may end up in the wrong language group which meant you could get lost in translation to borrow a title of a very good movie, from a few years ago. In my group there were ten people from Riyadh the capital of Saudi Arabia who spoke English and their own language - which at times I did wonder if I had died and gone to another Galaxy. These people were probably the biggest I have ever seen in my life and if they had been on the boat between Siem Reap and Battambang (sic) I don't think we would have made it. Having only visited a few grand house in the UK this one was more unique as all the trapping of an upper class family were mostly still in place, including gifts given to the King, over many years, including a piano played by the invisible man, near the end of the tour. On leaving the building and putting your shoes on you were then allowed to take photographs of the building it self. After this big adventure I visit one museum, in the grounds out of two that is dedicated to the current King's pictures taken over a life time. I am not an expert photograph but I thought that they were excellent, especially of his beautiful wife when she was young. This King who is also 80 seems to have many talents including playing nearly every instrument under the sun, I don't think the British Monarch can do this, do you? Before walking back to my digs, full of the joys of spring I have a lovely cup of coffee, for a very reasonable price. To finish the day off I have another wonderful massage with exotic Chor who afterwards I treated to a dinner for a staggering 429 Bart....just joking, of course, but as she was dressed in such a tight short sexy skirt I did think that perhaps I was dreaming, again. On my last day in Thailand this time I had another flash of genius inspiration when I decided that the whole world should read Noam Chomsky for at-least one day a month, as I did on this particular day at the pool side of the D&D Inn - which we could call a Noam Chomsky day of neo- enlightenment. What a brilliant idea Brian you deserve a knighthood and booker prize, now go back to sleep and stop dreaming. But in conclusion although I would love to come and live here if the State would have me, I do feel on reflection that perhaps like Columbus when he fist got to the new world that the people he met were 'lovable, tractable, peaceable, gentle, decorous' and 'the most guileless, the most devoid of wickedness and duplicity' (Chomsky 1993 p, 204). Which I would say about the vast majority of people I met in Thailand, but of course for a successful capitalist economy to work this can not be the case of everyone and of course the Spanish elite turned on the people Columbus met with ruthless brutality, like most Elites of this little planet, according to Chomsky.

Chapter Four

- Southern Asia - Vietnam

It's the 25th of September 2007 and I have just bought a ticket for Vietnam from Chris Sewell, in Bristol - no relation of Brian's the world's greatest art critic, so he just told me, from a cottage on the Moon. The reason for this course of action is to complete my final two chapters of this incredible book, so hopefully in a few weeks time the second part of this odyssey will begin at Heathrow airport and it did on the 5th November 2007 at terminal 3. Again leaving from this place was/is share hell. I was thinking to myself at the time that it did resemble my early life in the Falkland Islands when my stepfather was a shepherd. Dogs control the sheep in close formation but this time the masses/passengers were being controlled by security people. I was also very concerned that so many people were reading the Daily Mail, the nemesis of all Guardian readers, like me, especially the old hippy guy lounging on the floor reading such tripe - but also very pleased to see so many passengers reading the Guardian. The flight it self was not as comfortable as before as we were this time all jammed in like sardines in a can and the seats were as hard as a rock, the plane was quite old, so probably the reason, I guess. But the Malaysian crew were wonderful especially Joey Liew who was extremely beautiful, sexy and a bottom to kill for who seemed to have been allocated to our section of the aircraft too serve all our needs. Because I am a semi-vegetarian I always now have this type of meal on flights - as I always think it is much better than the alternative. Against all odds I even watched Die Hard 4 another stupid American movie with Bruce Wills who's story line was as surreal as seeing an old hippy reading the Daily Mail and as we all know if there is one grain of truth in this rightwing rag, it is like walking on water, a very unlikely experience. We landed at Kuala Lumpur the next morning were I had to wait for several hours for the on -going aircraft to Vietnam, whose current population is 84 million. While waiting I had a tasty little meal in one of the cleanest airports in the world, in this case having to go from one side of the airport to the other on a smart train, where according to my notes at the airport or on the aircraft going to Vietnam, it said 'love peace harmony & love', something you don't see in most countries anywhere, well most are run by neo-brutes, including the West. After another wonderful vegetarian meal in a smaller sardine can than the last one - we land at Hanoi, population at-least 3.5 million, apparently once called Thanh Long meaning the 'city of the Soaring Dragon' according to Lonely Planet. I was hoping to be met by Hanoi Jane (sic) one of my favourite actress of all time but according to her agent she was busy in Hollywood making jean adverts and as we all know she may be 70 but what a bottom. However

I was very lucky to meet Nicholas & Emma from Paris just outside the airport who was also going into the centre. Something I recommend to all backpackers is to come together at airports to try and prevent the great taxi scam at virtually everywhere in the world. Most good travel books will all always tell you about these scams or hustles, but not everyone has one. But some how probably because we were not really aware of the language of money in Vietnam we were nearly ripped-off again, by the time we got into the city centre, by the taxi firm. Hence, where in Lonely Planet it said it should only cost about 150,000 dong the taxi driver was trying too charge us 500,000 dong each. We stood our ground and told him to get lost and told him he was crook and conman, eventually by the time he dropped me off in the Old Quarter of the city he was starting to relent to our wishes, leaving on good terms with Nicholas and Emma that we had seen through his scam. The hotel I had picked out in the Lonely Planet was called City Gate, a slightly chaotic part of town, similar to Delhi, which was full - but got taken to a nearby one called the Prince for 25 dollars a night a bit dear for me, on a motorbike. Truly amazing and looked like a 5 star Hotel to me, completely spotless with satellite TV, double bed, hot water, shower, bath, beer & water in the fridge, etc. Before dropping off to sleep I was watching a TV documentary about camels, in Egypt, very interesting and a place I have yet to visit. I also was reading a book called The Essential Tao by Thomas Cleary all you need to know why Asian people are different than us, but with the essential needs of everyone, food and sex come to mind, for starters.

According to Lonely Planet this part of town is 'modern yet medieval, there is no better way to spend some time in Hanoi than walking the streets, simply soaking up the sites, sounds and smells' (LP p, 357). Which I did for a few days, even seeing artists doing paintings in the shops which is often an extension of their homes - after changing hotels close by to the Wing Hotel where I was booked in by gorgeous beautiful Wang which was excellent value - because there is 31,000 dong to the pound (November 2007), not the Thu Giang guesthouse I originally wanted, as again full, as was the Hanoi backpackers hostel so missing all the action on the rooftop bar, if Lonely Planet is to believed! The only trouble in Hanoi that I could see was that if you were not very careful you may end up dead very quickly by being run over by one of the millions of motor scooters in the city and Vietnam generally, if not very alert and of course the vast majority of women are again incredible in this part of the world.

My first adventure after changing hotels was to the Thap Rua (Tortoise Tower) on the lake of Hoan Kiem where I met Don from Perth. On the way meeting three lovely mature ladies from Sydney whose hotel was like a building site, being hassled by a book seller trying to sell me a book for 400,000 dong, but mainly noticing how clean Hanoi is compared with many cites around the globe. Again according to Lonely Planet the reason that this lake is so called is because heaven gave Emperor Ly Thai To a magical sword in the mid-15th century too drive the Chinese out of Vietnam. Apparently one day while out on the lake with the sword after this event he came upon a giant tortoise that grabbed the sword and disappeared beneath into the depths of the lake and ever since it has been known as the Ho Hoan Kiem...'Lake of the Restored Sword' because the tortoise returned the sword to its divine owners, so now you know, don't you? I should also note that Don and I got on like a house on fire probably because we were of a similar age and both loved Thailand. It seems that in Australia Don is a 'Land assessor' something like 'K' in the Castle written by Franz Kafka for those who are not well read, I presume - which I have been reading on and of for years, but still have not completed it; since first visiting Prague several years ago. Sadly Don's wife has had a stoke so lives in a nursing home, but most important we both agreed on what I have said on the chapters about Australia - that Western women all need to take a lesson on how to treat men from Thai women; especially the very stroppy ones who write for the Daily Mail and even the Guardian, for that matter....something I have been wanting to say for years. On the way back to the Hotel I had a cup of tea by the Lake and took my notes in very delightful surroundings. Reflecting on what Don had been saying to me that more than likely most Western women are dead jealous of how sexy Asian women really are to most males around the globe.

My next adventure was to get a bike/scooter for 40,000 dong double of what Lonely Planet said I should have paid to the Ethnology museum drove by Tran Van Dai a must do experience; just to get the adrenalin flowing through the veins. If you have a week heart I would not recommend it, as I don't want to be sued by some over weight moron. According to Lonely Planet again this is a place that 'should not be missed' on your expedition around the globe after reading this amazing book about my adventures, don't over do it Brian, it's not you. It was designed with assistance from Musee de I'Homme in Paris and is a real delight about the hill tribes and their cultures in Vietnam. According to a leaflet I picked up in the place 'the Viet (or Kinh) make up almost 87% of the population, comprising the largest of 54 ethnic groups belong to 5 ethnolinguistic families' and so on.

The grounds is all so worth a stroll around, as you can actually go into the huts that have been constructed and hopefully get some idea how this people live in their normal environment. With couples that had just been married getting some photo's taken, something that I had never seen before in my life. After my normal rest back at the Hotel I go to Gecko's for dinner just across the road from the Wing, a small but pleasant and spotless restaurant. Which is so famous that it is even mentioned in a leaflet on Hanoi that I was looking through while eating? Apparently I had Sweet and Sour Prawn with rice and a free glass of beer and very tasty it was with Johnny Cash belting out of the loud speakers. Slightly ironic, I thought, as on the TV in the corner there was one of Tom Hank's movies and if you think about it seriously it was only a few years ago the USA State was bombing this place with B52's. It was while I was in Gecko's that I could understand why everything in Hanoi seemed so clean, as even at 8pm at night women come around with a small cart cleaning the streets, more on this later. In my notes, I even mentioned that I thought Mrs Thatcher would love Vietnam now as everyone seems to be into making money, so if she did come her it would take her back to the corner shop in Grantham, Lincolnshire and her petty bourgeoisie upbringing. According to Huy Chinh who had an artist shop very close to the restaurant - it is better to own your business, as rent is very high in Hanoi. After the meal in Gecko's I walk up the street to Mike's Jazz club for a beer where on the way there a guy asked me if I wanted a women or some dope, I declined both. The beer was very pleasant but it was too early for any Jazz at that time of night, but as my old Mum may have said, it is very posh in here Brian?

On my second night in Hanoi I did not sleep well - perhaps because of the fumes from the bikes, so finished reading Thomas Cleary and start to read Ray Bradbury's Fahrenheit 451 a must read before you die. A futuristic story where it is a sin to read or own a book which may happen if Capitalism gets any more brutal in the future than it is already, especially in little class ridden hell holes like Britain and the USA, but of course in America they try and pretend that class does not matter, pure rubbish of the highest order. Strangely as it may seem I did meet Elliot (see below) from California who did not like Michael Moore because he seemed to be sticking up for the working class in the USA, presuming that as Elliot was a doing a degree he was not from this group and he also seemed well read, not a trait found in most working people around the globe, anywhere in fact.

After breakfast the next morning I am off to the amazing Temple of Literature where originally guests sometimes arrived on horseback. It would have been a long ride from the Falkland Islands but I did go to school on a horse so would have made it eventually, but today I am on the back of a motorbike. This Temple was dedicated to Confucius in 1070 by Emperor Ly Thanh Tong and was later established as a University of Mandarins. A few years ago I did read at-least four books about Indo -China and Confucius they were fascinating, as I was hoping to go there to teach English, but sadly turned down by the British Council and the VSO. There are five courtyards within the complex with a reflecting pool in the front section. Apparently in the 15th century 'Emperor Le Thang Tong ordered the establishment of stelae honouring the men who had received doctrines in triennial examinations dating back to 1442' (LP p, 356). Confucius (Kung Fu-tse) lived between 551 – 479 BC he was a native of the Kingdom of Lu in ancient China now in Qufu district who was a great politician, educator and philosopher, who foundered a doctrine. Somehow I don't think the ruthless philosophy of Mrs Thatcher's mainly taken from Hayek's, Popper's et al will live for as long as Confucius, do you? According to the leaflet I took this information from - 'virtue' seems to be the key element in training for high State employees, similar in essence to Plato famous axiom that knowledge should mean that you are virtues.

On leaving the complex I walk up the street and have a tradition Vietnamese lunch on a low level chair that all the locals seem to sit on when eating out on the pavement all for 10,000 dong and it was wonderful. Because I was limited for time I did not visit many of the other delights of Hanoi but hopefully on my next visit I will, for example Ho Chi Minh Mausoleum complex and so on. But while walking back to the hotel looking for a bank that may be open, I gave some money to a one legged lady, hoping that I would receive some good

Karma, but on the whole you don't see hardly anyone begging. Passing a bank that I thought was open but not for business as this was lunch time I saw two staff laying on the floor resting, considering that everyone seems to start work very early in Vietnam I thought that this made good sense, but this bank did not do traveller's cheques. Therefore, I had to wait for at-least 30 minutes for the lunch break to be over in another bank to cash a traveller's cheque, into some dong.

On my return from the Temple of Literature I book a trip to Halong Bay for 48 dollars at the Thu Giang guesthouse, the next morning. Then I venture up to the P Luong Ngoc Quyen road for a massage with a heavenly angel. It cost 70,000 dong but it was so good that I gave the angel another 20,000 dong on top because I felt 20 years younger - hopefully not being too mean. So to celebrate this unique event I treat myself to a beer in the same place as I did on the first day by the lake, thinking that if I could recover the sword, that I would be able to walk on the lake. Well in the 'Life of Brian' I was mistaken for the messiah. Before dinner in the Golden Drum I phone mother from the Internet café on Hang Non Street, well that's what it says in my notes so it must be true? The dinner was excellent as was the music thumping out a little too loud, for me. Ironically it was Credence Clearwater revival (one of my favourite bands, of all time) from 1969 one of the years that Nixon & Kissinger were knocking the shit out of Vietnam with B52's. However according to Noam Chomsky one of the worlds greatest living intellectuals and a real expert on the Vietnam war the American deliberately sabotaged the 1954 diplomatic settlement backing the French colonial thugs and afterwards committed massive crimes against South East Asia over a 13 year period until they were overthrown in 1975, based on some very dubious assumptions. More on this later in this travel book. Then had the cheek to turn reality on its head and blame the Vietnamese for crimes against the USA because of a few prisoners of war that were apparently being tortured in Hanoi. Which included John McCain and Mike Christian who he shared a cell with, McCain a Arizona senator is now running for the Presidency of the USA on the Republican side (The Guardian 28th December 2007). But amazingly tells the truth even if people don't like it, according to this article, is he real I ask myself?

On my return from the dinner, as I was leaving very early the next morning for Halong Bay I paid for the two night's board to lovely sexy Wang, who informed me that she was 22 and had a Japanese boyfriend who she is hoping to marry him, sometime in the future. But could not get a visa to Japan because I presume they were suspicion of her motives and according to her Vietnam is still very poor as perceived by Japan. Hence, they were concerned that she may stay if she was allowed in. I also asked her she thought all tourists were stupid and she replied no, good girl. Wishing I was 40 years younger before I went to sleep, I completely finished reading Fahrenheit 451, as I said before a must read before you get too old to appreciate brilliance and all written in nine days.

The next morning I up very early and make my way around to the Giang Guesthouse as the lady in charge said she would give me a free breakfast for booking the trip through them, which she did, a bread role and a cup of tea. Well we should all be grateful for small mercies, shouldn't we? The trip in the mini-bus ride to Halong city passed without any incidents apart from the process in Vietnam called driving on your horn which can drive you crazy after a while, because it never stops and Band was our helpful tourist guide. Once we got to the docks in Halong city we were separated again into a new group. The whole process does look slightly chaotic, something like market forces, on a bad day as there are so many ships looking out for tourists - but amazingly it all turns out okay and eight of us all arrive on one junk for a fantastic journey into the unknown. My group turns out to be five French, one Irish and one American and little old me from the Falklands Islands. Sean was from Galway in Southern Island a very well travelled bloke and computer programme. Elliot a mature student from San Diego in California but originally from New York and probably one of the most laid back blokes that I had ever met in my life and now teamed up with Sean and has only travelled in South East Asia. The French were made up of two young women, Lily & Vanessa and three young lads, one a spitting image of Brad Pitt. Who were on leave from there post graduate business course in BKK. JB (Jean Benjamin) the tallest lad out of the French group seemed to me to be the most rightwing, supporting Nicolas Sarkozy to the hilt - although from what I could understand/glean from them: the lot were all from upper middle class families. Lily even studied at the Sorbonne for two years. But why the hell do most French people smoke if so intelligent, all of these did. The answer so it seems comes to me from the Observer today

(30 December 2007) and apparently: 'Psychoanalyst Philippe Grimbert said smoking was suited to the French because they are a people in constant rebellion against authority'. To rub salt in to this concept on New Year's Day 2008 the French Government is going to ban smoking in 280,000 of its restaurants, bars and cafes, but will anyone comply with this decree, I ask myself? By about ten o'clock we are off into Halong bay on our junk, in my notes - I could not find enough adjectives in the dictionary to describe how incredible this part of the world really is. It may have been because the weather was perfect for such an adventure at this time of year and because I am reasonable well travelled, so could compare and contrast such beauty. According to the Lonely Planet there is 3000 or more Islands rise from the emerald waters of the Gulf of Tonkin a Unesco World Heritage site and very similar to the scenery of Jurassic Park, our guide said more than 2000 Islands. And strangely the myth of this place is nearly as silly as the movie where apparently a great dragon come out of the mountains and created Halong bay into its current form. In Little Britain we have many such myths which are just as silly, for example that there is a natural order from God to serf, because if true heaven can not be a communist paradise where we will all live in harmony, for ever, but very similar to societal arrangements at present, in little Britain. Halfway into the trip on the first day the Junk was tired up with a few other boats and we received a delicious lunch all included as part of the adventure for 48 dollars. Then on to a huge cave where we walked around for about an hour - where I was hoping to meet Osman Bin Laden, but there was no sign of him, anywhere, or any of Nixon's bombs. By

about five pm we weighed anchor close to one of the Islands and had a swim before dinner. I must also say that although in the past I have noted how stuck up most French travellers seem to be, or perhaps they just hate the English, who they have been at war with on and off for centuries. However my French travelling companions this time did not seem in the same vain probably because I did tell them early on I was writing my third book, this time about travelling. The dinner cooked by the crew, on the first night was a traditional Vietnamese meal made up of fish, rice and several assorted dished all washed down with a few cans of beer, which we had to pay for, like all the drinks. During dinner's casual conversation according to Elliott, in Japan they hang beef upside and feed them beer to keep them quite and calm, afterwards I did wonder if this was meant to be a joke. Because if true it is something the Western Elite world will probably do to the proletariat if they start to cause a fuss in the future about being treated like dirt, for most of their lives. In fact while making up my notes I did wonder if the Brad Pitt look a like; may have been the real thing trying to escape the madness of the epoch, but if not, his name is Sylvain.

I haven't slept on a boat for over 40 years, so this was a lovely experience sharing the room with our guide. As I have already said this place is so beautiful when the weather is good that it should be a 'must visit' before you die, to paraphrase Lonely Planet. The next morning after breakfast was just as good for the spectacular views, which are overpowering. Today I was very lucky if I had been a young woman as I went Kayaking in a two man one with Brad Pitt who I kept calling Ben, the other lad was called

Ben for over an hour getting lost in the process. Who may have been shorted sighted like me, so you could say it was the blind leading the blind, but his English is very good, as were the entire French group. On to Cat Ba Island we were allowed another swim before embarking for this wonderful Island that looks larger than you think. Much of the Island is a national park to protect its great diverse ecosystems and wildlife, including one of the rarest primates in the world, surely not the British Royal family, is it? After lunch in the Hotel we were treated to a two hour hike with guide Chan. An old man of 70 who could not speak English very well, but wrote it perfect, something like Band who had been to University to learn the lingo. We were taken in a mini-bus to meet Chan and then we were off up a hill, it was good job I am fit, being the oldest of the group by a mile as it was quite tough getting to the top and even getting down the other side, with smashing views of a little bit of the Island. After a rest on semi-circle of rocks and the chance to buy some drinks from Chan's wife, maybe or a close relative we walked through a small cave where according to Chan the locals had to hide from the B52's raids. It was while at dinner in the hotel afterwards that I gleaned from JB that he had extremely rightwing views, regularly visiting relatives in America. Even Lily did not like the railway workers in France going on strike as Daddy may have to drive for seven hours to get to the airport to visit her at Christmas, how terrible, old girl. You should not have cut off the heads of your aristocrats then should you…. only joking as I agreed with the French revolution, well I was not there and was not an Aristocrat, was I!

After dinner we all walked down to the Noble house for a drink and further conversations about the meaning of life and some played pool. The meaning of life for most men, maybe was sitting at the bar looking gorgeous in the form of two Danish girls who I found out the next morning on the min-bus were called Sarah & Celia, who were on there way back to Halong City. According to Sarah she loved travelling in India so could not wait to get back there for some nam bread, the last thing on my mind sitting next to them! While in the bar I also met Rachel and Scott who seemed about seven foot tall, who were on there way to Australia for a years travel and work experience. Rachel was very bright and apparently Scott had a brother in Perth doing okay for himself in the plumbing business and was hoping to get his brother to employ him so that he could stay if he liked the place, I suggested he would. After breakfast, where if you had a second cup of tea you had to pay extra and booking out of the Hotel - we all got on to several mini-bus and headed in a different direction to the harbour. This way in fact showed up the shear beauty of the Cat Ba Island, itself. I must come back some day and find the meaning of life, again...probably sitting on a bar stool. Going back to Ha Long city we went on a different boat with several other people including Kevin and Amy from North Carolina; who had adopted a baby girl from Danang, called Tessa. Kevin has a PhD in sports science and works at the University and Amy is a school teacher, both seemed like two lovely generous people too me, because it seems the whole process of adoption in this part of the world is a real nightmare, to go through. And they already have three young boys to look after, of their own.

During the boat ride, somewhere in the bay Sean who seemed so well travelled I did feel slightly embarrassed at times because I have only been to about 40 countries - had informed me that he belongs to the Pastafarian Flying Spaghetti Monster religion where heaven is a beer volcano and a stripper's factory. I believed every word of it, well wouldn't you? Back in Halong city we are taken from the boat to a restaurant for lunch, I sat with Kevin Amy and Sean. The lunch was again excellent like virtually everything about Vietnam, so far. At this point in my adventure is where I parted company with my new friends and Band, who I gave a small tip too. I got a motor scooter to the bus station for 25,000 dong. Rather ironic as the bus ride to Hai Phong was the same price which took at least four hours and not as bad as I thought it may have been and the scenery was very pleasant as well. We were even given a bottle of water and a wet flannel as part of the deal. One of the lovely things about travelling in the Third world is that when ever you get to a new town you have so many friends waiting - that it is always a delight. I think that this is meant to be a joke as the taxis and bikes all want to take you to their hotel where they will receive a small commission for taking you there. I had already decided that I would stay at the Hotel de Commerce, an old building from the French epoch, so got a motor scooter to this place, for 20,000 dong. So for one night only because of the size of the rooms Brian you are the King of France and all their dominions. In fact the bed is so large and room I could probably get the whole population of the Falkland Islands from 1982 (sic) in it. After a rest and shower I head for the mean streets of Hai Phong, well actually not very mean at all as this area of town is very pleasant and quite affluent and much more relaxed than Hanoi. As I walked up the street to the Carlsberg bar I pass an ATM machine with a guard outside without a gun. The Carlsberg bar was really chic, with My Way, how appropriate playing in the back ground and like most places in Vietnam spotless with lovely waitress, this time with two in very short tight sexy skirts. Noticing as usual beautiful sexy young women manipulating young men, so nothing that we don't see every where in the world, whatever feminist try to say women are women are women first - even before culture kicks in. Something you would never see under normal conditions in the Western world is real painting on the walls, in bars and hotels - because even without legs they would walk very quickly, but in this one there was several, and very pleasing to the eye they were, just like the women. Looking for somewhere to have dinner I ventured down the road into the Focus, a very up market restaurant cum-bar, apparently they serve 'meals for officers' but at outrageous prices and as I was only playing at being a King and not a real one for a night I declined the offer and just had a beer. Although having a degree I presume that I could be classified as an officer and if in the Forces would not have to do manual work. After this experience I look into an amazing shop that sells everything under the sun, from crockery to safes - open till late, all I bought was some batteries for my electric razor, at 20,000 dong. Still looking for a good meal at a reasonable price I venture into the BKK actually mentioned in the Lonely Planet for a Thai dish, which is highly recommended. 'The Ist and only Thai restaurant in town – Ideal for pleasure and business' (leaflet from the place). The meal was wonderful and all for about 60,000 dong with a drink of alcohol, what more can I say; eat Thai food and feel great afterwards. Back in the Hotel I did not make love to my Queen as she was only an abstraction tonight, but the next morning I did wake up with a head, probably because before going to sleep I could have watched two TVs in my room, but instead got stuck into a bit of Franz Kafka which is very good to activate the old brain cells, well so God told me!

In the morning I have breakfast in the hotel which was excellent, for a very reasonable price, 35.000 dong, as were a few the local guests who in female form came in – in very tight white jeans, which for an old man like me is not good for my heart-rate. As I have mentioned before in one of my other books, jeans were probably the one of the greatest invention since the wheel, with the bikini coming in a very close third. In fact several years ago I read that the bikini may have ended the fascist regime in Spain and the death of Franco. But to see an Asian woman on the back of a bike in very tight jeans is still an incredible sight to behold as is the process of a women riding a cycle here in what I called 'art in motion' because they seem so relaxed and graceful when doing it, even when there is chaos all around them on the roads.

Before leaving for the next town I go to the bank just down from the hotel to change a traveller's cheque which had open at 8am but could not change the cheque until 08:30. Whole of the staff was immaculate dressed in their winter uniforms, today the process did take sometime, but did not mind as the women are lovely to look at and they were in the majority. I was thinking at the time that it must be quite a job to impress a woman in Vietnam, as most are so extremely beautiful and sexy. I did mention this to one of the staff, suggesting in a cynical way, but polite with it - that perhaps it may be money too do the business, but she said 'no, it's not the case'. So, I presume that its not only Western women that lie through their teeth, but it may in fact be universal phenomena. However I went away feeling very happy because I had become a millionaire for the first and only time in my life, in local currency, of course.

At the bus station, where I have just bought a ticket for Thanh Hoa for 50,000 dong which I thought was very good value for money. While waiting for the bus I meet Richard & Karen from Toronto in Canada who had actually heard of the Falkland Islands because they had been to Chile and Argentina in South America. On meeting most people, when abroad I joke that I come from the Andromeda galaxy to lighten the mood and also to see if they are as stupid as a good percentage of the world's population – who are not really aware that there are billions of galaxies in the known universe…. an historical fact not fiction. The bus ride was uneventful, took four hours, the paddy fields plentiful and virtually everywhere you look something is growing and nothing is wasted but we did stop for a pee a drink and three eggs all for 10,000 dong, all in that order by the roadside. On arriving at Thanh Hoa I had decided to try a resort that Kevin & Amy had recommend in Halong bay, so I get a bus and then a bike and head towards it, through some of the poorer parts of town. Vani Chai turned out to be a very expensive complex built for very rich tourists, right by the sea and not relative poor backpackers like me and writing a travel book all at my own expense. The cheapest room was 45 dollars; I know it's not a fortune in English currency but quite dear for me on a tight budget, but Mr Son who ran the place was very polite and offered me a cup of Lipton tea for 20,000 dong. He also organised a bike-ride into Sam Son where I booked into the Knah San Bien Doi for 150,000 dong, roughly five pounds. Sam Son is also right by the sea just outside of Thanh Hoa so after a rest I venture down to the sea where I am accosted by a woman who wanted to sell me something, herself I think. I declined the offer as I was looking for something to eat; pussy (sic) I had decided was not on the menu tonight. I also saw a white Stallion on the beach I presume looking for a mare on heat. After a short walk up the beach I sat down in one of these little restaurants called Bia Lanh-Kem by the sea where I think that the owners actually sleep in when not flogging food. I had a fish dish with rice and a beer, explaining what rice was by pretending to plant some in a field. It seems to me that on the whole the only people who can speak English are the well educated ones in Vietnam. The meal was lovely as normal and I presume a lot better for you then Western junk food. On the way back to the hotel I watch some locals playing three card brag for money, the women seemed to be coming out on top, what's new I ask myself? In the morning at about 06:15 I pop out for a little exercise for thirty minutes where at 06:30 the loudspeakers came alive with something being broadcast for the locals, well I don't think it was for me and would you believe it some women were out cleaning up the streets. A constant theme of Vietnam for me was how clean the whole place was and how obsessed everybody seemed to be in this whole process. I was thinking when out jogging and walking that this idea getting up very early and cleaning the streets would be a wonderful idea for Little Britain where we could employ British women aristocrats who have never done anything in their whole life's, to-do. Many streets in the inner cities are a bloody disgrace in this little country, so what a fantastic idea for a future socialist government, to put into operation. Well if they lost their heads they would not be able too work, would they? Which may happen in the future, we can only hope if we keep on the present trend in this economic system, where even today in Bristol - where this book is being written. The Sunday Observer (13 January 2008) is suggesting that this place is the second most unequal city in the whole of the UK.

After a shower I venture back up the road to a another small restaurant where I have scrambled eggs, a bread role and a cup of tea, for 50,000 dong (he saw me coming, well I am a tourist) before heading back into Thanh Hoa, by bus to the station heading south. Getting the bus ticket for Hue was a little tricky as again I did have a little trouble getting the staff understanding what I wanted, no not egg on toast or a space ship to Mars but a bus ticket, it's that simple. In the end it cost me 240,000 dong for the sleeper to Hue, after speaking to a lovely lady who could speak a little English, on the phone. In essence probably the most strange bus that I have ever been in my life because you had to lay down if you were on a top bunk, like me and take your shoes off before going in. After several hours we stop for lunch and I sat next to heaven on earth, a very attractive young Vietnamese woman on her way to Vinh from Hanoi and Trang pronounced

Chang who had a higher degree from the USA. Back on the bus Trang and I had a good old chinwag about nearly everything under the sun, including different aspects of Asian culture, that all ways fascinates me. Especially the male female's dynamics from different perspectives and cultures. For example: Vietnamese women are becoming more assertive as they become better educated according to Trang. He also informed me that his wife works for Air France, so they get discounts on flights to travel and they have a maid, he works for the State as a public administrator.

While on the bus I also noticed several old men that were probably freedom fighters fighting the Americans in the 1960's and 1970's and even pop stars that could sing underwater on the TV, which was the more surreal I ask myself? In early evening we stop for another meal which was again all part of the package, by this time my two lunch time companions had left the bus and there was talk that because of the floods in the middle of Vietnam we may not make it through. While at dinner I was even given a little rice wine to taste, by a local gentleman who was amazed that without an interpreter - I could write about travelling in the Far East. By 11pm we had made it through to Hue where even at this time of night, a man on a bike appeared at the bus station, offering a taxi service to my hotel. The floods had affected some of the town so I had to settler for Truong Giang hotel for 15 dollars instead of the very cheap one I wanted, from the Lonely Planet. The hotel was very clean, had satellite TV like the vast majority, hot water and so on. According to Lonely Planet 'Hue is the intellectual, cultural and spiritual heart of Vietnam' and was the political capital of the country between 1802 and 1945. In the morning I changed my hotel to a cheaper one for 10 dollars a night, but nearly just as good. Then off to the Forbidden Purple city by my own effort, meaning walking for a change and getting harassed by motor bikes wanting to give you a lift. I walk over a bridge and decided that I better cash another traveller's cheque while on the way. This time the whole process hardly took fifteen minutes, but again the staff where immaculately dressed, however I did notice that some of the female staff was acting in the Thatcherite model of behaviour, a very worrying trend to all men of the world. But in my notes I had written that in this part of Vietnam I thought that these beautiful creatures, Vietnamese women looked more relaxed, so is there a contradiction here I ask myself! I also noted that it may be because this part of the world has not had fifteen generations of ruthless capitalism, like little Britain, where it all started.

You had to pay a few dong to get into the Forbidden City where we are all welcome now - but at one time the only people allowed in were eunuchs of the Emperor serving his every need, so very pleased that to get in I did not lose my testicles because I am still looking for a new wife who may even be a Queen. It seems that Emperor Tu Duc (1848-83) had 50 servants for every meal and 50 cooks who prepared 50 meals. The place itself still looked very impressive as if the Emperor could walk out to greet the tourists, like me at any moment. I spent nearly two hours wondering around the complex taking photos and thinking how amazing that a few countries like Little Britain who's royalty still live as if the were Emperor Tu Duc in the 21st century. In fact yesterday (7th January

2008) in one of the tabloids I was glancing through I saw that it still costs 30 million pounds to protect the British Royal family, a bloody disgrace when so many people still live in relative poverty, in this little country. On leaving the complex I buy myself a t-shirt as evidence that I been to Hue and then have a very lovely lunch sitting down with six beautiful local women, who all seemed to be checking out my bottom, or it may have been the size of my wallet. The meal was excellent, but when I thought about it later, I did think that it may have been big enough to feed a male mouse on Viagra.

On my return I get my hair cut for 50,000 dong, which was very reasonable, noting at the time how many men I saw smoking, but hardly any women. I also booked up for the Perfume River cruise for the next day, with lovely Linh in a travel agency next door to the Truong Giang hotel. In the evening I met Kevin and John from Perth accidental for dinner in the 'Why Not' restaurant cum-bar, both employed in working class skilled jobs. Who where minefields of information about the opposite sex, when it comes to marriage and its pitfalls when losing your head over such beauty and sex on legs in the Far East? It seems that one of them had read Fools Paradise and was very impressed with it, but would probably still marry heaven on legs from the Far East, some day in the future. Afterwards we stroll down one of the most affluent streets in Hue to view an art gallery and some of the most chic bars/restaurants in the whole of the city, which apparently had been bombed by the Americans, but now completely rebuilt.

The next day I am off on the Perfume River trip not far from the hotel, after a mechanic kick starts it with a spanner and a little knowledge of machines we are off on a tiny little boat called the Dragon boat trip, which a whole family lives on, with some other tourists and Han the local guide. Who were Tony and Marie from Melbourne, second generations Italians, Pierre & Myriam from Brussels, Rene was from Munich, Sophia was French from the Mediterranean region of France. I often think that backpackers is seeing the United Nations working in reality, because on the whole we do all get on, don't want to kill one another and if we were all educated to the same level, we may live on a planet that the great John Lennon sang about at the height of his fame – without boarders and so on. We visited Thieu Mu Pagoda one of the iconic structures in Vietnam according to Lonely Planet, the Tomb of Tu Duc, which we had to get to on a bike and the Tomb of Minh Mang with a lovely lunch thrown in as part of the deal. The trip took us from 8:00 to 16:30 so we had lots of time to get to know one another at a superficial level. Pierre & Myriam were a very friendly professional couple with an international outlook, on life. She was a lawyer and he was a graphic designer and they are on honeymoon, for several months. I also kept meeting them both as I progressed on my journey, which is always nice to meet a friendly face in foreign lands, but why do such wonderful intelligent people smoke? Tony and Maria had been together for two years and both have grown up children from previous relationships. Tony works for IBM in Melbourne and Maria is an administrator, Tony also told me that he thought that life was getting a bit more stressful in Big OZ, especially with the culture of the USA on the warpath, in big business. And both agreeing that the Vietnamese people are waking up to the fact that tourism is good for business, at many different levels and will go on increasing for the forcible future. At the last visit the boat owners left their dog behind so about 30 minutes on the way back home - we had to go back and collect him, from terra firma.

According to my notes in the evening I had a wonderful meal which was called a hot pot - the best so far in Vietnam in a restaurant called the DMZ Stop & Go, not far from my hotel, all for about 60,000 dong with two bottles of beer thrown in, served by Duyen. Afterwards I got speaking to two young women, next door to my hotel who tried to explain some of the complex processes of being a woman in Vietnam. These two young women shared a flat in this city and one had a boyfriend and the other did not, so they told me. And it would seem that in Vietnamese culture women should be virgins when they get married, if possible and having sex outside of marriage is frowned on by society as a whole. If this theory is in fact working with hard scientific empirical evidence may be a million miles from social reality because lets face it, most women in the far east are all incredible beautiful and very sexy and they all know it! To sum it up you could say the essence of this issue is: as told by a man on a scooter to me somewhere in Vietnam: 'that Vietnamese women are like cocktails: slim and sexy'. I also met Alan at the Lan Anh swimming club in Ho Chi Minh City from the UK but now working in Vietnam - who reckoned that in three months that he had 10 Vietnamese girlfriends, a bit of an Errol Flynn character I would have thought - because he also told me that he had a wife and children in Cyprus. But what the hell is so sexy about drinking water called La Vie as seen several times in ads in Vietnam, out of bottles?

The next morning I have breakfast at the DMZ Stop & GO establishment, who actually owed me 5000 dong from the night before in change, which they honestly deducted from the bill, a theme I noticed through Vietnam where the culture is one of bartering in many transactions, but once the agreement is finalised they carry it through to the letter and don't let you down. Then on to Danang (pop 1.1 million) by bus where we stopped at Lang Co Hotel for a break where I saw a huge ugly rat, probably Richard Nixon in a previous life, I wonder if somebody will shoot the bastard. Arriving in Danang at about 11am after a four hour trip where we passed through a very long tunnel that may have been built by the Japanese. We were dropped at a travel agency where they tried to sell me a hotel room for 10 dollars but instead I decided to stay in one of the cheapest rooms anywhere in Vietnam for 3 dollars and the motor bike driver only charged me 10,000 dong to take me there. You could not swing half a cat inside and had to share the shower and toilet but according to Lonely Planet it is the fourth biggest city in Vietnam. Perhaps, ironically this is also the city where the French and in theory the Americans landed when they invaded the place. As it is still relatively early in the day I venture into a large indoor market selling everything under the sun and then decide to walk to China beach. It is not a very pleasant day but according to Lonely Planet again it is only a hop skip and a jump away from the town centre. In fact according to this guide about 2km, but about 20 years later I arrive warn out and a lot older. I wonder around the sea area for sometime glancing in on some very posh restaurants, meant for rich tourists I presume; not many around today as raining and quite cold, with some old ones across the road for the locals and poor tourists where I spotted another huge rat. The only sign of life was a couple of locals digging up crabs, poor things and to think that this beach runs for 30kms south and north of the marble mountains, so quite a few crabs to dig up. For the exercise I decided to walk back to town; so by the time I got back I had aged about 40 years. To celebrate that I had reached 100 today I celebrate with a good cup of old Lipton's tea in the Heng Long little café who over charged me for the tea, at least in relative terms that is.

As I am a very political aware animal to paraphrase Aristotle I had decided to visit Christie's Cool Spot who has moved address in the evening, for a glass of beer and chat up the Americans who according to Lonely Planet visit this place, on a regular basis. Not true so it seems according to Barry who has been visiting the place for the last ten years. While drinking my beer served by lovely Jam Rue, Barry and Hong came into the bar. Barry was originally from Manchester but had lived in Sydney for years with two grown up children, so about my age. However has lived in Vietnam for over ten years with a Vietnamese wife and 9 year old daughter who apparently are going to be swapped for a new Vietnamese wife. I did notice straight away that Barry had strong views on many things perhaps because he refused to get drafted for the Vietnam War in the 1960's, when he was 19. Well done that's all I can say and now he is a manager on the 2 towers building project just a little distance from the bar and restaurant that we are in now, next to the river Han. Hong so it seems may have been in a labour camp after the old regime had been overthrown, by the new. According to Hong and Barry many of the poor now are from the previous regime that ended up broke and destitute or fled the country after 1975. Amazingly now according to these two the country is corrupt because of the one party system. Where a policeman on 100 dollars a month may have rented property and can afford to send his children abroad for schooling, in essence not really logical. Similar I presume to Tony Blair a pimp and deceiver who is now racking in the cash on all sorts of dodgy deals because he was the British Prime Minister for ten years and getting very rich in the process. Alan Johnson was parachuted in to a Hull constituency when it became available because he supported this con man, or as I prefer too call him a neo-priest of Modernity, when Prime Minister. I reached the conclusion that Barry thought eventually that there would be a massive legitimacy problem sometime in the future in Vietnam, as I believe that there is going to be one in the Western World, very shortly. In Vietnam only two million people are in the communist party and too join you must be invited into it according to him. Barry may have had an engineering degree I have a social science one. Also according to Barry very few Americans ever visit this bar and the ad in the Lonely Planet may have been paid for by the owners to entice tourists into the place, like me. He also praised the women of Vietnam who he said worked harder for him than the males on his building site. After Barry and Hong left I had a very enjoyable dinner in the place, making as many notes as I could about what Barry had just told me. Afterwards I venture into a lovely art gallery where I met sexy Kim who thought she was ugly, who worked in the place. Apparently because she wore traditionally dress to work where many young women now wear jeans to show off their beautiful assets, which most young men prefer, according to her. She also wanted to marry a foreigner and went to University to learn English - so I recommended my youngest son, as he is only 28 and without a wife.

The next day I travel on a local bus to Hoi An where it was the only time I spent in Vietnam that I was stupid enough to let the bus conductor rip me off deliberately. I had not checked the Lonely Planet to see how much it should roughly be - also it was raining so could not get off when he told me it would be 50,000 dong. I new straight away that it was the wrong figure but handed it over anyway and then looked it up to find out what it should be, which was about 8000 dong. The journey was also share hell because the driver was completely mad and drove like a lunatic. When I got to Hoi An I tried to get some money back from the conductor and driver but they would not let me have a penny back. So be warned when travelling on local buses, if you don't get a ticket in advance. However the town it self was a delight and I stayed in the Green Field Hotel which had a swimming pool, for three nights in a small dormitory for 15 dollars, fantastic value for money and has '60 well-appointed rooms'. It also had an excellent restaurant, satellite TV and free access to the internet and as normally all the young staff were wonderful and very helpful including Thuong who worked in the bar & restaurant.

According to Lonely Planet Hoi An (Faifo) is a living museum where trade has been going on with Europeans and others for centuries, which includes a gastronomic delight. As it was only lunch time I ventured just down the road to try this assertion out in the Viet café being chatted up by lovely Tu, who I presume was trying her English out on me. She is 22 years old and works from 10am to 3pm in the restaurant and went to college to train as an accountant. The lunch was very pleasant as was Tu, who I had a long chat to about everything under the sun. My next social action was to go for a bike ride on a hired pushbike (just like Norman Tebbitt once told the masses in Little Britain they should do to find a job) - around the town at first going in the wrong direction, reversing my direction a few miles down the road. Where I did see some poor people living as they may have done for generations - I head in to town to explore some of the wonders of this living museum where I popped my head around the Quan Cong Temple and the Japanese Covered Temple which was constructed in 1593 and my first visit to the market. For my efforts on this primitive form of transport, just like the ancient regime of Little Britain, I treat myself to a cup of tea across the river from the bridge. On my way back to the hotel I passed the Museum of trading ceramics and re-met Pierre & Myriam from Brussels, for a few minutes catching up on our travels, so far.

After my usual tea-time rest I go to the bar for my free cocktail in the Green Field hotel where I meet Steven from Naas in County Kildare who now lives in Australia. One of his most heart stopping moments in his whole life according to him in Sydney was when he went back to a new girlfriend's home. But was not was aware until the morning that she lived with her parents, so after a night of pure passion her father knocked on the bedroom door, in the morning. Thinking that he was going to have his head kicked in - all her Dad said was 'bacon and eggs mate' a lovely little story that many young men may have had over the last few decades, now that we all have become more lenient with our daughters in the Western world.

For dinner I went back to the Viet Café to see Tu and have a lovely meal of seafood and drinks; where I met Mike Sapp from Michigan who told me that he was a Vietnam vet, serving here for 12 months, even in Hanoi. At first I thought it may be true but after discussing this with other people I reached the conclusion the story was probably not true, but at least he saw through George W Bush's lies and said that he was 'a bit of shit'. Well at least something he got correct, don't you think? Whatever was the truth of Mike's assertion at-least the locals seemed to like him, as he had also been to a wedding in this area; so probably a decent human being in a sea of bastards.

In the morning, after a disturbed sleep as my indigenous college kept his lights on all night - I have an excellent breakfast in the hotel of omelette and tea all for 30,000 dong. I was thinking during the night, that my dormitory companion may have thought that I was an American and may have wanted kill me in the night. In the morning I discovered his name was Mr Tho and he was a guide from Hanoi for some foreign tourists. Today I wanted to go the very famous Cham city of My Son a world Unesco World Heritage site, but because of the flooding I could not go and over the next few days it stayed the same. So instead I went to explore Hoi An in more depth, the old town is a Unesco World Heritage site, for example I spent some time with lovely Ngayen Thi Thao in the Yaly fashion business, who is a guide in this establishment. In this specific place they make clothes, carpets, light shades and several other commodities, which you are allowed to see being made. The workers apparently work in a 3 hour rotation shift system of 8 hours per day. I was also informed by the guide that sir Mick Jagger and his wife's were here several years ago, I presume to buy wonderful made to measure clothes, in this town. I just hope he was very generous with his tips as he is worth more than 200 million pounds according to the Sunday Times Rich list (2007) and to think that last year I heard him complaining on the radio that he was fed up with American billionaires trying to rip the Rolling Stones off. I also saw silk worms in action making silk that are feed on mulberry leaves and according to lovely Thao the whole process only takes a few days and to think they do it all for nothing, the complete opposite to the Rolling Stones.

When looking around the hectic chaotic market, mostly run by women; I could not help but notice that some of the tourists lose their guides, who go around with arms raised; sometimes with an umbrella or flag as points of reference. In fact I did hear a story that an American Woman got lost on one occasion and was found 400 miles north of Darwin, Australia in an open boat fleeing from a ruthless One Party State but she was very confused if it was Vietnam or the USA. Hoi An is also renowned for its 200 tailor shop where they will make you up a shirt dress or suit in a couple of hours. In theory they are not meant to hassle you in to buying something, but some do. When I was there I got a lovely Japanese silk shirt made for 10 dollars. I also met Emerald who is 22 years old, very tall and beautiful from San Francisco California in my hotel; who came all this way just to get clothes made to measure. It would seem that she had been to Ecuador in South America and Cambodia but no ware else and my first impressions of her was that she only understood USA culture and not the significance of other peoples beliefs and cultures - although apparently having a degree in 'understanding history', seems like a good course for Blair and Bush, don't you think?

Strange as it may seem I did meet my second American and son in the Green Field hotel bar in Hoi An (only a small per cent of Americans have passports) and a complete different kettle of fish than Mike while enjoying another free cocktail in the bar. His name was Bob who was born in 1946 and he had a PhD in psychology with his own private practise in Nashville, but originally from New York. Well let's face it if Oliver James is correct many Americans like many in Little Britain need a lot of help in the department of mental health. I did get the clear impression that Bob did not like me as eye contact was not very regular; in fact he seemed pretty hostile towards me until his son Josh came in to join us. Who also has two degrees, but several tattoo's on his body, which you would not find on most middle class people in Britain. But was Bob really from this planet when he seemed to think that all Vietnamese people loved Americans, very unlikely Bob and when I was in India, he had been there 11 times, so he told me - I did not see anyone cleaning the streets, he said he did. The Induction method my friend is not always the best policy even if you have a PhD at least Karl Popper got that correct.

On my last day in Hoi An I again had a lovely day waiting for my made to measure shirt to be made and just wondering around this small town (pop 75,800) thinking and writing up my notes. I even gave a signed copy of my first book to a young beautiful female assistant in a book shop as I was so impressed with the shop cum-watch shop on the Tran Phu street where they were selling Michael Moore, J.K.Rowling - books about the Vietnam War and so on, but not Noam Chomsky. She was so amazed I think she nearly fainted, thinking that I was some one famous, I presume... perhaps when I am dead. I did note in my notes at the time that perhaps the great Noam Chomsky was thought of in the same way, or perhaps even banned in Vietnam. While picking up my shirt I explained to the assistants that I would love to marry a mature Asian lady because in essence they are still very sexy and attractive in later life, so one of them said to me that she would find me one for a commission fee. This may sum up what Vietnam is now all about, lets make money, what ever the Government may say about socialism, more on this later. Just outside of the 'Before and Now' bar cum-restaurant I met Travis from Melbourne who was filming a documentary with his family who apparently works on the Australian famous soap called Neighbours which I never watch because I think that I am far too intelligent for such total tosh. Sorry Travis. I went in and had a drink in the bar where you could drink between 5pm and 9pm – in the so-called the happy hour period at a cheaper price than normal, which I thought was quite amusing as

I did not realize that a happy hour could be extended for 4 hours. I did see this sign in several places, so each time I gave my self a small smile about this contradiction. In the Before and Now bar some of the young women bar staff had black T-shirts on with a wonderful message on for most men, which said: 'Night Wish – Angels there hell' so presuming it meant you may be better off with the complete opposite…personally I agree.

In the evening I had dinner in the Moon restaurant and lounge where I saw for the first time in Vietnam a chance to have a B52 cocktail and B53, this time I declined the offer. Afterwards I phoned my old Mother to see if she was okay, but apparently she could not find Vietnam on the map, so perhaps I am not here in reality, or the place does not exist, just like poor old Noam Chomsky (born 7th December 1928) in the book shop.

The next day I travel to Nha Trang (pop 315,200) on the overnight bus arriving in the morning about 6am after having two stops for the toilet buying a few bananas for 5000 dongs on the way. No doubt the great travel write Paul Theroux would have said something about this experience, but I could not think of nothing to report apart from meeting a very pretty doctor from Australia, sitting across from me. I got a bike around the corner to the excellent Phu Quy Hotel for 10 dollars with en-suite, satellite TV, hot water and so on. Before going to bed for a very well needed rest: I have some breakfast in the hotel, take a walk up the pavement adjacent to the sea. Straight away I felt that this was one of the more relaxed places in Vietnam, probably because it is right on the coast. In fact this place for me is a must visit place as there is a lot to do according to the Lonely Planet. Scuba diving, boat trips, mud baths and plenty places of interest and most male motor bike riders seem to be earning a little extra as pimps, well it is the oldest profession and whatever some feminists may say sex was the first commodity of all time. But reaching the conclusion when here that if I did try and do everything in Lonely Planet - I would be acting like a headless chicken, or very rich, which I am not. So acting in a rational way I head towards the Oceanographic Institute on a hired bike, it cost only 15,000 dong to get in but one of the best values for money you will ever spend. Pal who charged me 20,000 dong to get me here was the young man who told me that Vietnamese women are like cocktails, which I agreed completely. When walking around this wonderfully Institute where I took lots of photos and seeing many animals I had never seen in my life I kept thinking what Pal had told me and linking it the B52 cocktail which I discovered later was incredible. So would a B52 cocktail be more explosive than a B53 and so on, hoping that you understand the double metaphor, etc.

On the way back into town I have a swim in the stylish La louisiane Café swimming pool and a drink of original beer made on the premise and very tasty it was where I met Hans and Henrick from Sweden, who were in search of the sun. Hans works as a customer's office on the Norway border and Henrick works in Norway as a waiter, as there he can earn better money. They were both decrying Scandinavia countries for being too expensive a bit like Little Britain while having a small snack. I had yoghurt and fruit salad for 55, 000 dong a bit expensive but this place is certainly up market, as we would say in the West. While walking back to the hotel even a man who was with his wife and cooking food seafood on the street, I presume was trying to sell me a women for 10 dollars, I don't think it was his wife? There is no doubt about it that after the Vietnamese won the war in 1975 there was a Cambrian type of population explosion here. I don't know what the statistics are but so many young people are riding scooters cum-bikes that it is not hard to understand why, let's celebrate in the best way possible. And the impression I get is that most Vietnamese people seem happy and relaxed about life the complete opposite of most people in little Britain. For myself I also celebrate these facts by having a very pleasant cocktail in the Coconut bar cum-café adjacent to the sea, but not a B52 yet and thinking to myself that this may be the neo-epoch of capitalism with a smiling face. I have dinner in the Pasta House where I again meet Pierre & Myrianm from Brussels for a few moments before I have a delicious curry, highly recommended by my new friends. They told me that they were going to visit a micro bank project inland to see how it worked for normal people. While having my dinner I was watching a movie on DVD with the legendry Charlie Chaplin as the great Dictator, a real classic. I should also note that Brad Pitt may think that he is a world famous movie star but the few people I spoke to about him in Nha Trang, had never heard of him, when showing photos from my camera of his exact double.

The next day I go to in incredible Spa a few miles north of the hotel where I have a mud bath with two lads from Liverpool and all the staff where happy to see you. Who are Nick and Paul, Paul is a teacher doing research at University and Nick is a clinical nutritionist and has bought a house together. Paul takes a picture of me and Nick or vice-versa - hoping to have it published in the Nuts magazine as some where unusual to be photographed. The whole process took sometime as after the mud bath you had to have a shower and then enter another contraption and then another before having a swim in a very hot pool. But it was worth every penny as I had got myself a little stressed out before leaving for this Spa by booking an aircraft flight to Saigon for the next day, thinking afterwards that was it worth it, for 30 dollars. While at the Spa I also met Annli from the Capital of South Africa who thought the British Royal family were wonderful, and Tony & Theo who thought the complete opposite, like me...I think. Tony, who was the same age as me, was also very critical of Big Oz business practises. Having worked for 30 years for the Qantas airline but now retired with two lovely daughters. He was telling me that before retiring that trusted young people were often told to spy on their colleagues, about basic behaviour and even if you were well dressed, or not and ordering older work mates around as if they were kids. I think Nick Cohen should read this book (sic), don't you Mr Ken Livingstone? Afterwards resting in my room I was watching the Discovery channel - where the programme was discussing the possible genesis of the human race in the Congo. A fascinating story about our close cousins, other primates that act in different ways, for example some love sex others act brutally towards others and so on. Just like Homo sapiens. I also watched the Larry King show where the big story of the week was where a plastic surgeon walked out of an interview with

King. During it I kept thinking that in a world were 6.7 billion now live was this really important especially when about half live on two dollars a day and nearly one billion go hungry.

In the evening I have dinner in the Spot owned by Wilson from Scotland and married to a lovely mature Vietnam lady at 15 Hung Vuong Street, whose happy hour is between 3pm –10pm. I had a smashing fish supper and then afterwards got chatting to Wilson and his friend Shane from Canada. Shane like Wilson was well travelled so both had a better understanding of the world in all its complexities and very interesting to talk too. Shane had even been in South America at the time of the Falklands war, so new where I was born. Wilson who has a similar background to me seemed very political aware of the nonsense of the mass media in the Western world and how they (in all its forms) lie constantly about what is happening in the world. We were also Republicans united against the anachronism of the Monarchy in Little Britain, in the 21st century, Wilson who had passed very close to her when visiting an Island in Scotland, a few years ago. The assumption seemed to be according to Shane and Wilson that the Vatican may the riches organisation in Europe with the current unelected head of State in Britain in 2nd place. Shane was also very critical that the mass media in the UK whips up the hatred of foreigners on a regular basis, when having exploited at least one quarter of the world for profit, in the past, and to this day in some cases. We were even discussing if Scotland would become an independent country in the future, and quite ashamed that Sean Connery should accept a knighthood when he was such a nationalist, in the past.

Something that really amused me about Wilson's Business, which he has had for three years and only just starting to make a profit, was that the waitress would not do any manual work like cleaning the toilet, so he had to do it himself. And to think that in little Britain we often have stories about the working class, especially in the rightwing press - who will not cross over from one trade to another to help the management out. How shocking.

I got a private taxi to the Nha Trang airport, quite away out of town, where I met Kevin and John for the third time, having met them at the Spa on leaving. They had really enjoyed themselves from what they were telling me, both getting pissed out of their minds and involved with madams who robbed them. One on a beach with two girls and one in a hotel, or whatever, apparently the one inside was so clever because they did not take all his money but just a few dollars, while in the act. They did not seem to upset because they thought it was so hilarious how it was carried out. The flight to Ho Chi Minh City (Saigon) only took about 40 minutes and was very pleased that I got a motorbike driven by Hai in to town, via the HSBC bank, instead of a bloody taxi, my nemesis when travelling. He was going to charge me 5 dollars but I gave him 100,000 dong, hoping to get some good karma, and he was very pleased as well. I had picked out the Yellow house, in the Pham Ngu Lao area to stay in while in Saigon which turned out to be a very pleasant hotel run by beautiful exotic Anh, 38 years old with two daughters, who could speak very good English. The first night was a little noisy as the room was at the front of the hotel but for the rest of the stay I moved into the centre of the building where it was quiet. After booking in I ventured out for lunch to a small restaurant called the Cappuccino apparently since 1922, where I met the Anderson family from Brisbane again who were on the flight with me. Michael, Leanne and son Joseph had already been here before so were on there way to another county so was killing time before there next flight, out. Something that had upset them when in the city was the scam where you could be charged say 70,000 dong for a massage and then a compulsory 100,000 dong tip, before you were allowed to leave the building. So be warned Brian, so they told me. This never happened to me but in the evening before dinner I started to understand the complexities of the new market forces now operating in Vietnam, better in this city. Just two minutes from the hotel in a very noisy bar mainly used by Westerns, on the corner of the street I got charged 30,000 dong for a tiger beer, virtually an English pound, and another two minutes around the corner you could buy one a lot cheaper. But was thinking when having my beer that individualism as a belief will never catch on in places like Vietnam and Thailand because it seems to me that they love being a social being as Aristotle was well aware, too much. My first dinner in Ho Chi Minh City in a restaurant called Pizzerue was again excellent value for money, and was wondering what the great Irving Goffman would have thought of this place (sic). Afterwards on the way back to the hotel I had a drink on the street with a Swiss man who may have been a con-man and two of his local female friends, who also has a local girlfriend. The reason for my doubts that he is genuine person - is that he has been in Vietnam for sometime setting up a huge deal according to him and now he lives in Australia. And as the night wore on he also told me that all tourists visiting Saigon gets robbed, I did not and if so rich why was he living like a backpacker? However the two local ladies loved their beer and seemed very happy with very little, from what I could see and the Swiss man had done a little travelling so at-least aware that we are not all Caucasian and speak perfect English. The reason I did not get a good sleep on my first night became obvious when about 3am I woke up to a huge racket on the corner where I had, had the beer several hours before. Well we were all young at one time I think?

The next morning I have a lovely free breakfast in the Yellow house and then head back to the HSBC bank to cash another travels cheque and again the staff all looked immaculately dressed. Then on to the Notre Dame Cathedral which inside was much brighter than the original one in Paris, but still no sign of the invisible man. According to Lonely Planet it was built between 1877 and 1883 the year that Karl Marx died, in London. Then a stroll over to the Reunification Palace where in 30th April 1975 a communist tank 843 crashed through the gates and the old regime surrendered. According to the leaflet I was given when entering this splendid building the first stone was laid on the 23rd February 1868 by a French Governor called Lagrandiere and was completed in 1870. It seems today that this Palace is still used for receptions and loads of tourists' hopefully with tons of dosh and digital cameras. All the rooms that are open to the public are wonderful including the Cabinet meeting room and the dining room. I bought a few gifts in the small shop that sell nick knacks and so on in this place. Because I had not slept well on my first night in Saigon I go back to the hotel for well needed rest and then on to the fabulous War Remnants museum on the back of a bike; which is rather scary but a must do thing before you die. It only cost 15,000 dong to get in but a must do thing to do in Ho Chi Minh City if you visit the place. In the court yard there is captured tanks helicopters, etc from the war and inside lots of photos and so on about the brutality of war, including a list and mug shots of the journalists that died in this senseless war, mainly caused by ruthless colonist expansionist policies. In fact over the last five hundred years most trouble in the world has been caused by neo-brutes trying to take over the world, which includes the Ruling Elite of Little Britain, who's brutality over centuries, is only now starting to leak out (i.e. Chomsky, Pilger, Curtis, Mike Davis), which has always been legitimised by religion, in most cases. On the way back to the hotel I nip into the splendid Lan Anh club for a swim, which cost 20,000 dong to get in which included the free use of a towel and start to read the Quiet American, by Graham Greene, which I bought outside of the museum. In the evening before dinner I buy myself a wrist watch and then watch American Gangster with Denzil Washington playing a real gangster – so-called based on a true story. This was for a charity organisation well at-least in theory for nothing where you could buy/ have a beer or coffee while watching the movie. I gave a few thousand dongs on leaving and enjoying this excellent movie about trading in drugs from the Far East. The ironic twist to this tale was that not only were many

USA troops using drugs while fighting the Vietnam War - but the USA Military was also involved in the import of drugs into the USA main land, for this gangster as played by Denzil Washington.

The next day after another free breakfast in the Yellow house I go on a Cu Chi Tunnels and the Caodai Temple trip which takes all day, with an excellent guide but well worth it, first visiting a sort of factory where they make wonderful pictures with egg shells, etc. According to the leaflet I have in front of me given to me by wonderful Anh, who just by site I could fall madly in love with - this temple that was huge and magnificent is home to a unique religion where you can actually take photos while people are in the process of pray. While there I got talking to Megan from Minnesota who teaches English in Saigon and well paid for it so she told me and two young women who were seated right behind me, who I thought were upper class English ladies but turned out to be from Cape Town. Then on to lunch and the tunnels not far from the city, where you can actual walk through in a sort of fashion if you are not too tall, very creepy and for me would have been terrifying to travel through and live in. Before this process we were shown a short documentary about this whole sad business which started under the French heel and if you wanted to you could shoot a gun for a price of a bullet, I declined this offer. According to Lonely Planet and the guide this area we are in at the moment was one of the most important tunnel systems in Vietnam stretching from Saigon to Cambodian border and bombed to hell by the Americans. The guide Mr Minh, no relation to the great Vietnam Freedom fighter as far as I know - spoke quite good English and for the first 30 minutes of the tour leaving Saigon gave us a little talk about his life and how the city has changed over his 55 years on this little planet. Although I did not grasp everything he was saying at least when he was young he could swim in the river that we crossed, not now because it is too dirty and seemed to be suggesting that that the Vietnam War was about the Capitalist south verse the north and terrible shocking socialism. I don't think that this is what Noam Chomsky says about this whole process at all, but basically a nationalist encounter of Freedom fighters fighting a common enemy. His views seemed to me was very slanted towards the good south and the bad north, slightly ironic because what I could see that this whole country is now run on Capitalist lines. But Mr Minh was quite amusing at times and seemed to be a bit of a philosophy king as he kept saying that 'happiness should be the main gaol of life' and joking about the traps the Vietcong where making to injury the Americans, I presumed because they deserved it. For example, according to Chomsky: the destruction of forests and scraping the land bare so that crops could not grow causing starvation, the decision 'to pound South Vietnam to bits' which in essence was 'a record of war crimes and crimes against humanity' (Chomsky fb 1970 this addition 2003) and over thirteen years killing millions.

The next morning I again visit the HSCB bank to draw some money out of a safe ATM machine in the building before venturing over to the café opposite for a well deserved cup of tea. And while there I pick up the Sunday Vietnam news written in English to read and glance through. In it I read a fascinating little article about 'what it means to build a socialist home' built by Mr Sin. I was thinking that this would have been an excellent piece for that great socialist of the common people John Prescott (MP – I think it stands for mashed potatoes) too have read, in little Britain. Because at the bottom of the article it says 'there will be no gap among brothers and sisters', as a very dangerous Noam Chomsky disciple I could not agree more with this premise. And at-least in Vietnam you do not see many people begging on the streets where in little Britain, in the so-called fourth richest country (something Blair must have said a million times while Prime Minister) in the world it is quite a common sight too see and lets face it in Vietnam to me the whole place seemed spotless, and a wonderful trait in these people, where one day a year is set aside for 'teachers day'. Where in Britain it is pretty disgusting and dirty in many places in the inner cities apart from where the very rich live out there meaningless lives and to think that one day would be set aside for 'teachers day' - would be like seeing a man from earth walking on that very far away Planet called 'All mad Cows are free' (sic), because the last thing the British Ruling Elite want is for the masses to be educated. But in Vietnam I was quite amazed to read in a local magazine called the guide Almanai (Vietnam economics Times) in Nha Trang that tourist should be careful of scams that operate in Vietnam. Especially in places like Halong bay where some dodgy agents had sent some tourists on a non chartered Junk which sank with the loss of a life. It was also very up front about the average wage in Vietnam which is less than 2000 pounds a year, or in dollars 732 a year.

Before leaving Ho Chi Minh City I went back to the lovely Lan Anh Club for another swim where you could sit on a stool in the water and have a drink, something I have never seen anywhere in the world, where I have been - waitress even brought you food on request, by the pool side. I had also bought from lovely wonderful Anh a ticket for the so-called 2 day Mekong Delta trip fininshing in Phnom Penh by boat as I wanted to see a bit of the Mekong (where John Kerry may have won his purple hearts) and my next stop on this quest is Cambodia so killing two birds with one stone. In fact when reading Graham Greene at the pool side again I kept thinking that I must visit the Continental hotel to see if it was the same one as mentioned in the book - perhaps for dinner, but for some unforgotten reason I did not go but ended up in the Sa Sa café for an excellent fish supper with a few glasses of wine. Something I would highly recommend to other travellers is to venture of the beaten track when eating and so on, to taste what the locals eat; it is often a lot cheaper and just as tasty, even on a street like D Bui Vien where the Yellow House is situated with dozens of other cheap hotels. On the way back to my hotel for my last nights sleep, I slip into the Cappuccino for my last drink in Saigon meeting Aden from Columbia Ohio who like me seemed very cynical about Western civilisation.

The next morning after breakfast I take a few pictures of gorgeous Anh and say good bye to her and the staff and get directed on to a bus, just around the corner from the hotel. This time we had a much younger guide who was very amusing for at least 30 minutes while leaving Ho Chi Minh city telling us about his life and how young men act towards the opposite sex , etc. It seems that young men often have at- least four girlfriends on the go at the same time and also have two bikes, one made in China for work and a better one for taking their girlfriends out at night. Now we know why there are so many bikes in Vietnam, young men thinking about sex and from what I could see they never get drunk and unruly. He also informed us that at-least in theory you are meant to get permission from the State to move from region to another, but not every one does this and this is the reason that the big cities are now getting over crowded.

According to the leaflet that Anh gave me for this trip 'you can see green rice paddy fields stretching towards the horizon'. It is not far wrong as I said before nothing in Vietnam is wasted, but in the Mekong Delta where millions live there did seem to be quite a bit of poverty if compared with the West. On arriving at Cai Be we were taken on a boat where we went to see sweets being made, and than onto An Binh Island where we actually cycled the last mile to the restaurant on a bike, with another lovely young female guide this time. Two of my companies on this journey where Isabel from Britain and Jeroen from Holland, also Laura from Oxford and Mel from somewhere in the UK. The lunch was delicious and then back onto our bikes and boat and bus to Chau Doc, arriving about 18:30 at the hotel Tai Loi shattered, which I had to pay 3 extra dollars to sleep on my own. But was given dinner as part of the package in the hotel, which was very enjoyable although I did think originally that some of the staff did act in an authoritarian mode, with us.

According to lonely Planet this place has at least three ethnic minorities and even a hill that is called 'Two million

Dollar hill' because of the Americans bombing it relentless in 1963. After dinner I went for a small stroll and had a drink and wrote up my notes in a pretty little café affair, but not for long as we had to be up early for breakfast and the boat trip to Cambodia. In the morning breakfast was great and then loads of tourists from different hotels were taken to the dock to be put into different groups for the journey ahead, something like Halong bay but on a smaller scale. This trip was on a small boat, with a beautiful guide called Jane (24), where first of all we where taken to an incredible fish farm that is actually under a floating house, a truly amazing experience, which I have never seen before, however I don't want to come back as a fish. Well life can be a little short, don't you think? Then on to see a small village where some Islamic Cham people live, who centuries ago were a large part of Vietnam, but not any more - these people did look quite poor and to help subsidise their income, made clothes by weaving in the old fashion way and also selling knick knacks to tourists, including sweets. In fact the Chams were once so powerful that they attacked the Chinese and Vietnamese over centuries and even occupied the city of Angor for five years and it was not until 1792 that the Vietnamese annexed all of their lands.

According to Jane our wonderful guide on this part of the journey, whose boyfriend is a pop star, was explaining to me that because Asian women are not as well respected as they should be, by men. That often Korean girls are taken as wives by Vietnamese men and then sold on to there friends as a commodities for cash, if true quite shocking I thought. While we are on the boat, in the morning Jane takes all our passports and the

22 dollars each to get the visas at the Cambodian border. Where we have lunch on the Vietnam side while Jane is getting the passports processed, I sat next to my two new friends, mother and son from Australia called, Judy and Simon. Others on the boat where Callan and Tara from Ireland, three mature women from Spain, only one could speak English and a French couple who never stopped smoking. After lunch lovely Jane gave us our passports back and then we dragged our bags across both borders to get them looked at and stamped and then back on the boat, for a final journey. With a wave and a smile that was the last we seen of Jane who also had informed us of the 'spirits in the water' and other culture beliefs of Indochina. In fact she looked so good in jeans that she may even be Jane Fonda's daughter. Which leads me nicely into the last quote from Noam Chomsky in this chapter - which is not far from an axiom of most colonial powers throughout the last 500 years, as he asserts: 'despite the hyperbole, the rational core of policy making renamed in the early 1960's, and in fact can even be detected in the exaggerated doctrine of Vietnam as a "test case". In one sense, Vietnam was indeed to serve as a test case. Developing countries were to be taught a hash lesson. They must observe the rules of the international system as determined by the powerful – who, like many a stern disciplinarian, saw themselves as benign, even noble in intensions' (Chomsky fp 1970 - 2003 edition p, 44).

CHAPTER FIVE

- SOUTHERN ASIA - CAMBODIA

The rest of the journey on the boat was quite uneventful as this time we did not have a guide and in this part of the Mekong Delta is wide without a lot of shipping on it. However I think that there is something special about travelling on water in a very relaxed style, in such a small boat. About an hour out of Phnom Penh we are transferred onto a mini-bus which takes some time to arrive, but eventually comes. Then driven at breakneck speed on a very dusty road that gets dust over everything, coming into the city is a bit of a shock as there is no doubt about it that the outer areas do resemble the Third world, but the inner city is clean and modern. We are taken to the King's Hotel where we could choose too stay or go - as I was tired I decided to stay, but without hot water in my cheap room - well what can you expect for 5 dollars. I shared dinner with Isabel and Jeroen - who I took a real shine too. And in the morning I have breakfast with Sarah from Sweden who I had first met in Chau Doc and came on our boat when partly through the trip. Sarah was one of these very assured intelligent young women who had done a lot of travelling – as breakfast progressed I kept thinking that her body language was saying categorically too me (was old enough to be her father) or probably any man who may have tried it on with her - that if you mess with me boy I will chew both of your testicles off with one bite. Apparently she was some sort of chemist who knew a lot about food and what it does to us when we eat it. I said very little while eating my breakfast and kept my legs very tightly together. Sadly I never saw Sarah again as I decided to move to the very excellent Spring Guest house mentioned in the Lonely Planet where the staff are all wonderful and very friendly, slightly dearer but at-least I had hot water. After unpacking I venture out in to Phnom Penh for the first time and get a bike ride to the National museum, built between 1917 – 1920. Which is large and I thought slightly surreal as you are not allowed to take photos inside although I did see a few people doing it. The reason for this premise for me was that on entering the complex I saw two Americans on bikes that turned out to be Latter Day Saints from San Francisco, Elders Thomas and Rosdahl. Thinking to myself that what is worse falling bombs or false dogmas in both cases both invented by man, as there is no hard scientific empirical evidence to the contrary. The museum has treasures that go back centuries many looted from historic sights (LP) and well worth a visit. When I got speaking to these young men they told me that they do preaching and give English lessons free - but did not seem very aware of other cultures and beliefs although having lived in Cambodia for a year and insisting on calling me sir. After walking around for sometime I sit down relax, take notes and start to speak to a lovely little girl called Rilt aged 6 who could speak English, her Mum is selling flowers in the museum. When you buy some you give them as an offering to Buddha and I presume get some got karma in return. After leaving the museum I wonder up the road and when looking in a small bookshop I got talking to Jeff from Australia who now lives in Latin-America and Cambodia. Being my age he seemed like a mirror image of me who has reached the conclusion that man per se is a pretty stupid animal, which I agree completely with. In fact according to Jeff the Americans are paying Cambodians to go to church, which is causing a lot of tension in this mostly Buddhist country where he said that a church had been burned down recently because of this chicanery. Ironically when I was speaking to the two Elders in the Museum complex a high rate male American walked by and shouted out loud that there is only one God. I tried to speak to him after the young men left but he would not speak to me about what he had just said. Then on to Wat Phnom a very important religious site for the locals according to Lonely Planet. It is on the only hill in Phnom Penh and goes back to 1373 when the first temple was built by a lady named Penh. Who it seems built it to house four statues of Buddha swept in by the Mekong and if you visit it - it will bring you good fortune. At the entrance I tried to marry the beautiful mature receptions selling the tickets but she told me to get lost, but at least I gave some local currency to a poor man with a limb missing, so perhaps when I am dead I may become another Voltaire. What ever are the truths of these myths about Phnom Penh pales into insignificant when reading about the genesis of Cambodia if Francois

Ponchaud is correct. 'From 1841 to 1846, Cambodia no longer existed as a political entity to Vietnam and to Thailand' (Ponchaud 2007 p. 35), this about sums up the history of this State over centuries. In a Short History of Cambodia this historical fact and many others especially the dynamic tension between Cambodia, Vietnam and Thailand, which explains this process throughout time. The 'Spirits of Land and water' was the true meaning that the Khmer people called their country, originally from at-least the 4th B.C. Overtime Indian and Chinese cultures have impacted on the culture and beliefs of modern day Cambodia and its beautiful slightly darker people. In fact when reading this book for research purposes the recent Pol Pot regime crimes - although terrible and shocking is nothing new through out the history of this country or most of the world for that matter. The ironic fact being that if it was not for the French Cambodia may not have existed today but also they were partly responsible for the '3 years 8 months and 21 days' of the Pol Pot regime and the terrible dynamic tension in the 20th century between the Vietnamese and the Khmer people.

As far as I am concerned Cambodia today could be called the very tasty filling in the middle of a sandwich between Thailand and Vietnam. Voltaire's got nothing on me, what do you think good readers of the world? In my notes I wrote at the time in Phnom Penh and about this city (pop 1.5 million) - was that the first impressions of the place was that it did appear more relaxed than Hanoi or Saigon, but not forgetting that it is much smaller than either of these two cities. However with extremes of wealth and poverty, just like in little Britain and again like most of the world. As Lonely Planet suggests: 'the old adage of the rich getting richer and the poor getting poorer couldn't be more accurate description of Cambodia' (LP p, 186). In the Cambodia Daily (7th December 2007) written in English I read a very interesting little article about female construction workers, in Phnom Penh. Who only earn about (2 pound sterling) 4 dollars a day but according to this little piece they don't mind working with men on the whole but some can be crude, well nothing new here then!

Between '6th February 1963 and the 15th of August 1963' the Americans dropped '237,000 tons of bombs on Cambodia' mostly in the countryside swelling the population of Phnom Penh running from such terror and Battambang.

On my walk back towards the hotel from Wat Phnom I nip into the Green Vespa (on the river by the boat jetty) for lunch owned and run by Alan from Belfast, for the last three years who's got a fetish about scooters, so it would seem. With a real one stationed above the entrance to the restaurant, I had pasta and beef and a glass of carrot juice but was not cheap in relative terms (6.50 dollars) but very tasty. But in front of me I read on Alan's business card with pure delight that if I buy 4 meals I get one free.

In the afternoon I visit the Royal Palace which reminds me of the one in Bangkok with its splendour and architecture and cost 6.25 dollars to get in if you are a rich tourist, the locals pay 2 dollars. The first palace was built in 1434 and the present one in 1866 and stands to the present day - with some of the other structures erected in the 20th century, one of the buildings even celebrates the erection of the Suez canal, by Empress Eugenia, well she actual did not build, I don't think? 'The Royal Palace is regarded as a symbol of the whole nation and all the pavilions are adorned and painted yellow and white. The yellow represents Buddhism and the white represents Brahmanism'. So there, as this leaflet informs me that I am reading now - given to me while paying to go into the place. While in the place I got chatting to Eddie from Manchester who is a lawyer and has two sisters, the older one working very successfully for a publishing company. Also while in the Palace complex I got talking to five Buddhists monks who informed that the end of the world will happen when the monarchy in a far flung little Island sticking out in to the North Atlantic Ocean disappears for ever, so not tomorrow then! This may be a joke, but I did speak to five young Buddhists monks.

In the evening before dinner I walk across the main street to the VIP guest house for a beer and got talking to lovely Rotha. She is very friendly and engaging and tells me that this guest house has 8 rooms to rent and her family are making a good living out of this business. Then back to the Cherry restaurant cum-café for dinner where there was a controversy over what a bottle of wine cost, so I have a tiger beer for 1.50 dollar fifty cents instead, there was a suggestion that the wine could be 15 dollars a bottle. Lovely Dina serves me the main course, which if I was 30 years younger could have been her all served up on the plate too eat - or should that, be on a bed, searching for the G spot that really exists but not on all women, so it seems (Guardian 21st February 2008)…how cruel!

The next morning after breakfast in the same restaurant I take a bike ride to the so-called killing fields of Choeung Ek 14 kms southwest of Phnom Penh - where at least 17,000 prisoners from S-21 prison were murdered under horrendous circumstances. 8000 skulls are on display in a glass tower, sadly I kept thinking while there, taking loads of photos that this terrible crime was nothing new in the annals of recent and past history. Then on to Tuol Sleng or S-21 prison which was once a school where the classrooms were turned into torture chambers for the new enemies of the State. With lots of drawings and photos of the victims (mug shots) and how it was carried out, ironically one of the few survivors from this prison was a painter of portraits called Vann Nath. According to a book I bought about him while in Cambodia, with several others he only survived because he was an artist who could draw and paint pictures of 'Brother number One'. No not Richard Nixon, Henry Kissinger, George W Bush or Tony Blair but Pol Pot, Vann Nath returned after 1979 to paint many of the new paintings about how the torture was carried out from first hand experience. According to this book at least 200,000 Cambodians where classified as enemies of the State and murdered, with hundreds of thousands more dieing of overwork, disease and starvation. While I was leaving the last building within this complex I met Julie from Melbourne a young lady travelling on her own who had been to Sihanoukville and was very impressed with the place. But according to her, which may now be a myth it was too dangerous to travel to this small town on the coast at night, as you may get robbed by bandits. To recover from all this misery I nip into the Boddhi

Tree Umma (mentioned in the Lonely Planet) just across from S-21 for a cup of tea and to think about these whole mornings macabre visits. Just the shocking truth about how political power in Cambodia and world wide can go bonkers from time to time in its many forms.

Before dinner I decide that I would like a massage, so decide to go to the blind massage joint called Seeing Hands very close to the D Book shop, where I had bought several books from lovely dark exotic Chhay. Vi Rak, blind from birth gave me an excellent massage; he was 27 the same age at the time of my youngest son. After this wonderful experience I go to the Jungle bar right next to the river for dinner, where I had one of my favourite meals in Asia - Thai soup and rice. Served by an Angel in a very tight black outfit in red shoes, which nearly made believe that that the world is flat and Jesus if he ever existed walked on water, perhaps even the Mekong when flying around the world on a back of a Camel.

That night for some unknown reason I did not sleep too well, probably dreaming about the gorgeous angel and woke up about 4am deciding to put the satellite TV on and watched David Attenborough who was informing us that he fell in love with amber as a 12 year old lad, I was not convinced as it seems that a young girl of a similar age from Germany came and lived with his family with this substance. I was thinking it was probably the site of this young women and not the site of amber that made him fall in love, with it. After this process I did fall in love with my excellent breakfast in the Café Blue, just around the corner from my Guest house. Considering that it was called an America breakfast of bread, eggs, bacon savoury and some cold meat and free Chinese tea served before the main course. About an hour later I head down the road on the back of a bike to the very posh Raffles Hotel Le Royal where according to Lonely Planet I can have a swim for 3 dollars, not true folks. In fact according to John Spooner the guest and community Relations Manager from the hotel - told me the last thing we want in the world in this place is any form of riff raff with his dog in this upper class joint, or something very similar. John was from Sydney in Big Oz so after he told me this went back on what he had just said, then showed me what I would be missing if I was to buy a day ticket for 15 dollars, I declined the offer. Today apparently Royalty was present and some big fish from the United Nation, but the pool did look excellent and John was a very friendly Aussie.

So, after this rebuke I decided that I must visit Boeng Kak the large lake in the middle of Phnom Penh where cheap accommodation is plentiful and if stupid enough you could have a swim. Before seeing the lake I venture into the Lazy Gecko café where according to Lonely Planet in this place you can 'dine for a cause' and met accidental Fran Leigh who is trying to set up her own NGO. Who was kind enough to pay for my coffee, after informing me that she is a teacher and is setting up a drama group and staying for a year? According to Fran, who I was very impressed with - she is doing this as she wants to help the family and especially the young people who pick up the rubbish for a living in Phnom Penh. Two minutes from this café I walk into the No 9 guest house a much laid back backpackers establishment - look at the lake take several pictures, am accosted as a possible drug user (buyer of the weed) which I am not on the way in and think to myself isn't the British class system wonderful. When actually I really despise it but am reminded while writing this up by Beryl Bainbridge (desert Island disc 2nd February 2008) that it is a reality of Modernity, especially in this little Island.

Then on to the so-called Russian market an amazing in door establishment selling every thing under the sun, I think that I even saw Tony Blair and George W Bush selling weapons of mass destruction, on the cheap to an undercover Iraqi agent. I even bought a couple of gifts, a CD a DVD and a small digital radio for 7 dollars, but when I got home the CD worked very well but when I opened the DVD about S- 21 The Khmer Rouge Killing Machine, there was nothing inside, just like the WMD.

For lunch not far from the market I have an omelette and bread in the Nice to Meet You café run by a German playing with his laptop. Afterwards I walk back to Spring Guest house which took me at least one & half hours, which is always a good way to think and keep fit - about what you are trying to achieve when travelling and so on. For example, I kept thinking when in the Far East that if global warming is happening that the rich and powerful running around in their four wheel (4 x 4) drives, don't seem too concerned about it, or Tony Blair for that matter flying around the world constantly; pretending that he is such an important man. Having a rest I start to read Carol Livingstone's excellent book about Cambodia mostly from a women's point of view, working as a freelance journalist, which to me was/is very amusing in places. In the evening I had dinner in the Asian spice establishment just off the Sihanouk blvd, a soup type meal with a beer and a coffee, which apparently cost 3 dollars.

In the morning I am back in the Asian Spice for breakfast as I had decided that this place was excellent value for money in this part of town, if you are a hard up backpacker like me. At 11am I am on a bus to Sikanoukville (Kompong Som) where I sat next to Soun Kamsan who had travelled all the way to Phnom Penh the night before for one hours English lesson this morning before travelling all the way back home again, that is dedications to a good cause, people of the world. This road to Sihanoukville is one of the best in Cambodia and ironically may have been paid for by the Americans. While stopping for lunch I met John from Big Oz and when getting on the bus again there were several monks asking for money so that they could eat. Some how back in Little Britain I don't think that if I shaved my head put on an orange robe and put out a begging bowl for some money for food it would work. I may go very hungry indeed.

Arriving at the bus station at 4pm where I get a bike ride to Mich & Graig's guest house, for 7 dollars; after visiting several others who were all full. At the Reef where I am having a beer and writing up my notes it would have cost 40 dollars for one night, but they also have a swimming pool. It would seem that this is the high season, the reason that most hotels are full and a bit more expensive. Then back to my guest house for dinner which is not cheap, but excellent food. Sitting on the opposite table I met Humphrey, Leslie and gorgeous Tina a local young women and the girlfriend of Humphrey or Leslie; all living and working in Phnom Penh. The next morning after breakfast I hire a bike out for the day for 5 dollars from Chhour Sokneng (nice guy) just two minutes from the guest house called the Blue Dolphin internet café - as I had decided that I would visit Ream National park and probably a lot cheaper than a taxi. So today I am Che Guevara again, like I was in India or was that Thailand? The park itself is about 20 kilometres from Sihanoukville and as it was such a lovely day it was very enjoyable, indeed. I was charged two dollars by Noeun to get into the park only because I am such an honest bloke, most people probably don't pay and just drive straight past the entrance into the park. I drove to the beach which was very pleasant and down the road into the park, without seeing a lot of wildlife who according to Lonely Planet exists somewhere - instead I stopped and bought myself a bottle of water, without seeing Dolphins or Monkeys. On the way back I had to slow down for 6 buffaloes walking on the road who may have been British Aristocratics' in a previous life as they all seemed to bow their heads towards me...well I am Che Guevara for today! Back in Sihanoukville I pop into the Chez Popeye bar ale la Marine run by Johnny from Paris who has married a local girl and now very happy, for a cup of tea. In the afternoon I drive around other parts of Sihanoukville which has a population of just over 170,000 so not very large and I found a very laid back and relaxed little town. Having high tea (in little Britain only the very rich can afford this) in a small bookshop cum-café a delightful little place on the main street - afterwards I move into the Mohachai guesthouse cum restaurant-pub for two nights which had hot water and a little closer to the beach or as their business card informs me 'a stones throw from the beach, not only for divers'. Lovely Phory who booked in wanted to marry me so she said as I am a mature adult and as several women in the Far East told me 'young men are no good, I prefer older men who are great'. Before dinner I decide to have another Thai massage as being Che Guevara for the day is hard work with Tita Saraubuth.

The next morning I have a small breakfast by the beach and a day out on Bamboo Island all part of the package deal for the day including lunch, which I had booked with Nice Guy the day before. On the little boat going out to the Island I met two angels of mercy, Nicky & Sophia who had both worked in India for charity. On the way out to Bamboo Island, we were also allowed to go snorkelling which some us did near another very small Island. The whole day was a real delight and highly recommended if you ever visit Sihanoukville, including the snorkelling and the excellent lunch of fish & salad prepared for by our guide. You could say that this was like living in pure paradise for a day with out having to go through the whole process of doing 'desert Island discs' with gorgeous Kirsty (sic). Some local people actual live on Bamboo Island and sell and cook snacks and so on for the tourists. During the day I was lucky enough to chat to a very friendly Danish family, saw a large star fish while snorkelling. Nicky reckons she saw an Octopus, but may have been several young men trying to chat her up under water. Something I thought very amusing when there was that several of the cattle wondering around the Island probably thinking - why can't we have some lunch as well, actual tried to steal some of the leftovers as well as anything in a bag that may be food. For this cheek some of the foreign tourist took loads of pictures of these cattle doing these ghastly deeds and treating them as if they were real movie stars or celebrities… very strange in deed.

In the evening I meet John from Castle Maine near Melbourne in Australia again, having had several games of pool with him the night before in my new guest house, for dinner on the beach, called the Moon Shack. Probably the best meal I have had in my life, it was made up of several types of fish with vegetables (not most of Mrs Thatcher's cabinet) and rice all ordered by John, a bit of an expert on food so he told me. Also according to John he was a teacher before getting cancer in 2006, having one lung partly removed. He and his partner also loved jewellery so he bought some on the beach; apparently my faked Rolex watch looked cheap and nasty, which I had bought in Saigon for 20 dollars and which I could have bought for ten in Phnom Penh, so I man dealing in watches told me, at the Russian market. After dinner we walk along the beach to Alan's & Sue bar cum guest house were John was staying for a drink. Alan and Sue was from Yorkshire who had bought or rented this little place on the beach with their two grown up children and were very happy that they had moved from Britain. For some strange reason during the drink John got very upset with me, perhaps he just hated Poms; or because I kept saying what a bargain everything was in the Far East for tourists. Or perhaps thinking that I was bragging that we were ripping off the locals or vice versa – however because I am so poor in relative terms back home I was just pointing out that this place was real value for money - somehow I think that he got the wrong end of the stick. I even told him that I came from the Falkland Islands (so not a Pom) and having virtually walked on water to gain my educational qualifications because I had only 6 years formal education, two books published at my own expense, etc. Apparently between him and his partner Elizabeth they own three houses back in Big Oz, so perhaps in some strange way he thought that I had the same in the UK; not true John I own nothing.

The next morning at 06:30 I go to the beach before breakfast for a swim and on getting out I am accosted by Maggie from Australia who is pissed out of her tiny little mind like several other tourists on the beach, in the Dolphin Shack who tries to steal my towel belonging to the hotel. Walking back up to the guest house I kept thinking that this may have been some sort of sweet revenge for John getting so upset with me over virtually nothing, the night before. Her parents would have been most upset if they could have seen her and the reason I am putting it in this little project.

By 9am I am back at the bus station for my journey back to Phnom Penh. On the bus I got talking to Nick an only son from Wigan in little Britain who is a geologist going to a local wedding with exotic Nuth in Phnom Penh. It would seem that Nick did part of his MA in Abu Dhabai which was quite an adventure because of the danger factor. He now works for a firm in the UK and has been lucky enough too have ten weeks off to do some travelling, also informing me that working on a oil rig is hard work, if you do it - but after five years of suffering you are made. Geology is also not an exact science, according to Nick so nothing new here then, which is very strange because this something that another John from Cardiff University (1990 – 1991) kept telling me that it was in around about way when I was a postgraduate student there – doing my teaching training. Nick also told me that when the Americans were in Sihanoukville recently in a ship, not bombing the place this time, but I presume on a good will mission. They were not allowed to barter with the locals so in some case the taxi firms, Tut Tut drivers, etc made more in a week than they would in a whole year, out of the sailors.

Back in Phnom Penh I get a bike ride to the No 9 Guest House that I had visited before and booked in for one night only. Well it is very cheap and cheerful and very basic indeed after a short rest I go and see a short documentary about the Pol Pot regime that I had seen advertised before above a restaurant cum-café which may be still called the Mekong River establishment, or was when I was there. As I was the only one in the cinema and a little tired after travelling, I fell asleep, so missing some of this very important short little documentary, 'unique in Phnom Penh'…silly me. In my last evening in Phnom Penh before travelling to Siem Reap I find myself sitting on the floor in a lovely little bar cum-cafe drinking a Singha beer upstairs called the Wanderer, not far from the Guest house - well I may be because on the wall it says 'special cigarette 1 dollar' perhaps 'blue magic' (sic) what do you think? For dinner I have a wonderful vegetarian Korma with another beer, which is free this time, in the Indian Curry Pot, next door to the Wanderer.

While waiting for the bus to Siem Reap near my Guest house, the next morning I see a mature tourist so out of mind on drugs or alcohol he may actual be from another Galaxy, wandering around with a bottle of water in his hands. The bus driver may have also been on something illicit, because after about 45 minutes out of Phnom Penh we turn around and drive back in to get some fuel. I was very lucky on this trip because I was sitting next to gorgeous Heidi, now living in the USA but originally from Vietnam. Born in 1972, so the same age as my wonderful daughter and is a full-time accountant for Delloitt –Touche. Strangely as it may seem Heidi spent 7 dollars for this journey, Jane behind me spent 6 and I paid 10 hoping for a superior service. In my notes I wrote that the scenery was flat but interesting as was the soup I had for lunch for 1000 riel. Heidi was so friendly towards me, must have been the father persona in me that she let me use her ipod, for the first time in my life, I have ever used one - listening to Nora Jones went well with the long journey. On arriving at Siem Reap bus station in the evening, chaos seemed to rule as dozens of Tut Tut drivers where all wanting to take us to hotels for nothing. Not something that you would expect from most taxi firms world wide and as normally there was a catch. The basic idea being that if they took us to our hotels where ever we wanted to go, they could take us to Angkor Wat the next day or when ever you wanted to go. My very friendly Tut Tut driver Phon Savoeun took me to the River Star hotel who spoke near perfect English. The receptions was called Sopheak which means being happy and was 25 years old - a very bright young man who told me that he was not very happy as he was only being paid about 50 dollars a month but had to pay 40 dollars for accommodation near by, living with a Tut Tut driver. He came from another province so missing his family. After a shower I venture out into Siem Reap for the first time ever and the conclusion anyone with half a brain would notice that this is a boom town, on the make, as I was thinking while being drove to my hotel. During dinner in a near by restaurant I got speaking to probably one of the best travelled Americans of all times called Rick who said he had been to at-least 110 countries, is this a record I ask myself - and now a small businessman. Rick had been in the USA Air force in the admin section and was also aware that the Tonkin incident in the mid 1960's in the South China Sea, was a put up job by the USA establishment and just an excuse to accelerate the Vietnam War. This was one of the very important points that Alex Jones makes in one of his documentaries as well, hence the reason that I questioned Rick about this bit of disgraceful chicanery. But was very concerned in essence that he really understood anything about the Vietnam War - because according to him the so-called 'Viet Cong were a bunch of thugs' and the final assault on Saigon was an accident - not a thought out strategic process. To my knowledge from many different sources the conclusion in 1975 was no mishap but the final break through to end the war completely. Ho Chi Minh, like Nelson Mandela being two of the most important Freedom Fighters of the 20 century, Spartacus over 2000 years ago, being one of the first.

The next morning after breakfast in the River Star hotel I was hoping to meet the same Tut Tut driver as the night before, but not so. Instead he sent his younger brother Heng Sophat on a motor bike who could hardly speak English. So what do I do fly back to the Andromeda Galaxy on a broom stick or should that be a Nimbus 2000 or go with this young man to see some of the most famous ruins in the whole world. There was only one option and that was to head down the road on the back of a motor bike for several hours, of site seeing. On arriving a few kilometres from the main site you have to pay 20 dollars for one day or 40 dollars for 3 days or 60 dollars for a week site seeing, where hundreds of people are all trying to do the same thing. I chose one day as I am hoping to come back sometime in the future to see the place in more depth and a more leisurely pace and if caught without a ticket apparently you can be fined 30 dollars by the State. But what can a mere mortal say about Angkor Wat which is only a small part of the whole complex of Temples covering a circuit of roughly 13 square miles. Considering that some these Temples were built over 1000 years ago and at Angkor Wat 'the 5 magnificent towers representing the heavenly peaks of Mt Meru, the tallest of which was the home of Vishnu' (LP p, 208). The day I was there you were not allowed to climb up to the higher stages of the complex at Angkor Wat, but the share size and complexity of the whole place is mind blowing and I would suggest a must visit before you die if you could afford it. As my Lonely Planet asserts again 'Angkor Wat is more than just an astounding architectural feat, it is the national symbol, the source of fierce Khmer pride and the epicentre of their civilisation' and I don't think Bob the builder had anything to do with place (sic). To come down to earth after several hours of site seeing I wonder over to where you can get a drink and have a snack, if you want too, which I did, a smashing pancake. Then back to the main entrance to meet Heng Sophat who took me to several other sites, one which were Ta Prohm who was consecrated in 1186 by Jayavarman VII who dedicated it to his mother and the last being the very important Neak Pean site which may represent the idea of 'Anavatapta, the mythical Himalayan lake where the divine beings bathed and which was the fountainhead of the four great rivers of India' (The Treasures of Angkor by Marilia Albanses p, 195).

Then back on the bike for the return trip to Siem Reap with my very young guide, I gave him 12 dollars for all his efforts, which made him very happy. After a good rest I decide that to ease my very tired feet that I would treat myself to some reflexology, for the first time in my little life. Thinking to myself during this process that what I had just seen especially at Angkor Wat was something very similar to British society a very old State structure that is going to rack and ruins and hopefully will collapse a long time before this incredible structure, where Bob the builder is doing repairs, but not too sure what the estimate was and can Cambodian society afford it?

If you are lucky enough to read this incredible book, joke maybe you should have reached the conclusion that I love reading myself and in this project Asian women. The third love/desire/need in my life now is the B52 cocktail, which is the best cocktail I have ever had in my life. The reason for telling you this I am drinking one in the Blue Pumpkin a real smart establishment, just outside on the veranda while thinking about my wonderful day out at Angkor and taking notes. This is heaven in drink form and afterwards I have a beer in the Banana Leaf and dinner in the Temple Club - on Bar Street which is a real chic upmarket street that comes to life in the evening and the fresh fish meal was wonderful.

The next morning after breakfast in my hotel I am picked up by a mini–bus to take me to a luxury liner that is taking a few dozen backpackers to Battambang. Well that was what was on the leaflet I read when booking the trip and 'a must do' I was told on my journey around Cambodia. However as many of us know who were born at the bottom of the heap; what we are hoping and what actual happens in reality is two different things. The boat it self was no luxury liner but a rather old wreck that probably would not get across the English Channel if it ever tried. But lets face it Brian it was/is cheap and turned out to be a very enjoyable journey although very noisy as I was sitting at the back of the little boat. I was lucky enough to sit next too Rob & Catriona from Melbourne in Australia who were excellent company. The whole experience itself could be explained by suggesting that you had entered Kevin Costers Water World for a day and something that you would never see or experience again anywhere in the world especially for lovers of wetlands and birdlife where there lives some of the most rare species of birds in the world, I would have thought Bill Oddie's heaven on earth (sic). In fact this part of Cambodia is one of the most unique stretches of water systems in the whole world, as once a year the river reverses its flow because of the huge build up of water in the whole Mekong flooding a huge area of land. As Lonely Planet asserts, in reverse order of what I did: 'the fascinating boat trip up the Stung Sangker and down the Tonle Sap to Siem Reap is one of the most picturesque journeys through Cambodia' (P, 219). And for us the journey did turn out to be one off in a lifetime as it took a lot longer then it should have done, as we broke down with steering problems for three hours somewhere in the middle of it all. Within these water worlds there is whole villages built on it or should I say above it on stilts including schools, truly amazing. I was thinking that when we were broke down - that the young lad who seemed to be doing most of the hard repair work deserved a medal; as at the beginning the boat owner was shouting at him as if it was all his fault. But finally we did reach Battamburg and was taken to the wonderful Star hotel (probably 4 star in the West) free on another min-bus, although a bit pricey I was shattered, so decided to stay for one night. I was so tired that after a well deserved shower I fell asleep without a good meal inside of me. In the morning I have breakfast in the restaurant on the top floor of the hotel made up of omelette, bread and a cup of tea, booked out and walked down the street looking for somewhere cheaper to stay. I booked into the Chhaya hotel which was very far from being a 4 star establishment for only a few dollars less. Am I losing my marbles I did think afterwards, as the receptionist did try to talk me into staying at the Star Hotel for a few dollars less than I had paid the night before? But it was cheap and cheerful - and at times something like Charing Cross at rush hour with satellite TV and hot water and nearer to the centre or 'heart of town location' than the Star. Battambang has a population of 154,000 and between 1795 and the early 1940's was at times the centre of the dynamic tension between Cambodia and Thailand. It was also the home town of Vann Nath who did all those paintings of 'Brother Number One' while in S-21. According to him it was a peaceful province known as the country's rice bowel because the land was so fertile, before the event of the Pol Pot regime. Now it is just a normal but interesting small provincial peaceful town running along both sides of the Sanker River. In the first full day in the town I just wandered around the indoor market which seems to specialise in jewellery, John from Big Oz would have loved the place and did some site seeing; trying to recover from the boat trip and too burn up some flab. For lunch I had some excellent seafood soup in the well named Happy restaurant next door to the market after searching to hire a cycle on my journeys, which I never found anywhere. After a well deserved rest back in the hotel I venture down the road for a face massage and ear clean out given to me by Weli, who wanted to learn English so never stopped talking to me, for at least an hour. In theory it was only meant to last for about 30 minutes, so I got my moneys worth out of the whole experience, especially the cleaning of the ears that seemed to go on for ever. Now I can hear really clear when the locals call out Tut Tut sir or do you want a Motto sir, which is a lot rarer in this town, or my old Mother is given me some more words of wisdom, on the telephone! Before going to the Riverside bar for another B52 I was watching a little documentary on the Discovery Channel about China. It was very interesting although I was aware of the scandal and arrogance of the British Ruling class in the Far East, like must places they invaded, or should say planted a flag on and said that is mine. In Kenya even to this day the ramifications of this arrogance is very clear to any one who is not brain dead, while writing this book.

In essence I was not aware that the Chinese just thought the British were just 'barbarians', in the same way that the Romans thought about little Britain 2000 years before. The Riverside bar is an old wooden villa over looking the River which I never saw because it was dark, but it is a real delight and mentioned in Lonely Planet and the B52 was fantastic. Walking back into town from the bar I venture into the Phkay Proek restaurant for some seafood, I can't get enough of it and tonight it was in a curry form, washed down with two cans of Angkor beer. Before going to sleep I was lucky enough to see a little of a Richard Dawkins interview on BBC World, that carries adverts in the Far East, about his latest book The God Delusion. But seemed to me that he was going back on the whole idea that this is complete nonsense and the West should ditch it once and for all, if we are rational intelligent people and have a scientific mentality.

The next morning after a lovely breakfast in the Happy restaurant I am on the back of a motto with my 45 years old guide Thoeun to visit Phnom Sameau, who hangs out in the lobby of the Chhaya hotel. On the way we stopped for a drink, which was well needed as the walk up the hill which is quite strenuous, especially for an old man like me. The views from here are quite spectacular, but I did not come for this reason but to visit the caves which were used as slaughter chambers under the Pol Pot regime. Some of the human skulls remain in a dignified way apparently put in this order and displayed by the Monks, who also live on the hill. Another sad reminder of man's inhumanity too man. The guide Thoeun spoke quite good English and was telling me about his life as we walked up the hill and back down. According to him he was born in Battambang but at sometime in his life had to live in a refuge camp on the Thai border, I presume under the Pol Pot era. He also had a burning hatred of the Vietnamese where he suggested my digital camera was probably made, I bought it in Melbourne. In the afternoon I get taken to the Wat EK Phnom ruins by a very friendly young man called Ran Chanra (22 years of age) on his brother's motto who I had met the day before while having the face massage - which is a mini-version of the Angkor Wat complexes, built in the 11th century. The ruins are in a very peaceful picturesque area a few miles outside of Battamberg, where you are charged a small fee to view them. Ran Chanra is studying to be an English teacher and grew up in the Battamberg province, in a small village called Chrangbak in the Bovil district where his Mother & brother & sisters still live. While growing up he went to the Roung Chrey primary and secondary school, having moved into Battamberg in 2003, he now lives in a monastery while studying and only pays for the use of the water, electric and his food. On the way back to the hotel I take Ran to the Happy restaurant for a small meal for being such a nice and friendly young man and give him a few dollars for all his efforts and advice about Cambodia. Which was very similar to mine and the great Jean-Jacques Rousseau writing over 250 years ago (static society bad, true 'state of nature' good, freedom, etc) in that he thought that country people were the real people and not the false persona that is very thick too see through; that people put on in urban areas? Well done young man that's all I can say considering that his family grow rice, beans lemons and so on, out in the countryside.

On my last evening in Battambang I again go to the Riverside Balcony Bar for my last B52 in Cambodia but sadly it was closed because of Human Rights day. So instead I visit the Golden Night restaurant that did cocktails but not B52's. I had one with a delicious meal and then walked back to my hotel along the river. Where over the last few days the locals have been out celebrating on mass in the evening, with loud music, strobe lighting stalls of knick knacks, food being sold on the street ands so on. I even saw an event where you could throw a dart at a balloon to win a prize if you bust it, very jolly good fun indeed from what I could see and every body looked very happy and where all enjoying themselves. The smell of food was so strong although I had a lovely dinner in the restaurant that I bought myself a local dumpling for pudding and got one free - that I had tasted a few days before and I can report that they are probably the tastiest dumplings in the whole world. Which was a wonderful final experience too think and contemplate on when writing this chapter up about my travels in Cambodia?

Chapter Six

- Big Oz And New Zealand -
Part One

I have just boarded a very large 747 for the first time in my life in Singapore for Sydney having a few hours before I flew in from Bangkok. I am sitting next to Wayne and Fay his lovely wife from Wollongong who have just flown all the way from Japan, having done a fly and swim trip. Oops I mean fly and sail journey around a small part of the Pacific. He is a teacher and she does something only slightly less important - being roughly the same age as Wayne, who had also worked in the mining industry we got on very well and a very long chin-wag, about everything under the sun. Being at the back end of the plane on a 747 is quite an experience because on this trip it was so rough that a few times I thought that I had been swallowed by a whale or large shark as not only were we going up and down a lot but also sideways, as well. Basically I kept thinking to myself; are these planes safe and are we going to make it to Big OZ, in this life time.

The reason for this anxiety may have been the same as my new hero Bill Bryson (have read all his books) who also has been to Australia on several times and wrote a hilarious book about it called Down Under. In essence Australia is so dangerous that you may get eaten by a shark, eaten by a Yowie, killed by a spider, killed by several types of snakes, killed by a box jellyfish or worse still be attacked or eaten by a Larrikin, which may have been the baddy in Wolfe Creek. But what is a Larrikin, is it a wild animal, wild snake or some form of Homo sapiens or even a bottle of red wine? After I have been travelling around this huge Island - continent for two months, hopefully I will find out? It may be a word used to explain 'a fun-loving trouble maker who bucks authority and convention', but surely not another name for John Howard is it? The reason I am mentioning this neo- brute/bastard or 'Man of Steel' (Stalin was also called the same name and since first writing this he has been thrown out of office, even losing his seat in Sydney) is that I did phone him before the start of this part of the journey, for one simple answer. I had heard from the mass media that Australia is full, so would I be able to come and visit the place, if this was so. Hopefully I am a rational, intelligent, well read and logical man, because if Mumbai is not full with nearly 20 million and it's only a small strip of land mass, why is Australia full when it's the size of the USA with the same population? Is this logic, I ask myself? He did say I could come because you are a stupid tourist and we need to rip-you off, so please come Brian, thanks Yobbo. As it seems with over 5 million visitors a year it is not enough, so they want more, but not poor people - because if they try and come

they will probably end up as shark meat at the bottom
of the sea, so I was told by a friendly Aussie I met in
India – which may mean a 'flake' product sold in fish and
chip shop. Quite logical, I presume - if you feed them on
poor people they won't eat the rich tourists, will they?
I was also going to ask Howard why he spends about
860,000 Australian dollars (The Sydney Morning Herald
8th December 2006) on overseas travel a year when he
could swim around the Pacific for nothing. Apparently
he goes overseas to bring water bottles back in there
thousands - as there is not enough water in Australia
and that is the real reason that it is full, so a Larrikin
told me or it may have been lovely Leslie from Tasmania.
According to Mark Curtis Howard got elected in 2001
by seeking to curb the rights of asylum seekers who had
reached Australia, 'in blatant violation of International
refuge law' (Curtis 2003 p, 89). In other words get out
we don't want you; as you don't have any dosh too spend.
Amazingly according to the Guardian (23 August 2007)
'71,000' poms left little Britain to live in Aussie land in
2004/2005 to seek a better life in the sun, I presume if
you have some dosh to spend or a good job to go too.

So on arriving at Sydney airport I was very concerned
that I may not be able to get out of the airport, or
understand the language, if the place was chocker block.
But guess what not a soul in sight, only Steve the custom's
officer who wanted to look in my bag and a sign saying
'only 18 minutes to the outback'. The reason Steve and
his mates were suspicious of me was that I wrote on the
slip of paper, signed on the aircraft in advance - saying I
was going to a backpacker lodge when looking reasonable
well dressed. So I told him that I was a very famous

author, who he should look up on Google, from another galaxy at this rate and about to write my third book and have only come to do research, on the project. He said 'well that's okay then… it makes sense, does it not, its sounds logical' and Steve spoke such perfect 'strine'. I had picked the Woodduck Inn because according to Lonely Planet you get a free pick up from the airport and a free beer on arrival. Quite an inducement don't you think? But not actually true because the bus would drop you off at the Inn after you have paid 10 dollars for the privilege. The catch being that if you stayed for three nights we will reimburse the ten dollars, or pay ten dollars less when paying the bill.

The first impression of Australia was very positive apart from the weather and the industrial backdrop, just out of the airport; which looked like a piss poor day in little Britain, because the bus driver was a very friendly black man called Koffa from Ghana. As I have known several people from West Africa and lived with them, I think he took a liking to me and was very helpful for my search for some wood ducks. Well actually not one in site but he did drop me off near the Woodduck Inn. Why it is called this has been lost in the mist of time, because I certainly did not see a lot of wood or ducks for that matter. The process for getting in was a bit complicated as the actually living quarters was up stairs about a mile from the outside door. So you call a lovely young woman on an intercom system that does not always work and hopefully an angel will open the door if she can not press the correct button upstairs, to let you in. The angel, Lisa from Belgium let me in and after dragging my suit case up a million stairs I paid her for a full three days, in Aussie dollars. Being completely shattered after arriving at 6 in the morning, from Bangkok, I had a shower and a good rest on the top bunk bed of my little room.

After resting I ventured up William Street towards the city centre and straightaway had the feeling that you could breathe easy and feel relaxed in Australia. Even in this big city of 4 million people, it does seem that way walking through it, and at this time it all looked clean and tidy, but not as 'egalitarian' as wonderful Bill Bryson seems to believe, as we shall see. And of course most people speak a form of English, not a Russell Crowe version (BBC) as spoken in Master and Commander: the Far Side of the World - who in the movie apparently met Lord Nelson but something that we all can understand with a slight southern twang. First of all I bought a Guardian weekly, for 4.50 dollars in Thailand it was 450 Barts - one of the few objective newspapers in the world and then strolled in to Woolworths to buy some food. Back at the Backpackers I do wonder slightly that the description in the Lonely Planet and social reality may be two different things. They say 'the location's great and rooftop views are awesome 'watch the fruit bats commute at dusk'. First the rooftop views are not that spectacle and I did not see one fruit bat. But I did have a big idea on my first night which when I saw the gear stick tower (AMP), as the locals call it, for the first time - that I could rename it as the Rupert Murdoch tower, because it does look like a big knob. I hope that you get the joke and to think that he is now a USA citizen, so given up his Australian citizenship to make loads more dosh for him and his family. Some are never satisfied with their lot, just read Affluenza for the real evidence and the damage it does to you, especially in the English speaking world. In fact according to Oliver James the virus is so relevant in Sydney (he uses the metaphor of a virus to explain this phenomenon) that there is very little hope with people who have caught the virus. Considering that the first impression you get of Australia is that this is paradise on earth - but why is it that at least '1 million people are depressed'? Not forgetting that even the great Tony Hancock came here to commit suicide, but surely it's not that bad, is it! The fact may be as James notes that ironical it's the 'Americanisation of Sydney' that is the cause of this unhappiness. The reason is simple that ruthless Market capitalism tends to make every interaction between people a commodity, so if you are not useful to a person or family and vis-à-vis in an economic way; why do I want to be friends with you at all. Which is very cynical but very true, as some one who was born in a very small community and lived in one for the first sixteen years of my life and never really felt at ease in urban society, especially in a misanthropic hell-hole like the West Midlands in little Britain, where I unfortunately lived for 20 years.

The trouble with all humans if Oliver James is correct is that we have forgotten how to be children - as he explains about his beautiful little daughter on many pages but especially p, 281 (hardback edition) where she is the teacher with dada and the four teddies are the children. Two teddies are naughty so are singled out for corporal punishment; I wonder why it was not Rupert Murdoch 'the dirty digger', myself but apparently these two are so naughty that she spanks them, with a coal spade and metaphorical speaking she sets fire to them -

but keeps saying its only pretend dada. This is wonderful stuff, but I do get the point what he driving at, as I have a wonderful daughter as well, who is now 35. But I hope has not caught the virus although she has lived in London for 15 years, and travelled around Australia for seven months, with a boyfriend, and broke her arm in Perth - but still wants to buy a house sometime in the future, perhaps even in Sydney.

On my first full day in Sydney I decide that I must visit the Opera house, a 'don't miss' visit according to Lonely Planet - so after breakfast I walk down the parkway, St Mary's road, Prince Albert road and down past the art gallery into the Royal Botanic Gardens, which were very delightful a little bit of Britain on the other side of the world. Australians are on the whole very friendly people especially the middle class ones that I have met in Southern Africa, six years ago, who were mostly Vets, through out this journey over two months I did not meet, one Vet - but many other professions as I shall inform you as I progress. I am saying this because as I walk through these incredible Botanic Gardens even the birds seem relaxed and friendly. However near the great Shell type creature called the Sydney Opera house I meet a bronzed statue called the Devil in Bronze or 'Say Tar' who actually spoke to me and said something like 'what are you doing here peasant don't you know that I am Sir Lord Rupert Murdoch's father, in a new form and this is my resting place…go away and don't disturb me again'… 'No your holiness I won't'.

At the great Shell type creature called the Sydney Opera house I walk around it and try and think of something amusing that I can say about this wonderful structure, but surely not inspired by 'norks' were they? The only thing I could think of is that it does look a little like a tortoise or several who has been beached. Probably a few very short sighted females swimming up the harbour thinking that the Sydney Bridge was a male who wanted to mate, with them? But if this is not funny I did meet two very friendly guards called Richard and Scott who were interesting to talk to and helping to guard the great female tortoises for future prosperity and John Pilger. Because would you believe it this is what he says about this area – 'physically, there is no place like Sydney: the deep-water harbour, the tiara of Pacific beaches, the estuaries and secret bays where white eucalyptus, the giant gums, rise from the water's edge (2002 p, 158) etc. But, being wonderful John on the next page he returns to the harsh reality of life when he notes that when the IOC committee came to look around before making there mind up about the Olympic Games in 2000; the 'traffic lights were timed to green as their limousines approached'. Come on John, we all no that life is very cruel, for the majority - but at-least it worked, didn't it? Billy Connolly is also very impressed with Sydney as he walked to the top of the Harbour Bridge because he is in love with rivet's and got on top of the Opera house, some how.

The next port of call is the up market Portobello Coffee bar a few minutes walk from the Opera House, on the Quay side. Where I order a coffee latte; take out my note pad and drool over the sexy beautiful waitress from Slovakia, in the abstract, who delivered the coffee. The notes went well, the coffee was a rip-off, and the beautiful women from Eastern Europe had a very sexy bottom. The next stop is the area around Sydney called the Rocks, where I had my first argument/quarrel with an Aussie. This was quite a shock to me as I was under the false premise that Aussies were so laid back they never got uptight. Manual from Italy, with a New Zealand girlfriend also told me in another bar very close to the Portobello Coffee bar, he was the manager - that the local authority in Sydney was so authoritarian; as even if your chairs were not in the correct parameters, outside, you could be fined, I did think was this true or is this guy paranoid, about local government, like many small business people everywhere in the world.

So I walked into several shops viewing the goods on display, in one I noticed some boomerang, designed to kill being sold for '100 dollars' each, quite pricey I thought, in the Metcalf Arcade. So I suggested in a jokey way - what did he pay the indigenous people for their work, saying something like 'did you pay them 5 or 10 dollars, for them'. He went berserk with me, for being so rude; I just said 'I am a political satirist and trying to be funny'. I think the truth was that I hit a very raw nerve with this little businessman, who nearly threw me out of the shop and let's face it - even the great Aussie nation is now trying to come to terms with the way that Aborigine people have been treated in the past. The hard facts seem to be this in 1788 there may have been as many as '750,000' Aboriginal people and probably at least '600,000 have died' since the 'invasion' of their country (Pilger2002 p, 192). The ironic fact about this incident; according to a female German backpacker I spoke to about this small tiff, when I got back to the Woodduck Inn, run by gorgeous Cindy this time – 'was that more then likely these boomerangs were probably made in a factory in the Third World and not by the locals, at all'. Who are probably paid worse then the Aborigines for there goods, so if true, I did hit a very raw nerve with this little businessman. But ironically according to Bertrand Russell quoting Dr H. K. Fry about the aborigines, asserting 'a native in his wild state lives in constant danger, hostile spirits are about him constantly. Yet is light hearted and cheerful...indulgent to his children and kind to his aged parents' (Russell 1949 p, 19 & 20).

Phew that was a close shave, and I had one in the morning as well, so to calm me down I buy a few post cards, in the local shop and send them to a wonderful sexy lady I met in Thailand and another to my best friend Robert in the West Midlands. Then on to the nearest train, taking me to the Central Railway station; to buy a ticket to Canberra for the next part of this great adventure Downunder, in a few days time – on my return to the backpackers I meet my room mates for the first time. Who was Andy from Germany, Peter from Bruno in the Czech Republic and Jason from Plymouth, in little Britain the United Nations at work and play. Peter from the Czech Republic seemed the most serious of the three young men who did not want anything to do whatsoever with backpacking culture - but wanted to understand how the indigenous people of Australian lived and so on.

I also met Rupert, from the UK who on his second day in Australia fell off his top bunk bed and broke his back. If he was pissed out of his mind or on zolpidem, he never told me, but if the British Sunday Observer (04 02 07) is correct the second drug given on prescription sounds a bit dodgy to me. As it says 'the research, by Australia's Federal Health Department, found 16 cases of odd sleepwalking, 104 hallucinations and 62 of amnesia among users of the powerful sedative'. What about that for a bit of bad luck, but very lucky for him he can now walk and do everything else young backpackers do, which is…yes, what is it now? However he did seem like a very nice lad who's Dad were a doctor and his Mum who is not having a lot of luck with men - divorced twice and read History at UWE in Bristol, where I also was for a year several years ago. Rupert, having dropped out of University, was also a denier that 'social class' is an important issue in the world today. What I have noticed over several decades - it is always the 'established middle class' ''and the 'upper class' who lie and pretend that 'class' either does not exist or is now irrelevant, in this epoch; nothing could further from the truth. In fact reading Bill Bryson (mentioned several times in the book) who is a an American but married to a British nurse, in his books - you would never know that there is rich and poor in the world, although he did admit his wife's family did come from a less affluent family, in little Britain and the Southern part of the USA was so different from the rest, that it seems like another country.

But out of everyone I met at the Woodduck in probably Philippe from France seemed to be the most ambitions with clear objectives about life and a sense of purpose. He had already done numerous walks and was about to set out on another adventure, when I met him, armed with all the evidence, so very interesting to talk too. The next morning I have decided that I must visit Manley beach because again it's on the 'don't miss' visit in the Lonely Planet. So I walk the way I did yesterday morning through the Royal Botanic Gardens and on to the Ferry. For about 6 dollars I can have a small boat ride one-way through the harbour and on to the area near the beach. It was good to see that the Navy was in port, just in case they get invaded by the billions of poor people from up north and to protect Fort Denison and all those small Islands in the Pacific where some people don't know their position/station in the natural order of things. Once you have landed you walk across a small piece of ground, by the shops and then you see the sheer beauty of Manly beach, with lots of people trying to surf - which on the day I was there was quite rough. So I decided to walk around to the Cabbage tree beach, on the south side and although it was very windy I had a swim and nearly froze, to death because after Thailand this place, at this time of year the water is cold. The thought of being eaten by a shark is also at the back of your mind or being throttled alive by a Box jelly fish, one of the most dangerous animals on earth - which is never far from the surface of the active brain cells - that is if you have any at my age. Within the first few days Downunder I am enjoying the experience but already I have noticed that just underneath the surface of the so-called laid back Culture of Australia that there is a strong authoritarian streak in society. This would not be unusual, because the British ruling class and the Nazi were bedfellows, in my view - in fact I have read over the last few years that the Nazis loved the way the British ruling class treated the masses and admired them and tried too ape them. Things have not changed a lot in little Britain, but you would think that the Aussie would have seen through it, and probably the reason that nearly 30 to 50% of the population wants to leave little Britain. Later on I will be using sources from a book about the incredible Errol Flynn, born in Tasmania who would not be told what to do, by anyone and probably did not have to 'flog the log', too much as he had more women and men then most men would have in ten lives, it is called 'Satan's Angel' by David Bret, so go out and read it, you will not regret it. The reason I am telling you this is that at Manly beach I read a sign which said that you must not 'smoke or drink on the beach'. While there I also had a lovely fish and chip lunch in a local café and a relaxing hour on the beach with a book and I also sent a few emails from the local email shop run by a very friendly Muslim man. The only downside to Manly beach was the amount of flies that kept pestering you, but guess what I had another Albert Einstein moment, when there - where I did think that if we all become Muslim women we could wear a burka, for protection.....but would this mean that we were going back to the first billion years of life on earth, when we were only in female form.

The next day, after saying goodbye to the lovely friendly staff at the Woodduck Inn I am at the Central Railway station waiting in the local bar with some pigeons having a small breakfast, for the train to Canberra. Just before popping in to the loo for a leak and washing my hands with cold water, apparently I was told by a male pigeon, little John was his name - that the local government in Sydney are thinking of pumping in warm water from Thailand which would be quicker then waiting for private enterprise to do it for a fortunate...another hundred years sounds about correct. While in the bar I got reading the Sydney Morning Herald and was astounded to learn that perhaps the first life form to come out of the sea was probably in Australia. I think this may have been John Howard's grandfather, because if Howard and the Liberal party are on this Planet, they are not human and humane. If you are not aware how the Political system works here it is called a Federal structure and not an Unitary one like it is little Britain. In other words the seven States have some autonomy from the Central government in Canberra, while writing this the seven States are all controlled by Labour and the Liberal party control the ACT. In little Britain all the power is controlled from the centre. This has been especially relevant under the Thatcher regime and her surrogate son Tony Blair, who has now 5 houses to his name. This is why I am now saying/suggesting that we are now drifting into a ruthless One Party State in the UK. Because in essence who is representing the vast majority of 'wage slaves'. Think about it? Who are forced to sell their 'labour power' in the 'labour market' or starve? Pilger puts it this way: 'Like Britain and the USA, Australia is a single-ideology state with two competing factions, discernible largely by the personalities of their politicians' (2002 p, 168).

At 12:10 we are off on the Train to Canberra the Capital of Australia in the ACT - at the start I am on my own, so carried on reading the paper. After some time a young 'working class' man called Ben got on and sat next to me, he lived in Canberra and was on his way home. He told me that he had some sort of 'mental problem' and was on the dole but went to Sydney every so often to help his brother cut down trees, in Sydney... this process does not sound very eco-friendly to me. The scenery throughout was glorious as was Helen who booked me in, for four nights at the YHA on Akuna street, a very modern and new youth hostel with all the amenities required by a backpacker, including the smallest swimming pool in the world. So after having a swim and rest I nip down stairs, just outside of the hostel, for a drink and saw a young man being thrown out for being rude to the bar maid. I then venture out, in the big wide world for a walk around the shopping centre and try to find the local Chinese restaurant which I did not find, so instead I visited the Babar café cum bar cum restaurant for a wonderful meal, just around the corner from the YHA. Throughout I was thinking about the great Billy Connelly who made a fantastic TV documentary about Australia a few years ago. This is what he said about Canberra which according to him means 'meeting place' where apparently he has several relatives through his marriage to a very wonderful Aussie woman, now a professor. Nothing more than a place that Albert Speer would have been very proud off. A Teutonic paradise for the master race, oops the English ruling class, I presume - where there are at least 70 embassies in many different forms, run by 'pretentious pricks'. The next morning I did something that Billy Connelly or Billy Bryson did not do as far as we know; which was to hire a cycle for 20 dollars, from the hostel for a ride around Canberra. My objective for at least part of the journey was to cycle up the Black mountain about 860 meters high where the Telstra Tower is erected. So not having a compass I head off in the wrong direction, before I realize that I am heading in the complete opposite way that I should be cycling, so as soon as I see the mountain across the way. I turn around and head for the hills. The journey at my age was very hard work, indeed - but being a Capricorn I was determinate to do it at all cost. The view was very pleasant, but was it 'truly ecstatic' as Lonely Planet says, sex is; but views come on - as was my lunch in the Botanic gardens café at the bottom of the hill. Not leg over and chips but something not fatting and a tea. The next leg of the cycle ride took me over Lake Griffin to the Capital Hill area and on around the south side of the lake. Popping over to a small Island where there is a large statue but not built by the Governor General - however he may have laid the foundation stone, with some help. After about three hours of cycling I have had enough and rode back to the YHA for a good shower and a rest. Where I meet my new chums (room mates) for the first time, who is Bill from New Zealand, doing something, not sure what, John who is Government bureaucrat working in Sydney and Canberra, working on the tax system, but not at the same time, I hope and Sam who is a dentist with his own practise, from Taiwan. Surely the only man on earth who is a dentist and staying in a youth hostel, this was my supposition for sure. After doing my washing, I head back to the Babar café/bar/ restaurant for a good dinner, again with some two rivers wine, excellent and it went very well with the book I was reading. Back at the YHA I have a fantastic discussion about British Royalty and religion with my new chums. I was against both of these reactionary processes, they were not to sure - but Sam was certainly confused about class and how it impacts on all our lives even if we are not aware of it, or not. Getting tied up in knots about mental freedom and physically freedom, as if you can separate the two. Under normal circumstances I don't think you can without you are a Monk in Tibet or Thailand, who's sole objective is to reach Nirvana which means 'perfect bliss attained by the extinction of Individuality'. Surely the complete opposite to the crazy notion that we are all individuals, as proselytised in the Western world, I would have thought!

The very worrying aspect of this argument for me was how Sam is completely sure that life in Modernity is about ruthless Darwinism in the Herbert Spencer mode…very frightening, indeed. Nietzsche rules okay and perhaps he is more of a realist then I am - especially after reading 'Gangster Capitalism' by Michael Woodiwiss a UWE lecturer from Bristol. And reading in the Guardian today (8th Feb 2007) that 12billion USA dollars have disappeared down a great big hole in Iraqi…but if one single normal family gained out of it is very dubious proposition, so it seems. But when in the Babar having a drink after dinner I did have another Albert Einstein moment, that may be or not a brilliant hypothesis/proposition, that may be true - after observing three young men with Asian girlfriends who were getting on very well, just behind me, like I did in Thailand…with the new love of my life. Basically it goes like this that if Western women don't take an Asian course in manners about how to treat men in and out of bed, they are going to be doomed. In other words probably written out of evolutionary history, for good - I may be stoned to death by the Feminist movement (sorry ladies… upside down logic) for this terrible outrageous suggestion, 'how shocking can this little twit get'…I hear them all saying.

After breakfast the next morning I walk for sometime from the YHA to the 'National Museum of Australia', which is one of the newest in the world and which is on the site of a demolished hospital. Where when it was blown up 25 years ago, a poor young girl got killed, because instead of imploding inwards it went outwards, with tragic results - I was told this little story by a young women called Amy in another museum, who was born there - I visited the next day, close to the youth hostel. I spent two hours exploring this place and it was a very enjoyable experience, indeed. You could even drift/walk through the 'Garden of Australian Dreams' which has nothing whatsoever to do with the Protestant work ethnic, but probably not understood by most Western people who are now so brainwashed by the whole process that they don't question it! For once the Lonely Planet has got it correct about this structure, as it says about a part of the place; it 'seems to be more abstract Australian story–book than museum. Using humour, creativity, controversy and self-contradiction, the museum puts national identity in a blender, challenging visitors' ideas of Australian-ness' etc (p, 120). The small spinning cinema with a short history of Australia and its nationhood should not be missed…I thought in conclusion.

To recover I treat myself to a coffee before the long walk back to the youth hostel - trying not to stand on deadly snakes and spiders. While I was swimming in the youth hostel, I got talking to a teacher from the Northern Territory, who had brought some teenagers down to visit Canberra, from a boarding school, for a few weeks. What I thought was very nice, from what I saw was how the aborigine kids seemed to get on very well the white kids.

As I did with Jason from Plymouth who seemed to have followed me from Sydney when we had an evening drink in a local pub, where some young women seemed to be getting themselves, very pissed. Well what's new?

The next day I stroll up to the Australian War Museum which is a spectacle site but to what I ask myself, stupidity over generations, shall we say! As a pacifist I still find it amazing just like Lenin did many decades ago and Michael Moore very recently - how the Ruling Classes can still get the working class to kill one another, on very dubious assumptions and premises. What I wrote in my note book at the time was as most Museums in Australia are free and very good. So it can at least encourage some people to participate in the learning process and in the case of places like these perhaps question what our Masters of the Universe, say is really good for us, or not. Like the invasion of Turkey in the First World War, which went very bad for the allies and the loss of troops, was horrendous…another cock up you could say. In fact throughout most of my life there has always been lots of propaganda about Hitler - but never about the underlying causes of the First. Considering that all the Royal families of Europe were related, at one time and some even to this day the only real evidence seemed to be what the great John Reed said in 1918…Profit, and nothing else. After dinner in the evening I venture into the very compact small cinema by the Babar complex to watch the great Ken Loach's latest incredible movie called 'the Wind that Shakes the Barley'. Another story about the Irish uprising in the 1916-1920 periods and how the British brutes carried out their foreign polices which have not changed, a lot with a boot and a barrel of the gun in the face and stomach to anyone who opposes their thuggery.

I head for the Bus station the next morning and the open road to Melbourne, having purchased the ticket a few days before, Jason came along as well. It was a very long journey through baron land where it had not rained for a very long time, which is causing great concern in Big Oz, will I be able to run my swimming pool - after several hours we got off at a very small railway station at Albury, for a cup of tea and a snack. This place was so small we may have been the first visitors for a century or since Ned Kelly was alive. On arriving at Melbourne the birth place of Germaine Greer in the evening; Jason and I walk up the road to the Metro YHA probably one the friendliest cleanest and pleasant places I have ever stayed in and phone my new friend Sylda, who lives on the out skirts of this city. The next morning I wonder down into town, looking for some prescription sun glasses. I lost my old ones in Bangkok when either working on the net or dreaming about beautiful Thai women who are everywhere in Thailand. In fact where ever you move your head you see them and I presume that your testosterone level goes up with every move of your head until your testicles explode with the thought of making love to the lot. I find a respectable option that does not cost the earth and order a new pair from lovely young Christian from New Zealand. The cup of coffee a few doors down and the Sydney Morning Herald went well together, as well; but no handle on the cup, probably the first time in my life I have had a coffee without the cup and handle together. I did think to myself that I may have nipped over to the Andromeda Galaxy for a drink, while reading the paper. This may not be far from the truth as this is the city where Ned Kelly was hanged, and ever since has been a hero of the average Australian, who despises authority. This was also the city where the great Shane Warne was born and now when playing cricket for Hampshire, in little Britain advertises hair loss products while trying to bowl a maiden over, and in the Daily Mail. I never went this time to the jail in Melbourne where Ned Kelly was hanged but I must next time as Billy Connolly did and was in awe of the great man and the place, itself.

Back at the youth hostel I pick up my bags and trot off to the railway station to take a train to Diamond Creek. This is where my new friend Sylda lives and has for a few years. Like me she was born in the Falkland Islands and when we were babies were pushed around in prams together in Port Stanley and no doubt had very long conversations about the meaning of life, but have not seen one another since. Having got off the train we agreed to meet in the local Hilton, I mean fish and chips shop which I found after I had fell over the pavement and grazed both hands.

Having never seen me before apart from when babies she did think to herself how would she recognise me, she told me after the meeting - well I did have a suit case and two grazed hands. I am about two months older then Sylda so I think that we did get on and had a lot too talk about. She has a lovely bungalow in a very good neighbourhood and a married son called Ben, just down the road, with lots of books. After being shown where to lay my head I start dinner, my treat for my new friend which was a stir-fry, about the only thing I can cook without making a complete mess. Sylda is quite an interesting person because she was brought to Australia with her parent's brother and sister when she was 12, in 1960, on several ships. She married a local lad from Sydney had a son, worked for the central Government for ten years. Had lived in Newcastle, Canberra and South Africa as well as visiting the United Kingdom on holiday and now works for herself.

I stayed for five nights with Sylda, reading another book about 'the Falklands conflict' complete, by Dobson Miller Payne, swimming in the local pool visiting Melbourne on several occasions and doing the things that tourist do. Like going up the Rialto tower, listening to Vivaldi on the train station, having lunch on a boat on the Yarra River, visiting Federation Square where there was a demonstration about Darfur and pop groups getting in on the act, St Kilda's area, where apparently the red light district used to be, the Ian Potter Museum, etc. Noting that I am always very cynical when very rich people and pop stars who get involved in good causers myself - because in essence who are they promoting themselves or the cause. I also went to a local club with Sylda having a very long chat about Aussie culture and so on; with the locals…Mel very laid back, John et al. What I noticed above anything else was that the Protestant Work Ethic is alive and kicking in Australia and that those terrible Brits brought Union chaos to them in the 1960's. I am not convinced about this discourse because Australia was one of the first countries in the world to introduce the 8 hour day and Unions have always played a part in their culture (source, the great -John Pilger). I also noticed how sport is being used like most places in the world by the 'Ruling

Elite' to cement crude crass 'Nationalism'. However the highlight of my stay with Sylda was going with lovely son Ben for dinner and being taken around the Yarra valley tasting wine, with him and his mum, his wife was out of town. At one place, run by Ken who told us a lot about the whole process was also the local postmaster, wonderful stuff. I had never done this before but it seems to a part of the new culture that people are getting in on. Ben and his wife are both policeman in the Victoria State and lives in a house the size of Buck House. Ben is also an expert on wine, so I may have learnt something from the young man. He also represented Australia at Ice hockey, without an ice ring being anywhere near, so I presume he practised on an iceberg in Port Philip bay. We also had lunch in a very small village, where I ate crocodile pie and went to a Museum somewhere in the outback, which I had never done before and found it quite amusing, because to my knowledge there is not one on the Yorkshire Moors or must places where there is no people. For the last two nights in lovely Melbourne, or 'Toy Town' as I heard someone say - I stayed back in the wonderful Metro YHA while waiting for my new sun glasses to be completed by Optical City. Visiting the Melbourne Zoo for over two hours where I saw bears mating, what a disgraceful thing to do, what would Brenda (sic) think boys and girls. The Zoo is a magnificent place and worth a visit whatever you may think about locking up poor animals to stare at, what about the poor prols shut up in factories and officers for hours, isn't this a very similar phenomena, to the cruel Zoo? I was reading The Life of Pi at the time so very relevant to this visit. The four male Loins, living separate from the rest, also told me that they would love some female company, so come on owners of the Zoo let them have some lovely sex; they would enjoy it like most of us if we can get it! Or was this in this surreal book, I am reading? According to a brochure I picked up while there; there is over 36 different species in the Zoo and you could even have a sleep over with the animals. This is true I saw a sign on the way out, I am not too certain how it works but sounds very Aussie friendly to me. You would never see this in little Britain in a million years or the chance to see an Orang-utan, George W Bush nearest cousin - see Steve Bell's brilliant cartoons, in the Guardian; if you don't believe me. It seems that if you are 'in year 2 through to VCE' you can sleep over with the animals, but not George W Bush because he is such a dangerous animal, so God told me.

I also attended something new in the YHA on my last night in Melbourne that I had not been to before, with Eric (slightly deaf) and Gloria which was an auction, run by Safari Pete, but tonight he was away so we had Ivor dressed in Steve Irwin garb, who sadly got killed when I was travelling, for tours around Australia, with a free glass of wine. I bid for a trip from Alice Springs to Cairns on a bus, and got it, well it is a long way from Melbourne, folks. As evidence that not everyone backpacking and living in Youth Hostels are middle class. Eric told me that he had been to a pyjama party on the lawn outside a few nights ago - when some twit set fire to some furniture while smoking…meaning that they all had to leave the building in the middle of the night while the fire-brigade put out the fire. I was also told by a Victoria (the place not the era) lady in the YHA cafe that Asian women are very popular with Aussie men, perhaps I am a little clever than most publishers and agents think, in little Britain, what did I say a few pages ago! The next morning Gloria informed me that she was from New Zealand and that the Mafia run Australia, in fact she was so sure of this fact - they may even be in this place at this moment in time running the kitchen. At the time I did not see Rupert Murdoch in the place but you never know he may have been in the kitchen; cleaning the cooker around the back or should that be his beautiful sexy Asian wife.

After reading The Life of Pi all day in the YHA and thinking that this may be the biggest load of tosh I have read while waiting for the Ferry - I am informed on the BBC World Service many months later that this book has sold at least two million copies, not too sure why my self, probably because it won a prize several years ago, and people/masses can be manipulated by the mass media, very easy. As we know Australia is so full that there is no room for anyone apart from the 5 million plus tourists, so Howard has told the world and I think I know why now after being in wonderful Melbourne. It is called in little Britain the Nimby effect - which means 'not in my back yard' or in the case of Australia the whole continent. As Billy Connolly kept saying when he was on tour here that this place is a 'delightful country', even if the locals don't realise it - even in Newcastle that this place may be a bit 'rough' but it is still in 'paradise'. Noting that he also asserted about how most Aussies don't care to shits about 'class'; where if you go into a restaurant you would not worry too much if it was posh or whatever, it is irrelevant to their culture.

I arrive at the Ferry terminal, by tram after being told by a very well informed young back - packer that you just wonder on to it without booking up in advance, like most places in the world. A big mistake this is Aussie Land and they do things different here, or was I conned? As soon as I said I wanted a ticket for Tasmania to the young women behind the counter she said 'it is full'. Well actually it was not, if I paid nearly 200 dollars for a 'business ticket'. Having booked out and all the other rigmarole you go trough to get from A to B, I paid up and sighed, well what's money if you have not got it and this boat is called the 'Spirit of Tasmania', so may be worth travelling on and would I find the spirit of Errol Flynn in the people, or perhaps even the Princess and a Devil. And it was an all night journey in a very calm sea this time, but as you slept on a seat like an aircrafts, it was not that comfortable although according to the brochure I am looking at it has ten decks. So, a little larger than a dingy or the normal ferry crossing the English Channel, on a windy day and to think that Tasmania and little Britain were both part of the large continent about 10,000 years ago. According to a very recent Time Team special TV programme (24th April 2007) about the UK when it was attached to Europe, which it has been for the most of human history. Hunter Gatherers actual lived with some very strange animals thousands of years ago where the North Sea is now. Neanderthal man/women was also there apparently wearing Kate Moss garb, now worth 45 million pounds - so one old man told me from the other side last night, in my dreams. Brian those hot pants drove us mad, according to William who was King of one square mile.

The dinner was excellent as was the breakfast and very reasonable priced. I also met Professor Wilson Macmillan from Melbourne, but was born in Glasgow - who was travelling to Hobart for a conference of architects, not his favourite people, so he told me, as he was an Engineer by profession and they tend to speak in riddles, like Bush and Blair. If I was conned at least I made up for it by having a lift all the way to Hobart in his car for nothing and he dropped me off five minutes away from the youth hostel on Argyle Street. Hobart the birth place of Errol Flynn on the 20th June 1909 who 'nurtured a quite staggering appetite for young men and under-aged girls' - Wilson told me a very good joke about a parrot that lived most of his life in a brothel, a bit like Flynn. When the new owners bought him from a pet shop he made the huge slip up of recognising the new male owner when he came home in front of his wife. Oops no sex for a year Fred. He also informed me that he made loads of money in the TV colour revolution in Australia so was quite a successful businessman over the years as well as being a part time professor, at the University.

I had decided that I would spend about a week in Tasmania, 'the heart of Australia', can this be correct my heart near my feet, or is it my bottom - as my biological father if still alive, may live there. So after booking in I nip up to the Town Hall and see if I can trace him on the electoral register. No luck at all, anywhere in Australia, according to the register. But in the Quarry I did find 'brown sugar' for the first time in OZ for my tea and snack. When I return to the Youth Hostel I meet my new friends who were Sean, who I thought may be slightly bonkers but some time in the future he may be a very famous author. Who writes up stories every night, in his diary, after work and told me this axiom about women as he sees them – they are the 'gatherers the tenders and the executioners'. Not bad Sean! Leslie who was a little older then me and was an engineer from Melbourne and had never been out of Australia. But trying to save the heritage of the mining industry and Jonathan a young man training to be a plumber and very bright, from Tasmania. During the day I do some shopping, for food, buy the Melbourne Age for 1-80 dollars (extra cents for crossing the sea) and post a book back to little Britain after being forced to show my passport. The first time in my whole life that I have had to do this too post a package. Is this something to do with the Devil or should that be the Tasmania Princess? In the evening I went for a fantastic cheap Asian dinner with Leslie down in the Salamanca complex who informed me that it was probably a British conspiracy that got the Danish King's son to marry Mary, so as that the Australian people would never vote for being a Republican again. I just made this up, but in essence probably not far from the truth, what do you think folks?

While in Tasmania I walked up Mt Wellington from 'Fern Tree' or as my invisible guides the wonderful aboriginal peoples who were nearly wiped out by the white man told me; we called it 'Never again Mountain' because once you walked up there and back you would never do it again; I took 5 hours to walk up and back. I am only mentioning this because when walking back down I was listening to a wonderful old men called Paul who is now dead, on the radio - but had an amazing and tragic life because he was born half Aborigine, half Germen.

Apparently he was sent to a boarding school and treated like dirt while there, although a religious school so much for compassion. After he left school he went to where his Mother was born and suggested that he could feel the images of his own family jumping into the water and so on, very touching for an old cynical git like me. In fact Paul's father may have a very close relative of a youngish German Doctor who took a dislike to me for having my books published, I think in the Youth Hostel - or she may have met her match, intellectual, because I have spent 6 years at University as well. So to get my own back on her for being so stroppy, with me - I have decided to call her Rosy Keble's daughter out of 'From Russia with Love', (she was born in Germany in this book) the nasty piece of work with poison tips in her shoes, in the movie.

I also visited the Tasmania Museum & Art Gallery which was free and well worth a visit as I said earlier the Aussies are very good at presenting these places in a very aesthetic way. As they note, 'visitors to the Tasmania Museum and art Gallery experience a special interaction between art, history and science all within a cultural precinct steeped in history'. I also learnt what a devil really is, while in there - it is not Tony Blair but a little dog type creature that is very vicious with a powerful jaw. I never saw a live one while I was in Tasmania, but apparently they are a live and kicking somewhere. The crimes committed by the English Elite was also on display even stating that at one time there was '225 crimes against property' in little Britain. The reason that it was easy for them to send convicts to Australia for very minor offences in the nineteenth century, when stealing a sheep would have probably got you hung and stealing a apple a six weeks trip to Port Arthur, in a very dodgy old ship. There may be 500 crimes against property now that Thatcher et al and her son Blair have been in power for 28 years, for all I know? However the Police are not armed yet like Australia were in Hobart I saw a female Policeman with a gun on a pushbike, very scary. In fact it just goes to show how alert I had been because it was the first time that I had noticed that the Police carry guns downunder.

During the next day I have a very enjoyable trip around Hobart harbour sitting next to Noel and Tom two old men from around the Sydney area of Australia who had become widowers and were now free to do what ever they wanted to do - which was to see as much as possible before the 'coffin with no wheels' whisked them off to the grave as one told me. The commentary was also very honest about the Colonial days and the rigid British class system, that has not really changed a lot in little Britain for all the 'white propaganda' by the mass media, that it has. In the evening I met Kerrie from Rosebery who had slept in her car on the way down to Hobart to see a movie about the how the Capitalist West is becoming a very scary place, in the Activist centre on Murry Street. For some strange reason the system would not work with the stated movie so instead we saw a wonderful one about how Cuba has survived for over 40 years of sanctions from the USA and the collapse of the old Soviet Union and is still working. According to David Bret, Errol Flynn actual met Castro just after the revolution in 1959 and took a real shine to 'the dashing young Argentinean, Che Guevara' and seemed to think that the revolution was a good thing (BBC4 TV programme April 2006) the Americans in general, did not. The second one we saw with another glass of wine was about tree felling in Tasmania which was not to pleasant for the trees or the climate, for that matter - because it is made into wood pulp to make paper - so that the Ruling class and their cohorts can tell more lies about the world and sometimes the odd little bit of truth. Like the 7th November in the Melbourne Age (the cup cracked) when Jim Schembric wrote that the 'Melbourne cup day' had nothing to do with horse racing per se - but the whole rotten 'British class system' and certainly nothing to do with a so-called 'classless society' that Australians like to brag about. So the complete opposite of social reality for most and how the rich love it. When this was happening at 3 o'clock I was having my second swim in the big pool in Hobart so missed the great big event, when the whole country comes to a grinding halt (Lonely Planet) - but considering that I don't believe in the whole ruthless system per se, it did not bother me at all. I should also note that I was given a DVD at the Activist centre about how the Tasmania forests (a global treasure) are being destroyed at a rate of 44 football pitches per day with many indigenous animals losing their habitats.

I visited the Museum for a second helping, the next day. I also visited the Divisional Headquarters of the Salvation Army to see Meg who was helping me to trace my real father's movements and in the afternoon went for a walk with Leslie et al under Hobart, a very stimulating experience not mentioned in Lonely Planet., being an Engineer Leslie gets very excited at seeing anything mechanical as he did several nights before when taking me for a walk around the harbour and seeing the fishing boats and so on. In fact I was telling Leslie that when I was swimming in the local pool, in the morning that it was so big that at one moment I thought I saw a whale but it was a very large lady stuffing her self, with a big Mac, so another whale told me. In the evening I had a glass of wine in the Hadley Hotel, a very up market hotel for a treat after talking to the statute of Edward VII who apparently was a 'peace maker', but strangely 4 years later Europe went to war and butchered millions, very peaceful, I must say, Sir…he did not reply. His relatives also went to war with Hitler 20 years later and some were even best mates and married to officers who worked with the Nazis (The Royals by Kitty Kelly 1997…a booked banned in the UK, so much for freedom of speech).

Hobart was the second city of Australia because of what I have mentioned above, so Port Arthur is a must do thing when you visit this place, I presume that 'Brenda and Keith' may have done the same thing when they came here in 1963, or she may have been trying to find Errol Flynn as a part-time lover, so Keith told me - unfortunately by the time they came; he had died of too much sex and drugs…lucky bastard. The next day I was going to go by ship but because the weather was so rough we all went on a very enjoyable bus ride with Kevin the very amusing guide. He took us around this famous site that had been renamed and the returned to what it was original. In essence because of the nature of the place the ruling groups were trying to brush history under the carpet. However this was never going to be possible and now it is a must see place for all tourists, accept Billy Bryson and Billy Connelly. The model of this place was taken from Jeremy Bentham who apparently designed his prisons for reforming the convicts in every way: through 'discipline punishment, religious and moral instructions' or as he noted they are Penitentiary as 'a machine for grinding rogues honest'. Paradoxically according to a little pamphlet that the Sunday Observer had made up (22nd April 2007) about Geniuses, Jeremy Bentham was a 'fierce atheist' just like me.

When having lunch and a glass of wine there I was joined by Gene from Indianan who was an academic, teaching English at University. Discussing why we did not see Bush, Blair, Thatcher, mother and son and all the other 'rouges' of history in the place. After lunch we went for a boat ride around the famous harbour and stopped off on the 'Isle of the Dead' to visit a grave yard with a guide who was very good and informative. The weather however was beastly and very cold and wet. The most famous prison of all time here was probably William Smith O'Brien who 'was member of a revolutionary group formed to fight for Ireland's independence from Britain'...in 1856 he was allowed to return to Ireland. According to Victoria Wood (BBC TV 13 May 2007) when a few of the convicts escaped during this period they ran out of food and had to turn to cannibalism, very gruesome but true apparently. On the way back home I was sitting next to another American - they are not all power-mad and stupid. She was called Ardis Dickey, married at least three times and was from California and had been in the movie 'Sleeping Beauty'. Not the cartoon version; but a real one so it seems.

CHAPTER SEVEN

- BIG OZ AND NEW ZEALAND - PART TWO

It's the 9th of November 2006 and I am at the International Tasmania airport (this may be a joke) after catching the bus from just down the road from the Youth Hostel, on Argyle Street. Where I meet Rose Keble's daughter for the last time in my life, I hope isn't Modernity wonderful? But what a figure and bottom, on her, especially in those tight blue jeans! That day was to be quite unusual because on my trip over to Melbourne on a Virgin Blue aircraft I was sitting next to Patricia who was 77 and just about to visit her son and daughter in law, in Melbourne who I don't think she got on very well with, so she told me… it's something like 'walking on egg shells' when she was with them. The ironic twist to this little story is that she had had a son killed in an accident before he was 20 and Kath 87 who I met (sat across from) on the flight from Melbourne to Perth also had a son killed before he was twenty. Kath for her age was quite an amazing old lady who seemed to have had a long and happy life and loved having very long lunches with vicars. Not my cup of tea, as I would probably end up throwing the bottles of wine and the food over their stupid heads, but she must love them. Kath also told me that she had worked as a Matron/nurse in a school in Tasmania and also was a nanny in the UK for a few weeks and flew to Zurich in 1957 when you had to peddle the engines to make them fly, I think. Well it was 50 years ago, when writing this up.

Perth which is sometimes called the 'Cinderella city' (Billy Connolly) can be very expensive as I found out on my first few hours in this city and the birth place of Heath Ledger. First of all the backpackers I first went to - thinking it was the Youth Hostel mentioned in Lonely Planet wanted at least 100 dollars up front to use my visa card and then when I went out after booking into the new wonderful one on Wellington Road to buy some bread and milk, they were nearly 7 dollars. Being tired after travelling can get you upset and this certainly got my back up, had I landed in a parallel Universe, I did think! Kevin with an 'attitude problem' also was not that friendly the young man who booked me into the YHA... perhaps he just disliked poms, which original meant 'Poms of Milbank' (source - BBC Radio 4 - autumn 2007). These little problems of mine do however pale into insignificance when you have travelled in the Developing world or if you were born an indigenous person in OZ - as according to John Pilger; Western Australia has the highest death rate of Aborigines in this State than in Bangladesh (2001 p, 162). Western Australia, Perth and Coogee (just outside of Freemantle) in this case, was also the place that Susan Tickner and her brother Roy was sent to from Britain in 1951 - as her stepfather and mother did not want her in 1951. On the notorious so-called Child Migration scheme at the age of nine years old, her brother was sent to another State in Australia and he is older than her. Having just read 'Goodbye, Mummy Darling' by Susan, (august 2007) this is a must read for all women everywhere which explains these experiences in Perth and many others about her life in the UK.

The lovely Asian meal later on the evening just up the road made up for my original pessimism about Western Australia and Asian women are so sexy...don't you think? The next morning I get the train, clean and spotless to Freemantle (pop 25,000), a small little town now virtually part of greater Perth on the south side of the city. Where I have a good look around and a coffee and light lunch in the shopping complex. I also buy myself a new suit case as the second one bought in Melbourne had lost its wheels. In the evening I go into the main shopping complex near Wellington road for dinner and a drink of wine. The experience this time was quite unique as this was the 10th of November 2006 and they were starting to celebrate Christmas, in this part of the Universe. Yes, its true - the celebration was called the 'Spirit of Christmas' and it was a little a strange to me as it was a mix of singing religious songs with gags and stories about the farming world and so on. I was a little confused as I only worship: food, good authors and sexy women; so it did not really make sense too me. The dinner however was wonderful as was the young black man I met and spoke to - on my back to the YHA who was guarding a small plane that was going to be in a show in the next few days. Like me for most of my life; forced to do crap stupid jobs when he was a very well educated person - who had decided that Australia was a better bet than his own country.

The next morning I board a 'Western Exposure' bus with 15 others mostly lovely young back-packers, from around the globe for a four day return trip to Monkey Mia, 12 were going on a seven day round trip and three of us, just four. Rachel from New Zealand was the guide and driver; the unsung heroes of the tourist business which is huge in Australia. If you ever do this when in the middle time/age of your life, like me you will find that pop music is always on the agenda, most of the time, which could be very young or very old music and even the odd funny rude joke, may be told. As Anna said during the trip she had seen a 'monkey having a wank' (sic) I didn't know they did it, did you? The first day was mostly going up a very long road called the Brand Hwy heading north, where there is very few people so if you see a vehicle or a person the driver waves just in case you never see another one again. Lunch was in a little town called Jurien and then onto the Kalbarri area stopping to see some strange natural phenomenon, called the Pinnacles and then on to the YHA for the night. It was at the Pinnacles that Billy Connolly stripped off and run around naked, for a bit of fun, well done Billy that's all I can say. On these trips everyone gates involved in the whole process of cooking, which can be good fun and helps people get to know one another. Drinking and good conversation went on for several hours, even if I had heard it all before. According to my notes I was not impressed with the sleeping accommodation, which may have been designed for convicts for the first night were Sebastian and myself shared a dorm with the young women: Gina, who was very amusing Emma, Carrie who hated men, so would I have my testiculars in the morning, Allison et al. The next day we visited a gorge had a long walk around it saw the 'nature's window', had some very long conversations with some insects walking around my window, I may have been an insect in a previous life and so on. I tried to find out why in Australia they are such a pest to humans, but they would not answer the questions. We also visited the stromatolites phenomena the same place that Bill Bryson visited in Down Under and was amazed that such a simple life form could have helped too create Jeffery Archer. The second night was at a place called Denham in the Shark Bay area which is a World Heritage site (Francois Peron National Park) and it was wonderful. We even went for a swim before dinner, in the warm wonderful sea, for an hour.

After another early rise and breakfast we are off to see the wild Dolphins at Monkey Mia. In fact I am going to tell you something that no one knows apart from me and the Dolphins this is an Aussie State secret, so don't tell anyone, will you. After they had a small breakfast and a million photographs taken off them - the alpha male told me that to keep the tourist coming to Monkey Mia the Australian Government have given all of them special bank accounts and at night they sneak up to the ATM machine and draw out their dosh, because apparently nothing is free with 'the hidden hand of the market' so they have to pay for their breakfasts. After seeing these wonderful creatures, which come right up to the beach - we have a choice go out on a boat or meet Darren Capes an indigenous Australian. For me and six others, there was only one choice and that was to meet Darren and have a one and half walk with him around a small part of the area with him. Darren is truly an amazing and intelligent man who seems not only to understand his own culture in full but also the white-mans complexities. The first thing that struck me was the complete opposites that the Western World believes in and what the Aboriginal people believe in. In other words you respect your environment - when you are born an Aborigine and are in harmony with nature. The white man does not care a dam, and may end up killing the Planet, through naked greed and destruction of our environment. A few times during the walk I did think that Darren may have been pulling our legs, but probably not and just being completely honest about his culture. My only regret was that I did not bring my tape recorder with me so that I could have put down everything he told us. From the fauna the tracking skills, how they interact with animals to find food, the 14 different culture groups, and their languages and beliefs and so on, around this area. We had to pay a small sum for our walk with Darren, known as Capes but it was worth every penny and even Rachel our guide was very pleased with the reaction from everyone who had met him in the past… it was 'awesome' that's all I can say - as many young people say in Australia. I did ask him if it was impolite to look an Aboriginal person in their eyes when you speak to them as Capes did, or was Germane Greer right when she critiqued Bill Bryson for not understanding their culture when speaking to them direct. She may have been correct, so it seems which I did notice later on in my journey, as we shall see.

The time with the whole group was very stimulating to me as I just love listening in on conversations, for example

I noticed that the young women were often taking the piss out of other tourists on there journeys around the globe, especially the Americans although there was one lovely young man from the USA on our trip. Anna who had been to Southern Africa like me, 19 and was going to University this year (2007) and kept referring back to her 'Dad' in casual conversation – and was very paranoid about young men who wore underpants that were not 'boxer shorts'; apparently Speedo swimming trunks should be 'banned'. I was also threatened that if I said anything about her that was not true in this book she would sue me…so there! I presume because she was born 'middle class' or higher and I was not? But at least Gina who has a degree in Sociology, said that she was going to 'Google me', which is a lovely thought as she may some time in the future, buy one of my books.

During the day Sebastian, Sophia and I are dropped off at a café cum garage where we are picked up by Reg's right hand man and drove all the way to his farm, called Northbrook - just off the Brand Hwy, heading south. The rest of the young people are on there way to Exmouth up the same highway, heading north. So it would be several days before I hear 'cool' again, repeated about a million times a day by most young people and 'guys' used as an collective noun for men and women in Australia. Reg a very jovial friendly Aussie who hadn't long been into the tourist industry - so was still expanding the business. After we had booked in Sebastian and I went for a swim and Sophia wrote out some post cards. For dinner, cooked by Reg and family we were joined by another gang of backpackers. The dinner was delicious and a very happy occasion, served in a small type hanger, I did not see an aircraft but it was nearly big enough for one. After the meal we all congregated around a camp fire sang songs, well some did - eat a cake cooked by Reg and drank some beer. The sheep were not amused, so they told me and one even got caught up in a fence and had to be released by one of the other backpackers. It was while I was in Western Australia that I read in the local paper that 'one million Australians are depressed' and one way to cure it is to have more 'fish oil'. In the same paper we were all so informed that a male Panda living in Thailand that was not interested in sex was going to be shown some porn (sic) to get him randy, the things you read in newspapers, are incredible, don't you think?

After breakfast, the next day and all the other backpackers are on there way to some where Reg picks up: Sebastian, Sophia and me and we head towards Perth. About a million miles down the highway a slight exaggeration but hopefully you all get the drift, Australia is a big place. Reg turned out to be a wonderful guide for the day and fully of knowledge and wisdom to disseminate. First of all we visited a wheat processing planet where Reg used to take his own wheat when he was in the business to be sorted tested and stored. While there he also informed us that at one time if the 'end-user did not pay'; say for example, Saddam Hussein - 'the producers did not get paid'. I told him that this was very ironic because to my knowledge in little Britain and it may be the same in Big Oz that if you were selling arms and the 'end-user' did not pay the Government and the State would bail you out. I must admit that I did think that this was rather pathetic and just shows were the proprieties are in this epoch. Killing people is more important and profitable, then feeding people. The USA spends at least 400 billion dollars on the arms industry each year; when nearly 1 billion people go hungry every day because 'poor people have no money to secure a constant food supply, and no resources to grow their own food' (Jessica Williams 2004 p, 161).

We also visited a private Zoo where we feed Kangaroos, a camel and some other animals and birds and then were shown a variety of snakes that we could handle if we wanted to by the owners. A very delightful experience that's all I can say, which I think we all enjoyed. Then on to a fishing village down the coast for lunch where Reg used to have a crayfish business via a memorial to an Australian war ship that disappeared very mysteriously, in the Second World War. While having lunch, with some very friendly birds, on a pleasant piece of open grass near the sea. I asked Reg about this whole process at Monkey Mia where you are not allowed to swim with the Dolphins in certain parameters, because this seemed slightly strange to me - as I know for sure that in some other regions of the world you can. What he said was that some of the less educated types 'would put cigarette ends in there blow holes' and so on and often hurt the animals, so that was the reason the guides protected them. I presume; that these horrible people were the 'proles' who 'used scent' out of '1984'? The rest of the journey went by very quick with Reg giving us some of the more quaint little nuances about Australian culture and how most of the individual States seem to be in competition with the rest. For example 'VB beer' stands for 'very bitter' and not the name of the State where it comes from, etc. What I noticed about Reg more then anything else was how he liked to disseminate his knowledge, gained in a life time, this may one of the main differences between Australia and British culture. He was also not amused about how agents in the middle of the tourist business take their cut for basically nothing, perhaps in some cases 30% of the total bill. By the time we got to Perth it was tea time, so I said my goodbyes to Reg, Sebastian and Sofia and booked back into the YHA on Wellington Road.

The next day I am off on the Train to Fremantle to get a Ferry across to Rottnest Island for several hours where I hire out a cycle and 'get on my bike' (sic) to visit Lord Norman Tebbitt, Thatcher's Rottweiler, if possible. During the cycle ride I meet several Quokka, take a few pictures of them - small rat type creatures; which is unique to this Island and enjoy the experience of this lovely little place. When Billy Connolly visited the place on a private boat he was sea sick - apparently revenge I think for the treatment of Aboriginal people who where imprisoned here in the nineteenth century. While waiting for the Ferry back home, I have a swim and saw several small fishing boats coming right up on the beech, where the primary objective seemed to be buying beer/drink and relax on the beech, before their return. My thoughts during this process, and being on an Island where about Robert Hughes (art critic) who apparently said that the only good thing he would do for Australia 'is to tow it out to sea and sink it'. What a bloody cheek that's all I can say; because first of the size of the place it would need a very big boat and secondly what would happen too the Kangaroos, can they swim, I wonder?

It's the morning of the 16th November 2006 and I am off to the airport for my flight to Ulura (Ayers Rock) 'the world's biggest monolith' with Qantas which is a much better airline then Virgin Blue because at least you get a free meal and a drink of orange juice. And if Private Eye is correct and you are lucky enough to be Ralph Fiennes, you may be treated for something very special in the loo with one of the hostess. They say it goes with the new PR from this wonderful airline if you are a business class passenger, according to Lisa Robertson. During the flight you do wonder because of the size of the place will the Pilot actually find the airport which is a very small strip of tarmac in the centre of this incredible land. After several hours we land on the tarmac and is picked up by a small bus and I am dropped off at the Outback Pioneer Hotel & Lodge. I am booked into a dormitory with 20 others, from all around the globe. This place is everything you hope in the middle of know where, a nice restaurant, entertainment in the bar and a smashing swimming pool where I spent a few hours reading, swimming and relaxing after my flight and the site of Ulura is 'awesome'. Dinner in the 'Bough house restaurant' where I met gorgeous Michelle who is apparently 'in love', is she real I wonder, was excellent, a very up market little place on the site and cool beer and a good old chin-wag with other tourist from around the world in the bar area after and the singer doing his thing, made my day. In the morning I return to the Bough house restaurant for breakfast the reason for this course of action is that I am now getting a little low on funds so I am using my Visa card for the little things in life, like easting and travelling. Noting that I was thinking that Australia favourite meal is not barbecues per se - but visa cards, for breakfast, lunch and dinner they can't get enough of them, well at least for gullible tourists, that is! After breakfast I pack up and wait around for the bus that is going to take me/us for a three day tour around Ulura some other large Rocks and on to Alice Springs. The 'Rock Tour' bus arrives with Micah our very friendly guide and driver and the other 9 who are going to share this experience. I am the only Brit on this trip, with other mature people - so hopefully I will not be met with those ubiquitous words of young people everywhere, that's 'cool'. Young Micah was a revelation apparently in another life he had tamed horse and camels, in the outback and was one eighth Aborigine, so he told me. On the first day we all walked around Ulura after the visit to the National Park Culture centre close by. 'Australia's favourite postcard image is 3.6km long and rises a towering 348m from the surrounding sandy scrubland' (LP p, 429). It took two and half hours to walk around so a lot bigger then it looks from a distance. Hence, passing very close to where in 1980 Michael and Lindy Chamberlain a Seventh Day Adventist had their baby daughter taken by wild Dingo's, from their Tent. This was their story but not believed by the government, so Lindy was charged with murder, though later acquitted. A few years later Sam Neil and Meryl Streep made a very good movie about the whole event, I still blame an Alien from the Andromeda Galaxy, myself.

Before we have dinner and sleep under the stars in a swag (sic) we view the huge rock from a distance as the sun is setting and what was amazing to me was that there were hundreds possible thousands of people in coaches doing the same thing, well actually having a drink of champagne outside, but had come on coaches - a very unusual sight indeed. Micah did the cooking which was fabulous and the sleep under the starts was truly amazing, seeing all those stars and galaxies without the contamination of light. On the second day just before breakfast we viewed the opposite effect, the sunrise coming up over Ulura and also the Olgas as Kata Tjuta which was just across the way. Where we had a long walk in the Valley of the Winds after breakfast, which was magnificent especially the view of a huge pass which I renamed the Elizabeth Taylor pass as it looked like her beautiful full breasts. After all this exercise we went to a camp site for a swim, relaxation and dinner, where you could buy beer, food and so on and another sleep under the stars in the swag. These camp sites in Big OZ are really well organised as they supply the cooking equipment free, which you would never see in little Britain if you looked for a thousand years. Basically it's for the laid back culture of the outdoor lifestyle, when not working.

On rising early the next day we are served up a delicious breakfast, by Micah and then go for a very long walk in Kings Canyon, with Jeff from Canada, Caroline from Switzerland, Thorsten and Nicola from Germany, Rianne & Hans from Holland and Magnus and Victoria from Sweden.. Where you need to be quite fit or you would never do it. During the walk we go down into a huge gorge called the Garden of Eden but not really as Micah said because if this was the Garden of Eden the Aborigines would have 'eaten the snake first'. Where we were allowed to have a swim in a small lagoon with our other backpackers friends, from another group, which was a rare treat when you are hot and sweaty. After the walk Micah does a lunch and then we are off to Alice Springs about another few hundred miles down the road. I am dropped off at the local YHA which was friendly but a little cramped with their facilities. In the evening we all meet up for a pleasant dinner and drink in a local bar. In fact it was when we were relaxing in the bar after dinner that Hans told me that he had won 'Who wants to a Millionaire' in Holland and that was why he could take his lovely girlfriend on such a big adventure.

I had booked into the YHA for two nights as I was going to meet another organised tour the following morning. So hoping that my mode of thought is very similar to Bill Bryson, a sort of get up and go mentality, I am off to the Desert Park - exactly like he did several years before, but while waiting for my pick up I got talking to a young women in the Arrero hotel entrance - who was trying to inform me about some of the culture aspects of Aborigine culture from her perspective, living in Alice Springs. She informed me that there is a high percentage of unemployment in the local community and some even sleep out on the dry River Todd, at night. Also some of the men get quite aggressive at night and can be dangerous, so probably she has never visited an inner city, in little Britain on a weekend? They also break into homes but normally don't steal anything valuable, apart from a little food.

The first objective was to see a short movie about the evolution of Australia a very interesting bit of knowledge, we should all watch, because Errol Flynn was not mentioned once. Also while in the park I saw an Emu red Kangaroos many types of birds and an incredible out door bird show with Sharon and her colleagues, with wild birds - I must admit that I had never seen one of these shows before in my whole life and it was very impressive. While there I could have cooked an Emu as there was an instruction of how you go about it. But it would have been too bigger a lunch for one, and I would have had to invite my neighbours around - which are not really a-part as British culture anymore, so it seems.

This is completely different from Aboriginal culture, or may even be to Aussie culture per se today, as I noted before - for example it seems that 'during the Altyerre, pronounced ul-cheer-ra (or Dreamtime) spiritual ancestors created the landscape and all living things? The Law and culture of Aboriginal people were set down in the Altyerre. The ceremonies, songs and relationships needed to maintain this Law have been passed down from generation to generation'. On this little plate that I photographed at Alice Springs it is suggests that in this area of Australia the indigenous people may have been here for '30,000 years' and in other regions '150,000 years'. So a very long time before James Cook was even thought of and being a social-being is what life should really be about. According to my notes I also listened to a tape about the Quoll which was an animal which looks like a large Rat – and may have lived in trees and eat meat; like many others related to 'dream time' a sort of 'Totem God' and 'sacred' to the Aborigines. Which 'taught you to be good' certainly nothing that Bush and Blair worshiped then?

On a very recent Ray Mears adventure series on BBC 2 (4th January 2007) in little Britain, he went to Australia, to learn how the Aboriginal women collected their plants etc, as a template of how we may have done it in Britain, only about 7000 years ago. One lady said that she spent at least '8 years' learning this knowledge from her elders. And in the last series of three about food and how we went about this whole process in those times to support life he roasted a hog and got everyone involved in the series to taste it and join in, and said something that I thought was very ironic in this day and age and that was what he liked to think about was how 'eating food' would have been a very 'social occasion', for all concerned, well done Ray.

For the next part of today's adventure, after watching a DVD about the outback and the audacity that the Aborigine people may have lied to the white-man about water...how shocking - I am picked up, by a young woman in a bus and taken to one of the Culture centres. Where I view a lot of art in the Araluen Arts centre, look around the Museum of Central Australia an eclectic mix of just about everything under the sun including some insights into how brave the early white settlers were, or either very fool hardy. A look around a small aviation museum and again how the early pioneers were a lot braver then most people would ever be today. Walking back from this museum you can walk through some indigenous art forms - like I did and past some local people who completely ignored me if I did not exist (no eye contact whatsoever), perhaps I don't...well have you ever tried to get an agent interested in you if they can not make money out of you. However in the evening after dinner I went for a walk to see if I could buy some beer in the main shopping complex of Alice Springs and was lucky enough to get talking to June Sutton, with eye contact, a local Aborigine very friendly lady in her 50's who had went to a Catholic school in the town, but now lives up north somewhere. She was trying to sell her 13 year old daughters art work that was magnificent, on a grass area, near the shops. She spoke perfect English and told me that the Catholic school was very strict and the local art galleries would not let the local people sell their art during the day. Apparently she also has two other daughters 14 and 33, her father was from Afghanistan and her mother was an Aborigine, but sadly now both dead. He may have been a relative of Osama bin Laden (my hypothesis, well anything is possible in this surreal epoch) so a 'freedom fighter' when fighting the nasty Russian and now a 'terrorist' because he wants to get rid of the Western menace, from the middle east, etc. The reason that she is now in Alice Springs is because her daughter spends a month every so often in the year, here and then returns home for the rest of the year. This was a real treat for me because from what I can see it was hard to get into conversation with the local people without being in a proper organised trip. This may have been quite ironic because I read in one of the papers while there that not enough tourists stay very long in Alice Springs...so there! In the evening after dinner I had a very long and interesting chat to Robert Tompkins a Palaeontologist from the USA, with a PhD. Who has discovered that the all Tories from little Britain were originally related to the Neanderthal, which may include the Liberals from Australia. Billy Connolly also came here and visited the

Todd River looking for water unfortunately he never found any - but according to him every year there is a boat race on the river without water…bizarre but true apparently.

I am off on a large bus with 31 other mostly young people the next morning and Graeme the driver and tourist guide, in his middle thirties to Cairns. These two nights and three days trip is called 'the Desert Adventure' and I won it in Melbourne for a couple of hundred dollars in a competition, at the YHA. So hoping that it will be worth my hard earned cash that it cost me - on board it was really like the United Nations, on tour. People from: Brazil - Anna a real treat, if you could eat her, Scotland, Ireland, Japan, South Korea, Sweden, Belgium, little England, Germany, Australia - Dan the pop star in the 'Fuel Economy' and the USA. And only one woman from the USA was not very friendly, did not speak once too me - although Glenn from New York was. In fact I think she may have been writing a book or article for a newspaper so perhaps when she learned that I was doing the same thing she may have not liked the competition. For a lot of the time we were just travelling east through the Simpson desert at quite a speed although there was hundreds of miles that were not tarmaced. I kept thinking that if we break down here we could be in the shit; while talking to Yumiko from Japan and Sarah from Ireland. Martina also from Ireland was a make up artist on movies and had met many big stars over the years; including working on Ken Loach movie called 'the Wind that Shakes the Barley' (see above). While on the Bus we saw the movies 'Rabbit Proof Fence' made in 2002 which is a fantastic movie about some racial scandals that the Aborigine people suffered only a few years ago and a story called the Dish about how in 1969 at the time of the Moon landing a few very bright Aussies were involved in this adventure, at a signal base, that all went wrong…very amusing I thought. Just like seeing Billy Connolly feeding crocs in the Northern Territories, a site to behold I thought. The next time I come here I am hoping too feed the British Aristocracy to the big 300 million year old beasts. I think it is probably more humane then the Guillotine, don't you?

What I really liked about Graeme the driver and guide, apart from all the stories he told us - was that he seemed to be very sympathetic to the indigenous people and how they have had a real raw deal from the White settlers over generations. Something that I thought was a complete scandal, according to Graeme the Aborigines people as such really did not exist and were called 'Native Fauna' right up until '1967' with very few 'rights' and being nomadic it was not fashionable or the right way to behave - with the white ruling class up to about '1977'. Power and tight social control has always been an axiom of this group; just come too little Britain at this very moment to understand this phenomena, especially from 1979 when Thatcher et al took over the reins of power. There may be as many as a half a million people who are being monitored, looking into their e-mails and listening into phone calls. I am probably one - for the crimes that I have committed against the ruling class and the established middle class (sic). Read my real CV for the hard evidence.

What is so ironic about the conditions of the Aborigines, at least in the Northern Territory's if Barbara

McMahon is correct in the Sunday Observer (24th June 2007) is that Australia is now so rich as a State that it has a 13 billion dollar surplus, 'but there's a 2 billion to 3 billion dollar deficit around Aboriginal communities'. With 'overcrowding, unemployment, disease and truancy are rife in Wadeye where there are an average of 17 people per home', the community that she visited.

The meals again were a delight with everyone mucking in with the whole process. We could have had termites as apparently they are very nutritious, but we didn't as well as a good cure to get rid of mosquitoes. There is in fact more termites in Australia then people by about a 200,000 billion or more, the most successful animals there apart from Larrikins, so I have been told. It was a shame we did not meet one on this bus journey because he could have helped Graeme with the bus whose air-conditioning kept going on the blink. On one night we stayed at a cattle ranch called the Wirrelyana, the size of New York run by Trevor and Eatha and on the second we stayed in a little town cum hotel called Hughenden that only had about two showers for 40 people. But the meal was excellent as was Trevor's and the little game of killer pool after with the gang. At the cattle ranch the guys who run and own the place had a small pet Kangaroo called Mary; who drank beer and had toast and coffee for breakfast. A very tame little animal that took a nasty turn in the morning after breakfast and attacked me, after taking some photos and another couple of the group. I could not make up my mind if it was the wrong time of the month or she had a hangover from the beer or had a bad hair day…well you can not be too sure with the opposite sex, is that not so ladies? Eatha told me before leaving that they had 4000 head of cattle and 300 sheep, apparently the nearest town called Boulia was about 50 kms down the road, where Trevor was the Mayor and the local Landlord. I was also wondering when I was at this cattle ranch that this may have been the same place where Errol Flynn had to bite off sheep's testicles with his teeth, well you never know? 'I was getting big money, but my jaws started to freeze up', so he wrote and to think that they where called 'prairie oysters', because they where so 'delicious to eat'.

We also called into possible the loneliest and most isolated pub/hotel on the planet called the Middleton Hotel run by Leslie for a drink. He was a world expert with the whip, so very good company for Nannies and goodtime girls everywhere. In Winton we had lunch on the second day - a very famous little town where there was some very ugly industrial disputes at the end of the nineteenth century and the town where Waltzing Matilda was born and sung in about 1895, by Ben Patterson a lawyer who wrote this rebellious diatribe against the time, so Graeme told us. And as we also know because I saw the signs you can go on a dinosaur dig and dig Mrs Thatcher and her friends up. There may even be opals just over the hill as well, so well worth a visit and dig, I would say. In the afternoon we went for a swim under the Millaa, Millaa falls, can this be correct Brian? But we all had a wonderful time and then off to Cairns on the coast and another YHA, this time an oasis in the desert of time. In the evening we all meet up for dinner in the Woolshed and because of the hassle with the air-conditioning on the bus - the big boss of the firm let us all have a few free drinks on the company. The highlight however for me this evening was not the meal but the entertainment where a bartender cum compare compared a game of Blind Date. The questions asked were direct and to the point for example 'have you ever faked an orgasm' and so on. Also the young woman had to pretend she was having oral sex with a bar of chocolate, although slightly crude - I just think that Education is good for you and can take many forms, anyone for a bar of chocolate girls? The reason for suggesting this is according to the Australian newspaper that I am reading while taking notes at the outdoor swimming pool in Cairns – suggest, that young male chimpanzee prefer older females, which is the complete opposite in the main to home sapiens. At this very moment I am thinking of wonderful sexy Anna from Sao Paulo in Brazil, who according to her she is a trained architect, I wonder why? May be because of her beautiful shaped gorgeous bottom, or is it those lovely shapes in her mind, surely not… and I am in very close eye shot of two young women in bikinis, as well. After exploring the Town and dinner I ventured across the road to see the fantastic movie called Borat with a couple young people off the Desert Adventure across half of Australia. This was probably one of the most outrageous films ever made, so virtually everyone you meet says how incredible and amusing it really was, but very unlikely to be perceived like that, by the good folk of Royal Tonbridge Wells. Borat did not go across Big OZ but the USA instead - not pretending to be a author like me - but pretending to come from Kazakstan and be a TV news reporter tricking many people as he went to find Pamela Anderson the final objective of his desire who was in on the act.

I am up early the next morning and off to meet Pete the Captain of the Seastar II and his smashing young crew - but will it get us out the Great Barrier Reef and back in this century as it looks very old indeed, was it built before the Ark, I was wondering to myself. But considering that I hoping to see one of the greatest natural wonders on earth, for 80 dollars which includes lunch; I decide to stay on and see what will happen. When buying the ticket from Margaret in the travel agency she did not mention that it actually gets quite rough on the way out to the reef, so what happens is that all the Asian people on the trip are as sick as dogs. I am lucky that I just sat still and admired the sheer beauty of the place and Anna's bum, from Poland, this time. When we get out to a very small Island called Michaelmas cay (MC) with 20, 000 sea birds we get our snorkel gear on and off we go on a little boat, with Pete. I learnt to snorkel as a young man in Cyprus between 1968 and 1970 while in the Royal Air Force. So still feel confident that I know what I am doing after all this time a bit like riding a bike you never forget once you learn. If you wanted to you - you could also dive, some did. In the brochure it says 'exotic MC, an unspoilt natural coral Island. World renowned bird nesting sanctuary, home to over 20,000 sea birds'. And it was a truly amazing experience snorkelling around the incredible coral and seeing the wildlife in all its glory and actually touching the coral. Some of the fish were so big they looked like small sharks around the hull of the boat and of course so laid back just like the Aussie culture. Then back on the Seastar II for lunch and a soft drink, while the Captain takes us out to the next part of this incredible day out, I am only rubbing this in because my hero Bill Bryson did not do this when he went around big OZ. The next snorkel was at 'Hastings Reef' near the 'Fish Bowl' on the outer edge of the Great Barrier Reef. This time you did need to be confident in the water as on this day it was quite rough. However what did shock me a little was how lovely Anna from Poland only told us before going on the second snorkel - not to touch some of the shells as they could kill you, which may have been Cone Shells, a very dangerous species that can kill you dead, with one nip of their tentacles. It was also quite hard to concentrate on the wonders of the place when swimming with at least two angels - one from Poland and the other from Wales, with bodies too kill for. According to the brochure I have in front of me 'Seastar cruises' has been going on these trips since '1956', so just before the Ark then. It is also a family run business and I thought a very friendly staff, so if you want to be treated in the same relaxed manner as us at Cairns, for a very reasonable price on this wonderful full day out just email: info@seastarcruises.com.au.

Back at the Hanging gardens of Babylon as I have renamed the YHA Central in Cairns, may be slightly over the top, so God told me - but this is a very nice youth hostel, run by David, Amy et al. When I think about the glorious nature of Anna's bum, sorry I mean the sheer beauty of the whole Great Barrie Reef and a must is too proselytize this experience to the whole world before man and his ruthless elk destroys it all. This is very unlikely to happen too Kuranda a wonderful little village a 34 kilometres north of Cairns. I got there on the small train that runs up the hill, the next day, with the commentary being a little confusing as I was not to sure which side of the Train you should look out if you were sitting in the opposite direction to the man speaking through the speakers. The little markets were a real treat where I bought some original Aborigine art and two boomerangs and had a little chat to a local man playing the didgeridoo. After buying a newspaper I sit down read it and have a lovely little lunch and a cup of tea. The rest of the time was spent walking around this delightful little place and my return on the amazing Skyrail. Another 'must do' if you ever visit this part of the world. The sheer beauty of this ride was beyond belief, but also to me a little scary as I don't specifically like heights. At the bottom you get picked up by the local bus and returned to your accommodation. Where I meet Mark from Oz and Chris from the UK who is working in Singapore, just hoping that he will bring another bank to its knees like Nick Lesson did several years ago, well we must take our revenge every so often, on these powerful institutions, should we not? Before going to bed I have a little drink of beer in the Hogs Breath, just around the corner from the hostel. It tasted lovely and not like a hog at-tall and the young people serving behind the bar and the restaurant were working really hard.

I have another swim at the smashing outdoor swimming pool, the next day and a little light lunch and a walk to the strangest Zoo in the world. The Cairns Wildlife Dome – Your Zoo in the City above the big Casino is perhaps the weirdest place on earth because if the big Croc does not get you a Shark in the Casino may. I spent several hours in this small place thinking and just enjoying the animals and birds - which included Frogs, Koalas (very similar to the British Aristocracy very slow and very stupid), Turtles, Snakes and the Goliath 4 meter crocodile which was brought into the Dome by a crane. Well come on ladies and gentleman he could hardly have been brought up the stairs in a shopping trolley could he? Afterwards I slip into the Casino to observe how lots of people many Asians losing their hard earned cash and a little try on a machine with lots of buttons and lights flashing. On the way back to the YHA I pop into the Landmark Art Galley where there were some very expensive pictures on show and for sale. But was there any pictures painted by the great Jimmy Pike on show; I wondered after seeing again the Billy Connolly DVD in action, who actually saw this incredible man paint. In the evening I treat myself to a special dinner at the Oliver's restaurant run by very friendly Oliver Schreiber from Hanover in German and then off to bed for the last night in Cairns where most people like and some Australians despise. Well this is a tourist trap and a lot of money is being made here, according to the paper I was reading while on the bus from Alice Springs.

CHAPTER EIGHT

- BIG OZ AND NEW ZEALAND -
PART THREE

At 6am I am up early for a home cooked breakfast of weetabix and tea as the check in time at the Railway Station just around the corner from the YHA is 07:45. I have my luggage weighed; apparently this is so that when the staff handles it they will know how heavy it is. As it was over the standard level I had to take out several books and put them in my back-pack. If you were wondering what books are; it is something very secret that the 'established middle class' do with them, that is so dangerous - but not the working class as according to George Orwell, it may be a seditious act after 1984, if they do the same thing - so I have been told by God, again or was that Tony and George from the Ministry of Truth. What a useful bloke God really is, don't you think? The Sunlander Train leaves at 08:35 for Brisbane and I am in car J seat 44 as I have been reading books against the laws of 1984 my old brain is not working properly and I decide that just having a normal seat may have been a silly thing to do, as apparently the Train will take 31 hours and not 13 as I thought, silly me, so I ask the Crew if I could upgrade my ticket for a sleeper which they agreed on. Thanks again fellows who were/are Julius, Andrew et al; all wonderful friendly guys who made our trip a real treat. Considering that the gauge is so small on these trains it is a wonder that they can go around corners without coming off the track and straight into the Great Barrier Reef for a top up of water. Where the great wonderful Billy Connolly, went flying in a beaver aircraft - just like I did in the Falkland Islands in 1962 on the way to my first job in Port Stanley from Goose Green, when he was still an unknown welder in Glasgow.

My companion for the whole journey was called Ray an older guy, well actually not much older then me - who was born in the UK but had lived a lot of his life in Australia and was on his way to Brisbane to see one of his children and a friend. I take out Down Under for the second time and start to read another master-piece by Bill Bryson. What can you say when you are travelling stress free on a very long journey with regular stops to stretch you legs and Bryson in one hand and an old man of the land and the sea beside you to talk too, heaven on earth? It would have been nicer with Kim Basinger beside me in her birthday suit - but lets face it you can not have everything, can we. The scenery on the trip was not bad either, on leaving Cairns it is very tropical; and then you could not really tell the difference between old Blighty and this part of the world as they are very similar, in nature. Even Daisy the cow gives milk and not beer, as some may think about Australia, well come on - where does Foster's come from the Toad river or is that Paul Hogan's bath water?

Ray turned out to be a very good travelling companion as of similar age; you do have more in common. So we had tea breaks together dinner together and lunch the next day together. On coming to Australia in the year dot he bought a boat and travelled around the Pacific something like Errol Flynn did - but to my knowledge he did not get into fights, get the pox and other sexual transmitted diseases or meet head hunters in Papua New Guinea. After reading Down Under he lends me one of his books about a bisexual tribe in South America, a very strange story indeed, slightly confusing and about as real as a Tony Blair or a John Howard speech, I would have thought. In fact last night I was watching a very interesting and controversial TV programme (Channel 4 - 8th March 2007) about Globe Warming called 'the Great Global Warming Swindle' and if true we are all being conned again. Well nothing new here then, although because I am a 'Political dissident' I have was always wondered the opposite to most peoples views and this is again about making more dosh for the rich, for example 'carbon trading' and more social control of the lower orders. Where at one time the Wealthy (upper class) were blaming the 'Left' that they were using this as a tool to smash Capitalism - where according to last nights programme it was suggested that the sciences involved in this whole process was not being looked at in a holistic approach to the problem, if it exists? Which may be completely true, for once?

On arriving at Brisbane Ray get his old car off the Train and drops me off at the local YHA, I say goodbye and will see you next time I come to Big OZ - where lots of new building work was being done and if I wanted I could have 'rented a fence' for the first time in my life. While in the hostel I saw a little TV and was quite amused how open Aussie culture is compared with British, where there is a lot of laughter, I also noticed this on the Radio as well and some of the things that they say, you would never hear in little Britain for a thousand years too come. On one day a TV reporter was talking about the Test Cricket matches being played while I was there and how some English people were getting sick of being called 'poms'. This guy said well they call us 'sheep shaggiers' and other pejorative terms and we don't mind that so what is wrong calling the Brits, 'poms'. As I am not a moaning 'pom' it does not worry me what you call them….a load of stupid 'wage slaves', is okay by me. With 'Brenda' and 'Keith' ruling the roost and owning most of the land with a few hundred other rich aristocrats who think they control the known universe. If only they knew what is going to happen too them at the guillotine party on top of the Tor, in the next few years.

Brisbane is the third largest city in Australia and has a population of at least 1.5 million people, but no more room for poor people, only rich tourist with visa cards. The next morning after a good night's sleep I walked into town and can not help but notice the building made of Lego with a water tank or maybe a King's coffin on top, I kept thinking what does this mean? May even be a coffin for all of Kylie Minogue money, sometime in the future, well she is worth at-least 100 million Australia dollars.

At the bottom some one has dropped all his balls, or this may have been a mass castration of dinosaurs a few years ago, just across from the Treasury building. The reason I would suggest this may be the case because they had to castrate the dinosaur in the museum on the river before they stuffed him...I just made this up. Museum-ites is really getting to me as this may have been at least a hundred museums I have visited in the last few months. So I keep seeing surreal things, like speeches made by Politicians that tell the truth, pictures of Sir Cyril Radcliffe dividing India in 36 days. Stuffed animals that don't exist, other things like - for example models of Cherrie Blair/Booth not leaving an Australia shops without free goods under her arms, Pete Foster telling the truth, in paint and so on. I calculated a few years ago that Mr & Mrs Blair probably earn at least 15,000 pounds (UK sterling) a week, in fact this may be a very conservative estimate as they use Chequers free with servants, as well. So if she comes to Australia again on the, cadge; tell to her too get stuffed, and put her in the museum for good, with the dinosaur. And to think that I recently attended an interview for collecting Government statistics on a freelance basis, in little Britain (March 2007) and the pay was going to be just over six pounds an hour. The two women who interviewed me may not even have a degree between them, or an A' level for that matter - so I was turned down, thank God. Well to me this place is a world of make believe if you don't understand the logic of my conclusion.

Joking aside the museum was great like all of them in Australia and the work that is put into them is beyond belief. From the believable to the unbelievable in one day, this is what happened to me on the 30th November 2006 when across the river I saw a demonstration of hundreds/ thousands of workers against John Howard's latest scam against the working class. Being an inquisitive sort of guy I walk across the bridge and join the demo - are given some leaflets buy a couple of papers and assimilate what is going on. The Green Left Weekly being one of the better ones I have bought over the years and this is what the great John Pilger says about it: 'there are few other news papers that draw together news and analysis that is as well informed, credible and non-sectarian…Green Left Weekly is a beacon to those who believe the press ought to be an agent of people, not power'.

In essence, what this was all about is that the Howard's Federal Government has introduced an act of Parliament called 'Work Choices', or 'IR laws'…since the introduction of these rightwing measures weekly earnings have fallen by about '1.2%' in real terms. Which has very little to do with choices but social control over your own life - whenever there is a down turn in the economy your Employer can send you home without pay, etc. Crimes of the powerful have always been cruel for centuries but this bit of chicanery just about tips this rotten epoch off the cliff – for once and for all. If you think that I am over the top here this is what was said in 1982 by a 'capitalist think tank'. 'To restore adequate profit margins – to provide an incentive for investment and the resources to finance it…real wages (must) be kept below productivity gains for several years' (Striking back at Howard – pamphlet, 2005). In good old Aussie slang you could also say this statement in this way: 'don't come the raw prawn with me, mate!' I enjoyed the demo as I did Pete Paul and

Mary a pop group that certainly looked like the original, from the 1960's.

After breakfast the next day I went for a swim and sun-bath near the river called the South Bank Beach, man/woman made, free and wonderful, but always a little afraid a croc from the river may jump on you for a free lunch. For lunch I met my daughter's best friend, on the other side of the river - who has moved to Australia called Kelly and her daughter Sophie, in the main shopping complex. The lunch was delicious and meeting Kelly was very nice because my daughter has been talking about her for years, but I had never met her. She told me that her younger daughter had settled in well but not Sophie who had been bullied and the difference in culture between little Britain and Australia that she had noticed. After lunch I nip in to the local Hertz higher car garage, to hire a car for the next day and on the return to the YHA I pop into the largest second hand bookshop in the Southern hemisphere, in   40 Charlotte street, with over a million books on every topic. My sort of heaven, books from Ian Fleming to Michael Moore, where all on display. During this process I was listening to the Cricket, on my head phones as I was in Cairns a few days before and although I don't really understand it, being like Bryson I do find it is very entertaining while doing nothing in particular. Like walking around Brisbane and the good news was that the English were being beaten by the Aussie's, if it was when the maiden was being bowled over, I never knew. Apparently this was on World's Aids day as well so sad and good news all in one day.

I pick up a fantastic car from Hertz the next morning and try and find my way out of Brisbane, not always easy if you are a stranger from another Galaxy, like me. Especially when travelling down the Gold Coast Hwy looking for gold on the streets as you go along. I did not see any, but it was a very pleasant drive and in the evening I stopped in a bit of a hell hole, Surfers Paradise it may have been called - something like Blackpool, I thought. The El Rancho Motel was okay run by Pat and Joe but very authoritarian couple from what I could see, but spotless. For example, although it cost me 100 dollars, for one night - I was not allowed 'to entertain anyone in my room'. I presume if I dragged someone of the streets to have a drink with, it would have been against the law. But amazingly Pat and Joe did have a sense of humour - as this is what it said on the wall in the Motel, on a plaque "A man and his ever-nagging wife went on vacation to Jerusalem. While they were there the wife passed away. The undertaker told the husband, 'You can have her shipped home for 5000 dollars, or you can bury her here in the Holy Land, for 150 dollars'. The man thought about it and told him he would just have her shipped home. The undertaker asked, 'Why would you spend 5000 dollars to ship your wife home, when it would be wonderful to be buried here and you would only 150 dollars' The man replied, 'Long ago a man died here, was buried here, and three days later he rose from the dead. I just can't take that chance'" Not bad at all, that's all I can say. . But reached the conclusion that TV in Big Oz like little Britain is total crap and nothing more than 'prolefeed' for the masses. Although on this particular night there was an interesting documentary about the 'First Emperor of China', which I watched.

The breakfast cost extra so this must be Blackpool, but was very pleasant, as I had poached eggs on toast my favourite meal, after the swim in the little pool. The next part of this incredible journey was a look around a little museum cum café down the highway - which this time was Italian in origin - trying to avoid any hungry Crocs that may have been in the rivers; if I fell asleep at the wheel, while listening into a Religious radio station 99.9. Today I am on my way to visit the oldest person on the Planet, one of my Aunts, who lives in a little place called Kemsey. Well actually she is only 80 in July, but as a young man at the Darwin Boarding school in the 1950's & 60's I probably thought of her as a very old woman when in fact now I have children older then she was at the time. I pull up at the local swimming pool at 4pm, and go in for a swim, 'sorry sir it is now 5pm and we are closed. But my watch says 4pm; it is in Queensland but not New South Wales, sir'. Well I never, now I know why some people say that in Queensland they live on another Planet and fly around on the backs of Archeaopteryx's to get from A to B. So off I go down to the coast for a little swim in the rough red sea to freshen up and a shower. On the way back I pick up some favourite alcohol of my Aunt's and casket of wine for me and phone her to see where she lives as the map says that her address does not exist.

I had not seen this particular Aunt Sis since 1960 which is a very long time indeed - so automatically she did seem a lot older then I remember her and a little shorter in height. Probably that is what she thought of me, as well - I was only 12 the last time she saw me. She shows me around her splendid huge house and cooks a very pleasant dinner, but without corgis and servants. Over the wine and meal we discuss everything, well nearly everything that has happed over the last 46 years. Did we really get to the Moon and so on? If not, the jury is still out in my neck of the woods, she did marry Maori royalty in New Zealand; after divorcing my uncle a few years ago, so she told me – without the two hundred servants, plus - that the current anachronistic British Monarchy has. The next morning I go for a swim in the local pool which is awe-inspiring considering that Kemsey is such a very small place. Afterwards I meet Candy (a very sexy, long lost relative, born in South Georgia) and Colin her current boyfriend who comes around, so that we call go and have lunch in the local ex-services club. The fish lunch was delicious and not a bad price for what we had, although we nearly froze as the air-conditioning was on full. In the evening I watch 'the Road to Perdition' with Tom Hanks and Daniel Craig; for the second time and understood it this time. The next morning after breakfast I take some pictures of my Aunt's house and say goodbye too her, climb in the wonderful hire car and head down the highway again, calling in to Port Macquarie where lovely Candy lives for a quick look at the beach and the town. I was going to have a coffee on the beach - but at 4 dollars a shot, I declined their offer. This place is also the headquarters of Radio Station 99.9 so I was looking for people with two heads but did not see any. The reason may have been as according to this station closely linked to the Americans, Jesus was a businessman for a few years of his life, that's if he ever existed? And let's face it the real hard scientific empirical evidence is lacking in credence, according to at least some scholars (Abuse Your Illusions

Notes from a Small Planet: Volume 1

2003). Further down the highway I have a drive around Newcastle, I was not impressed the West Midlands by the sea - was what came into my mind, straight away. Billy Connolly loves the place and even caught a sea salmon when he was here. With dozens and dozens of ships anchored waiting to be loaded or unloaded. However I did notice something that amused me on the coast in this industrial town, and this was that you could learn to fly with wings just like Jesus, but without a parachute. I took some photos in-case my friends did not believe me when I explain this phenomena to them, on my return to Blighty. A must I would have thought for the next earthquake whenever it comes to Newcastle. By the time I got to the Blue Mountains YHA another incredible hostel, for poor people like me, but this time nearly as good as a five star hotel, it was 'high tea' time. The very rich in little Britain can spend at least 60 pounds on this tea, so I have been told, by Socrates (sic). After 'high tea' I venture down to see the three sisters, which was awesome - part of the seven sisters at 'Echo Point' for the first time and they were very sexy, and delightful. I always wanted a sister, so perhaps I can one of these back home....just joking, just in-case an Aboriginal person should ever read this book. When I was at the YHA, having dinner I think I may have sat just across from Princess Mary her Danish bloke and the baby, this maybe a State secret. So please don't tell anyone, will you!

The next day after a good breakfast full of carbohydrates, hopefully I venture again down to Echo Point for a small walk in the Blue Mountains National Park. I walked down the Giant Stairway very cautiously as I don't like heights, walk under the Three Sisters and head up the Federal pass walking track. Down here you could be in Queensland or another Galaxy as it is very unlikely that you would have walked in such a delightful surroundings and very different to what you may have done before. I walk all the way to the Ruined Castle pass the old coal mines the lift to the top and back up the Golden stairs, five hours in all. By the time I got back to the top I was shattered completely, well I am nearly 59. However just before I got to the top of the Golden Stairs I met a lovely English couple called Andrew and Caroline who had sold up at home; bought a Yacht and sailed it all the way to Australia. Who had also travelled around OZ quite a bit and had noticed that Australians when holidaying at home don't seem to go far. The reason for telling you this is that they were very kind to me and dropped me off by my car about a half a mile down the road, in their car. Apparently they were so impressed with the people they met on the Islands, coming across the Pacific and the kindest the local people showed too them that they did not mind doing a little favour for me. This to me seems to be what all humans should try to achieve, doing something for others instead of being so selfish. The complete opposite to how the system works at present, especially based on very dubious assumptions of F. A. Hayek et al and Australia is not really any different from little Britain. The only difference is that young Aussies are probably better educated and better travelled - this was the conclusion I reached at the end of two months, travelling all over the place.

After all that walking, the next morning I go for a swim at the local pool and completely relax. I must admit when out walking in the National Park it did cross my mind, on several occasions, that if enough dingoes attacked you - you could end up as a doggy barbeques. This may have also applied to those strange creatures called Larrikins. For the rest of the day I explored the local area went to 'Orange' for an apple, a walk in Cook Park where I saw a cage for humans and relaxed in the YHA reading a book and the Sydney Morning Herald. Noticing that there were coffins on the ceilings, well actually lights shaped as coffins, very strange indeed. The reason for this state of affairs may have been that I read in the newspaper 'that 60% of men' in Big Oz 'believe in God' and '72% of women'. On a sliding scale the less intelligent seemed to believe in the concept more then the rich. So not as intelligent as I thought then - although the sample where this tosh came from was quite a small one, so it said. If Kevin's Rudd sexy redheaded deputy believed in this balderdash I don't know but according to the paper 'she did once have a boyfriend who was a hairdresser' and now has a new hair do. This is so shocking to me that it is if our Deputy Prime Minster was a waiter on a ship who has thrown ever principle he ever believed in overboard. So perhaps he was a waiter after all?

I explore a bit more of the Blue Mountains which is very beautiful and delightful the next day. On the road to Lithgow in the Hartley Valley - I stopped at a café cum Museum cum Art Galley and shop selling art, in the middle of nowhere. This is one reason that Australia is so unusual and appealing in some ways from Europe or most places on the Planet, I would have thought; as the chance of seeing a little place like this would be a big fat O. To finish the day off I stayed in a Log cabin well a building modelled on one still in the Blue Mountain area, called the 'Cedar Lodge Cabins'. The owner was a very attractive mature lady called Carol and this little house had everything from a microwave oven to the kitchen sink, as we say in good old Blighty. I cooked a Hog on a spit for dinner, after killing it in the woods no I didn't just made this up, instead I had macaroni on cheese and a bottle of wine and watched a little bit of 'prolefeed'.

I leave the wonderful Blue Mountains in the morning and have a very causal drive into Sydney, as the car has to back before 4pm. I must admit that I was a little apprehensive about driving in Sydney as I had never drove there before, would I get lost and ever find the Hertz garage? Having driven for so many years I can relax when driving even in a big city like this one. So on entering I top up with petrol and ask directions to the correct part of town. I found the place with ease and lots of spare time before it was due back, in fact just around the corner from where I had stayed in the Woodduck Inn all those weeks before. On the way I popped into the YHA near the main Railway Station to see if I could book in for a few nights, unfortunately I would have to wait two nights before I could get in. And as the Woodduck Inn was also fully booked - I booked into a scruffy old Hotel for two nights. Had my hair cut by a very friendly gay guy for a fortunate - read some more books, wrote up my notes, did not take 'ice' and did a 'bludger' for a few days...is this a contradiction in Australia, I wonder?

For my last five days in Sydney and Australia I was lucky enough to stay in the YHA just stated and it is lovely and relaxing place and probably one of the largest in the world. However I was in room 317 and one night while staying there I was pissed on literally by a drunken young Australian, at 5am, I was on the bottom bunk bed, he was on the top - probably the only man in the world who has had this experience and can tell the world about it. I was lucky because in the room there was a spare bunk bed; so for safety sake I took the top one across the way for the rest of the stay. As he was only a young lad I did not get too upset, and by 6am he was gone - as a young man I never pissed the bed but did get drunk on several occasions.

During my last few days in Sydney I went for a cruise around the harbour, saw where Nicole Kidman lives in her 30 million dollar house, very egalitarian and went to the awe-inspiring Aquarium, across from where there were some submarines. Bought Bill Bryson latest book the Thunderbolt kid and read it, walked to Bondi beach via an Art Galley where there were very large naked ladies, with their legs open. Rubens with pubic hair, we could say, but if this is modern art; God help us and I am an atheist. I was not impressed with Bondi beach as it was a very cold day - this may have been the reason, but had a pleasant lunch and a look around the incredible bookshop cum café, near the beach and paid. Where according to David Bret again Errol Flynn had the cheek when recovering from a 'venereal disease' in Sydney would often have meals in restaurants and do a runny without paying. Saw Charlotte's Webb and the latest James Bond epic with Daniel Craig, at the movies. Got caught up in a march against the Howard Government where a young Australian man has been in prison at Guantanamo bay for several years without a trail. Howard was in a cage in an orange jump suit, which would be the best place for him along with Thatcher, Major and Blair - the last three are all multi-millionaires now, bastards...my conjecture. Nothing more then getting very rich - while screwing the masses into the ground with polices that were always very suspect from day one (The Trap: What Happened to our Dreams of Freedom - BBC 2 11th March 2007). And what is left for the masses another bloody War Memorial, like the magnificent one in Sydney and heaven is a communist paradise. Get lost you bastards! Will this little 'nuclei' get 'marked down by the Thought Police and eliminated'...just a thought (George Orwell 1984 p, 218 Penguin paperback modern classic)!

I also went to the NSW State library for a few hours to read, but before you get in you go through quite a procedure, you take off all your clothes, put them in a locker, just made this up - but heaven help us it is a bloody long rigmarole to go through just to borrow a book. And having started to read 'Satan's Angel' about Errol Flynn in Tasmania I just had to keep going with it, as it is an incredible read. For example; the idea of Cary Cooper being tired up by a sex manic called Lupe Velez for hours or was that days and 'losing 35 lbs' when saving a small town in High Noon from the bad guys is too disturbing a thought to be contemplated rational. Completed the book in April 2007 and reached the conclusion that Errol Flynn was the greatest Larrikin that has ever lived with the great Billy Connolly only a few mill-seconds behind him in a similar way to the incredible John Lennon, who once said he thought he was a genius. The Red wine is not bad either coming from the Flinders Realm, simply called the Larrikin. As was a movie I saw in the YHA right at the top of the building where two men who were slightly bonkers/mad/insane got on the train from the Perth area to Fremantle, the one I had been on weeks before and was mental tormenting a young woman, very disturbing but incredible acting from the actors.

The only conclusion that I can reach about Sydney and Australia as a whole - is that it a wonderful place and would be very nice too live, if you could afford it and was not full up? But it is not as egalitarian as Bryson et al assert, if you look close enough through the trees, or across the harbour. In fact according to David Glanz neo liberalism known as 'economic rationalism' down under has been on the march in Australia since 1983 where now the richest 10% owns about half of all the private wealth and the poorest 30% has basically none, or very little (Anti Capitalism p, 257).

I would also agree with John Dike from Tasmania who I have mentioned in the chapters on India that in little Britain there is terrible tension meaning an 'edgy and angry feeling just underneath the surface of society' where in Big Oz you do not feel this so much and people in general are more 'laid back'. A few years ago in Trieste I was told by a lovely old man called Orlando, in a restaurant - who was born in Italy but had lived in Australia since 1954 with his wife, six children and nine grandchildren that 'God made man free but put free men into OZ'. I presume that this is how most immigrants now, may feel about the place - but probably not the original convicts from little Britain.

Never forgetting that if Paul Krassner is correct Scientology was once kicked out of Australia (Abuse Your Illusions p, 333) but now back with vengeance. I noted this phenomenon on the streets of Sydney on one of my last days there when some young people were trying to sell Ron L Hubbard most famous book and they were doing strange relaxing experiences on the masses, with a small machine. Also in the cinema they were promoting his most famous book again.

On arrival at Auckland airport I get a bus into the city and dropped off on Queen Street just across from Turner Street where the Auckland international YHA is based. Sounds very impressive, don't you think as if it may be on the Moon, or even Mars, especially if I could find a live Moa before I leave. This in fact may be the case because according to the Lonely Planet New Zealanders can do anything with 'a bit of Kiwi ingenuity and some number-eight wire – the gauge used for making fences' (Lonely Planet) and we should never forget that this is the place where the great athletic coach Arthur Lydiard was born and helped train my hero Lasse Viren to win four gold medals (Observer August 2007) in the early 1970's. Also up until the 1950's 'it was illegal for farmers to allow their cattle to mate in fields fronting public roads'. Not sure why but 'Sunday papers were also illegal until 1969'. Russell Crowe was born here and Pavlova was invented here and the Maoris probably arrived about 850 years before the white man and were not a push over. Like most of the governments since 1984 that carried out ruthless neo-liberal polices and especially in 1991 when the Employment Contracts Act destroyed entire trade unions, again according to David Glanz (ibid). This may have been the reason that Ken Jones could not afford a 400 NZ dollar satellite dish or at-least thought they were a bit expensive. So being a New Zealander he decided to buy a wok for 10 dollars so he could provide wireless broadband for his house. Isn't ingenuity wonderful stuff especially that now Ken has his own television station that beams out signals using woks (Private Eye p, 16 - 1185) to the whole of Oamaru.

According to my very attractive first cousin Tessa - Pavlova is a cake made out of egg white and sugar and a Hangi is a Maori way of cooking. The YHA was very clean and pleasant with all the amenities you need to survive as a back-packer. So after a rest I venture down Queen Street for my first look around Auckland the biggest city in New Zealand with a population of 1.2 million people, built on several Volcanoes. The first impression is very favourable especially now that I have discovered the shear beauty and sex appeal of Asian women, who seem to be everywhere. On my return to the YHA I treat myself to a Chinese take-away for about 6 dollars, peanuts for me as the exchange rate is very good for the Brits and a few cans of beer.

I have a good swim, sauna and spa in a local pool the next day - before having a one and half hours cruise around the harbour with a free drink. The thousands of boats in the harbour were very impressive, including the Navy and especially Graham Hart's (the richest man in NZ) which is called Ulysses and would take '250,000 NZ dollars' to fill it up, another contradiction here I think, if the basic culture is similar to OZ? We also saw some idiots bungee jumping off the bridge, considering that it was upper class twits who first jumped of the Clifton Suspension bridge in Bristol - about 1979, the year that Thatcher came to power in little Britain, is there a connection here I wonder. I often wonder why sane people do it and now made famous by A J Hackett who apparently jumped off the Eiffel Tower in 1986 and let's face it - it is not cheap, for a 30 second thrill, at least with sex you normally see someone naked. According to Lonely Planet A. J. Hackett started the first commercial bungee jump in 1988 and its '43metres' high not far from Queenstown. Never forgetting that it was in Auckland harbour on the evening of July 11th 1985 that the Rainbow Warrior was sunk deliberately by the French State and a Portuguese photographer was killed. Something I would have thought that the wonderful French people were not really very proud of.

Before I went for the Harbour cruise I had popped into the Sky Tower complex and thought well I must do this, but chickened out, at the last minute. It is awesome and takes quite a bit of courage if you don't like heights like me. By the time I walked up from the harbour after the cruise I had decided that this time I must do it. So I paid the money and on the way up froze in fright at being so close to a huge drop, on the way up. Shaking at the knees, as if I was a young Elvis; I venture out to the awe-inspiring site of Auckland from a great height, where the great sir Edmund Hillary lives (did). I walk around several times observing all the sites and then do what any sane English man would do - buy a pot of tea, sit down and think, especially at this time of day. There will not be an earthquake today, will there Great One in the sky? With that settled I do what any sane man would do get talking to one of the young Asian ladies serving the tourists. Before leaving I watched a fascinating documentary about Mario culture and how the North

Island was dragged up by a super human being from the South, may even have been Errol Flynn in a previous life. In the evening I have a delicious Japanese dinner, in a restaurant, with four young women right across from me.... but it was so small that I am still looking for it, in Aussie land this would have been called a 'skerrick' portion. No wonder that Asian women are so slim and sexy.

On the morning of the 17th December 2006 I get picked up from the YHA and get taken to a hire car company, just down the road - that have let me have a car for a week. On my way out of Auckland I visit my lovely first cousin Tessa, for the first time ever - get my schedule sorted for the next 14 days and I am off to Cambridge. I am on my way there to meet my surrogate Uncle for the first time in about 42 years. It was smashing to meet John after such a long time, having first met him as a very young kid (which I don't remember) and then in 1962 when I first started employment for the Falkland Island Government. He has a very nice nearly new bungalow and is still working at 70 and has an adopted son in Latin America. But is very cynical like me about the Falklands war in 1982 and let's face if it never happed or could have been settled peaceful with out the death of nearly 1000 people too save 1800 - we would never have had all those cruel social polices that her Government carried out against the working class, or Blair et al too carry on her legacy. And according to the Sunday Observer (18th March 2007 – p, 43) it now costs the British tax payer 75 million pounds a year to keep the British forces there (may be 100 million), suggesting that the Franks inquiry/report was basically a sham. What's new? After dinner

John invited Jennifer & John Luxton over who lives five minute away from him and are also from the Falkland Islands. So for the rest of the evening we chewed over all the old gossip about everything and everybody we knew. In the morning after breakfast I drop John, who was a very amusing host - at his work-place and headed towards the great unknown. Fiery monsters and what ever else there was in Lord of the Rings to terrify us all rotten. It was only fiction, was it not?

In fact I headed towards Lake Taupo, New Zealand largest lake, calling into some natural hot water actives, called the Wairakei Natural Thermal Valley on the way. I never visited them because the very amusing owner of the 'Rustic Café' where you go from - wanted money for seeing a natural experience. I told him to get lost, but did have a lovely fresh mug of coffee and when four young local girls came in they were allowed to see them for nothing, what a bloody cheek, that's what I thought. So instead of that I went for a swim in the local pool in Taupo, which was very refreshing and eat my sandwiches close to the lake. Then on to Napier at Hawke's bay a delightful little town where in 1931 it was destroyed by Mrs Thatcher, err I mean an earthquake. There is no doubt about New Zealand is a very beautiful place and in theory it is not full; only 4 million people and millions of sheep and they speak English, well a sort of English, with a Southern hemisphere twang. Only Russell Crowe speaks perfect BBC English…see above. After booking into the local YHA and a rest I venture out, walk up on to the hill for a good view of the Town, take a few pictures and then have dinner where according to my notes I had a fantastic Prawn meal, in a local restaurant.

Yes it is coming back, those old brain cells are working after all - in fact it was in a pub/bar with a lovely open fire and not a Dinosaur in site.

The next morning after a good breakfast I have another swim in the local outdoor pool called the Ocean Spa. This was an excellent complex with a sauna, a hot and cold pools and a spa. While in the sauna I got talking to a local mature man called Tim who was a Union rep and was having trouble at the docks with his employers – well nothing new there then. Then on the wonderful Hawke's Bay Museum, on several levels where 'there are exhibitions on Maori art and culture, including artefacts from the East Coast's Ngati Kahunguna tribe, and displays on the early colonial settlers'. However I did not see one photo of Jack Hawkins who I remembered as a young kid - was fighting the Maori's in a movie about New Zealand. But the memory of some old people on screen, who was in Napier in 1931, was truly awe-inspiring, when the quake hit and destroyed the place. One I liked especially was about the Cows who would not go into their sheds a day before the quake hit. In other words they had sixth sense and new it was too dangerous. There we have the real evidence Cows are more intelligent then humans and they don't write for the Times of London or read books, do they? You may not believe this but it is true I actual know an ex- Academic who has never heard of Tom Paine, I wonder if the cows had ever heard of the great man who had to flee for his life to France after writing The Rights of Man at the time of the French Revolution.

But would they find there way to Wellington in a car, I wonder in the 21st century. I did and it was a very special journey through lovely countryside and the museums were wonderful. I didn't stop in any on this part of the trip, as they were not always visible from the road. Reaching the conclusion that even in a place where there was half a sheep and one building there would be a sign for another museum. Never forgetting that New Zealand is positioned very dangerously on two platonic plates so at any time you could slip into the great South Pacific and never be-heard of again. Hence, I recommend from what I have saw so far - with a lot more to come that you all visit the place before this happens. I got to the capital of New Zealand by teatime, who has a population of 205,500 (LP) and booked into the Wellington City YHA for one night. After my normal rest, without Radio 4 (sic), I venture out into the city - got talking to a very friendly guy who was helping out with the local athletes, on their training jog. Sport is very big in New Zealand like Australia and is used as a tool of social control by the Ruling Elite. So never tell a Kiwi that the 'All Blacks' are crap without you want a very large black eye. When there I even saw an advert on TV where the great John Walker was being shown as a positive role model, for the young of today. Seeing all this physically activates stimulated my juices in my empty stomach that wanted to be feed. Just as I was approaching a Chinese restaurant where I entered and had a glorious hotpot, at a very reasonable price. I could not say that about the bar I visited straight after where they charged me 5 dollars for half a pint of something, it may even have been beer.

I am up early the next morning as I am booked on the Interislander ferry that takes you from Wellington to Picton. The trip takes just over three hours so I had lots of time to have a very pleasant breakfast, rest, read and a think. Picton has a population of 3600 people so Lonely Planet informs me, just a little speck of dust in the big Universe, at the head of Queen Charlotte sound. By the time I had got off I had decided that I would head towards Westport on the west coast of the South Island. A few miles out of Picton I got one of those where am I moments - as I had not seen any signs for a few miles, so I stopped by a large man on a large bike to ask the way. Before I had hardly opened my mouth he told me that he was 'an ex-chief of Police' and has a 'MacDonald's franchise in Nelson'. The bike was his 'mid-life crises', I told him mine was my greying hair. The drive to Westport was an incredible experience as the South Island is more beautiful then the North - well that's my view so it must be correct. In fact you could drift off, while driving and think that you are on another Planet or perhaps a galaxy as the views are magnificent, including the spectacular coastal view where I stopped and took some photos. Westport is a very small sleepy laid back little town of a few thousand people where Ron the cat runs the local YHA. Well actual this is a joke; I think - Ron might not like it. Vicky a very friendly young lady actual runs the place who is married with three children. She told me a very naughty joke about stupid tourists that should not really be repeated, but as I am I trying to be a modern day Voltaire, here goes. Basically it goes like this; because tourists are so overawed by the shear beauty of the place they are all over the road and drive very slowly especially when in Camper Vans. So the locals have a name for them which is 'Road Maggots'; but is it funny I ask myself? The YHA even had a outdoor fire to keep the place warm at

night, so something very special I thought in that very
unusual old fashioned cosy way. My room was very spick
and span with a TV, I normal have a shared room but
tonight I thought that I would treat myself to my very
own, which I did. After a little rest I drive down the main
beach which is huge for an hours walk along it and think
of my new Aphrodite from Thailand. Am I starting to
be like Forest Gump, I ask myself, who kept thinking
of Jenny, as did Marx who he eventually married? On
the way back I pop into the local market for some food,
being served at the counter, by a very alienated young
woman. Dinner was delicious washed down with some
very nice New Zealand wine. The TV and most of the
radio in New Zealand to my eyes and ears is total tosh,
not forgetting that I am getting very close to the big 60.
So I just watched a little TV and read the paper, before
the big sleep in nod land.

The next morning after breakfast I say goodbye to
lovely Vicky and Ron the Cat and head down the road
towards 'Arthur's pass'. Having only climbed small hills
in the wonderful Lake District and really enjoyed the
experience and seeing these glorious mountains you do
get the urge to climb them. However when your higher
senses in the cortex kick in - in that very rational way,
if you are on Planet earth and not in a Cult which may
mean you have lost it (Abuse Your Illusions 2003), if you
are! Hence, especially on your own it would very fool
hardy to venture out alone on them. In fact according
to Lonely Planet at least '200' people have died climbing
over the last one hundred years around the Aoraka/Mt
Cook National Park alone. Not something that Sir Ian
McKellen will be telling the two million stupid tourists,

who visit New Zealand, I would have thought. Driving through Arthur's pass is an incredible experience and a little scary in places, which makes it all worthwhile. The highest mountain that you pass, at close range is called Mt Murchison which is 2400 metres high which is in the Craigieburn Forest Park. Coming down the other side you pass Porters Pass at 945metres high. On arriving in Christchurch I book into the Rolleston House YHA, just across from the Arts centre for several days, as I had booked a Camper Van on a relocation package deal, from Christchurch to Auckland over a four day period - which means that you don't pay for it but just the petrol, over a four day time scale. Christchurch was the births place of Kate Webb probably the most famous female New Zealand journalists of all time and a very brave one at that; according to the Guardian (15th May 2007) who has sadly died of bowel cancer. In 1971 she was captured by North Vietnamese army in the Kirirom Mountains and thought to have been killed by the Khmer Rouge, 23 days later she walked out and nearly died of malaria. This obituary of her is so touching it really warms your heart and a real fantastic role model for all young women everywhere.

Over the next few days I relax by reading Lance Armstrong's (with Sally Jenkins) It's not about the Bike an incredible story of bravery, visiting the new Christchurch Art Galley which is spectacle but was told by one of the hostess that it cost 42 million NZ dollars to build. Which apparently is good value for money as it helps too make the people happy and builds up their moral - well I never, so I was told by the same hostess? The admission is free for seven days a week; it was opened in May 2003 and is the largest Museum to be built in New Zealand for 50 years. I visited the local cinema and saw Brenda the movie (sic) with gorgeous Helen Mirren and could have had a drink of alcohol when watching the movie, something that is banned in little Britain and most of Australia. So don't tell anyone this little secret as if the masses here of this in little Britain they may want to do the same thing, and we can't have the masses enjoying Nirvana in Blighty, can we Mr Tony? Slightly ironic I thought because according to Lonely Planet again Christchurch was built around the concept of the Church of England and the gentry in little Britain and the ruling class structure to go with it, including the river Avon. And as we know from the Queen (the movie) there is a natural order from God to serf, total bullshit of the highest order, but still believed by many people, so it seems. Legitimacy and deference are two very important concepts to understand in this epoch, because without it working in the abstract - the system would probably collapse.

I had a walk for a few hours to the top of Mt Vernon just south of the main city in pouring rain but it was worth it as I had a lovely view of the Le Bons Bay area. Several causal walks around the city, a swim in the local pool, did not go on the Tramway first introduced in 1905 and a good look around the excellent Arts Centre. In this place, it was the first time ever that I had heard of the concept of painting and music as a symbiotic invention joined together. Will it catch on I wonder? I also met a very friendly female artist/ painter, who may be called Sabella Gauthier on one of the small bridges over the river Avon, who was collecting money for a good cause and is an artist in residence, whatever that means.

The next move was to become a 'Road Maggot' in New Zealand by collecting a camper van from near the airport - it sounds lovely doesn't it; soft, warm, very slow and very tasty if you are hungry or a member of the SAS. As I had never drove one of these wonderful vehicles before I was shown all the complexes of the process by a young women. Then on to the local shops to top up with all the necessities of life - for example: some teabags, milk, carbohydrates, proteins and so on. With about 10 hours to go before I catch the ferry to Wellington from Picton - I head up the road towards Blenheim. This was a delightful drive as most of it is very close to the coast and I loved being a Maggot - stopping to take pictures, having a cup of tea when ever it is convenient to you and so on. I got to Picton earlier then I thought; so went for a very pleasant swim in the sheep shed. Well actual it was not a woolshed as such but where you undressed and left your clothes, which was called a shed. This was Christmas Eve and amazing I got talking to some German female tourist in the pool who was going to spend Christmas day in Picton. What you do in Picton on Christmas day is beyond me but being very attractive young women there must have been a very good reason for this project. Surely not a sheep farmer with money was it – just a good old fashioned cynical thought young people. I got the PM ferry and settled down to a bit of rough ride across the water, as the wind was blowing quite hard. It is at these times I wish I was Jesus; because I could walk on the water and get across for nothing, where in this case it was free anyway. I would have liked to stayed in Wellington for another night - but because I wanted to be at another first cousins for Christmas lunch in Wanganui. I had decided that I must go up the West coast, a little way, before settling down for the night. So after getting lost by going up the wrong road, where I should have turned left, I go back a little way and head in the correct direction, pull off the road, close to the shore and have good nights sleep. In the morning I have a walk along a very windy beach, shave and shower and head up the road. The scenery in this part of the world is very similar to little Britain and on this Christmas day it was also raining, so nothing new here then... perhaps I am not in New Zealand after all.

I had been invited for Christmas lunch with Stella and family, another first cousin, Tessa's big sister - so I arrived about midday in Wanganui. Stella seemed really pleased to see me after such a long time of 46 years. The last time I had seen her and Michael her brother was in 1960 at the Darwin Boarding School, Goose Green – now sadly a burned out wreck...a bit like me, after travelling for nearly four and half months in the Far East. Within half an hour, Roger her husband two daughters, son-in-law and two beautiful little granddaughters had all arrived, for a glorious lunch and good old chin-wag. Whacked with all that food inside me I excuse myself and have a little siesta in the back of the camper van, for several hours, falling asleep without realizing how long I had dropped off, for. At 4pm I get up and have a cup of tea, a few biscuits and another long chat with Stella and Roger, before venturing over to Lisa's (oldest daughter) and Shane's home for a smashing barbeque. With Cherry (second daughter) Shane's brother girlfriend and old Uncle Tom Cobbley and all - Shane and Lisa being lovely host and Shane a very amusing young man with enough land that I thought I was in Buck house visiting Brenda and Keith (sic).

Arise Sir Brian, because you are now as famous as Voltaire was in his day - so we thought we would knight you, err I am still asleep in the camper van, sorry about that, just dreaming. Plus I would not join the British Establishment for all the tea in china and the rice to go with it. That very dangerous radical pop star called Mick Jagger worth 215million is even a knight now and to think that he once had a very close shave with a mars bar in a very unusual place. After several hours of eating and merriment and sad goodbyes, I am off in the Road Maggot for the New Plymouth area - hoping to climb Mt Taranaki/Mt Egmont on the way. By about 9pm I pull up very near a camp site by the sea and get into bed. About 30 minutes later I hear a very loud bang on the Road Maggot and am told by a woman in a very pejorative way – 'it is against the local by-laws to park here'. What illegal to park by the sea, in a car park? Not wanting to cause a fuss on Christmas night I decided not to question her pack of lies, and very Christian principles so moved on down the road. She wanted me to spend money in the camping site, I would have thought! The next morning, wanting to be Sir Edmund Hillary I venture outside to see if I could see Mt Taranaki, nothing but fog as far as the eye could see. Hence, Plan B had to be put into operations - forget about climbing mountains and keep going along the coast and back into the heart of New Zealand's North Island again. I had decided to visit a very rural place by the sea called Kawhia, which also has a huge harbour, anyway - not wanting to be knocked up again by Mama Cas, in the middle of the night - I decide to visit the little campsite for the night, as well...for 20 dollars. Today was very good for me because not long after parking up and paying the dosh, John and Dawn a mature couple from South Africa now living in New Zealand pulled up right next to me and parked their huge exotic Road Maggot. After a rest I walk into the little town, take some pictures watch the locals swimming and fishing on the pier and visit another small history museum, with no sheep in site. Where it tells me everything I wanted to know about this place and who has run it since year dot – which were the Maoris originally and are still here, from what I could see and really enjoying themselves, especially in the dark muddy sand.

Being only about two meters away from John and Dawn I get invited to join them for dinner with a few bottles of beer. John was basically a businessman/salesman, in the Holiday business and had only been in New Zealand for a few years but seemed to be enjoying their experience. Especially driving around the country in their large camper van and also having a boat to explore the coast and so on. Like me he also seemed to think that at least the established middle class in New Zealand are doing very nicely thank you very much. So like the Aussies in my mind they have pulled up the draw bridge to keep everyone else out, without you have a very good profession - that they can exploit and in New Zealand they hardly can say that there is not enough water for more people, can they? They may be letting more people in compared with Australia and this is what I was told by several people, who said it was easier to come here then anywhere else - but I don't think anyone can say the place is full; full of sheep and cattle, yes but not Homo sapiens. After my breakfast the next morning I say good bye to my new found friends and head up the road to Auckland, where it is full. On the way I saw gay Bulls, cows climbing hills with their walking boots on and being lead by Sir Hillary - probably practising for their next attack on Everest and lets face it – they may be cheaper then Sherpa's? The first book that real inspired me into reading seriously was a book about Hillary and Tenzing climbing Everest when I was a young lad at the Darwin Boarding School, in the 1950's so perhaps I should not make small jokes at his expense, who has sadly died while writing this little book. But being an intelligent mature man that can do anything with a No 8 fencing wire and a pair of walking boots I don't think he will mind too much, do you? He was in fact a simple bee keeper in real life while climbing all those wonderful mountains in New Zealand. I had arranged with my wonderful first cousin Tessa that I could spend my last few days in Auckland with her and her son Jared, before flying back to Blighty on the 30th December 2006, so with a little help from the road map; I am back from where I set off from 11 days ago. After a fine cooked dinner with Tessa and Jared - I phone Les Gledhill my first boss from the Falkland Islands in 1962 with his name on the banknotes to see if it would be okay to visit him in the morning on the way to dropping off the Road Maggot, near the airport. He was the Colonial Treasure in Port Stanley. It was and it was lovely to see him and his lovely wife an ex-nurse/ sister after 42 years, he could not remember me from Adam, but it was lovely to see such a fit old man who's mannerisms had not changed one little bit, it brought lots of happy memories back for me, I can assure you. I also found it completely fascinating when he was telling me about his early life in the Falkland Islands before the Second World War and during the war, which was very amusing. He still plays golf makes toys for charity and with his wife deliver lunches to the older generation, at least once a month. After dropping the camper van off I decide to do something completely mad and walk back to Tessa's home - a slight mistake as it took me over four hours through a huge industrial estate where the working class work, I would have thought, who would not have 250, 000 dollars in their back pocket to fill up a boat, with fuel! But by the time I got back I did have a good tan as it was a glorious day for a walk and an hours recover before I cooked Jared and myself a stir fry for dinner. Tessa did not have any as she has got something wrong with her eyes and did not want to risk eating my efforts. She is listing everything down on paper that she eats and does, so as too see - if she can diagnose the problem.

During the next few days I play chess with Jared several times, he is very good and smashing young man, have a swim, cycle up One Tree Hill on Tessa's bike, cycle around Auckland for one and half hours. Have a very pleasant lunch out with my hosts, near the harbour and a long chat with Tessa about the meaning of life. For example; amazingly she agreed with some of my analysis about the power that women have over men and going up in the Western world - but in the main will never admit it. In fact if I am ever asked if I have been to University by a women and I tell her that I studied Politics and Sociology 99.9% while there - they will always tell you that they nothing about Politics. Nothing could further from the truth folks, Politics is mostly about 'Power' at many different levels and very little else and as I noted at the very beginning of this project if a so-called very important man believes the 'Moon is made of cheese', many others may also. Which can even mean gang warfare that apparently even happens in Auckland according to the BBC Radio 4 (31st March 2007) which may be caused because of the 24/7 work revolution/culture around the globe which includes New Zealand…parents are not at home when needed. All the great men of History who has wrote about the subject from, Plato, Aristotle, Voltaire, Jean-Jacques Rousseau, Tom Paine, Karl Mark, Noam Chomsky et al all wrote about this process in great detail, so if you don't understand it go out and read them all, it may change your life.

My flight was at 2300 hour on the 30th December so at 19:30 on the day in question Tessa and Jared took me to the airport via her Mum's old home for the very long flight home. Before leaving I had to pay 25 dollars to leave New Zealand and as I was by now out of dosh (money) Tessa paid it for me, I was very grateful. It had been a lovely last few days, with Tessa and Jared - on a four and half months venture cum quest for further evidence for the meaning of life. I think I have found it, get out of little Britain for good and live the rest of my life in beautiful Thailand, or somewhere in the Far East writing books - so there! You have been warned.

Bibliograph And Sources

The Sunday Observer – various editions

The Guardian - ditto

The Daily Mail - ditto

Sydney Morning Herald

Melbourne Age

Private Eye – Various copies

International Times

Hindustan Times

Indian Times

Herald Tribune

Sunday Times Rich List

The Green left weekly – OZ version.

George Orwell: Nineteen Eight-Four – Penguin classic paper back.

John Gribbon: The Birth of Time - 1999

Carl Zimmer: Evolution - The Triumph of an Idea - 1988

Bill Bryson: Down Under - 2000

Bill Bryson: Short History of Nearly Everything - 2003

Bill Bryson: Walk in the Woods - 1997

Bill Bryson: Thunderbolt Kid – 2006

Marilia Albanese: The Treasures of Angkor - 2006

David McLellan: Marx - 1975

Mark Tulley: India in Slow Motion

Anthony Giddens: Human Societies 1992

Michael Parenti: Democracy for the Few 1988

Arundhati Roy: An Ordinary Person's Guide to Empire 2005

Arundhati Roy: The God of Small Things – 1997

Arundhati Roy & David Barsamian: The Chequebook & the Cruise Missile - 2004

Jones et al: Politics UK second Edition -1994

Michael Woodiwiss: Gangster Capitalism - 2005

Fredrick Engel's: The Conditions of the Working Class in England.

Robert Nisbet: The Sociological Tradition 1967

The Pears Cyclopaedia 2003 – 2003

Mark Thomas: As Used on the Famous Nelson Mandela - 2006

Jessica Williams: 50 Facts that should change the World - 2004

Plato: The Republic – Penguin Classics

Bertrand Russell: Authority and the Individual -fp. 1949.

Steve Jones: Y: The Decent of Man - 2002

Noam Chomsky: Hegemony or Survival – 2003

Noam Chomsky: Year 501 – 1993

Noam Chomsky: For Reasons of State 2003 – fp 1970

John Pilger: The New Rulers of the World – 2002

John Pilger: Freedom Next Time - 2007

Aristotle: The Politics

Lonely Planet: Australia & New Zealand on a shoestring (LP)

Lonely Planet: India (LP)

Lonely Planet: Vietnam, Cambodia, Laos & the Greater Mekong.

Yann Martel: The life of Pi – 2002

David Bret: Errol Flynn Satan's Angel – 2000 – a must read before you die, for all men of the world!

Aussie Slang Dictionary -2002

Striking Back at Howard – The struggle to Defend Our Unions -2005

The Economist 23rd – 29th September 2006

Oliver James: Affluenza – 2006

Dobson Miller Payne: The Falklands Conflict

Kitty Kelly: The Royals – 1997

Graham Greene: The Quiet American

Vann Nath: A Cambodia Prison Portrait – One Year in the Khmer Rouge's S-21

Francois Ponchaud: A Short History of Cambodia

Thomas Cleary: The Essential Tao

Marilia Albanese: The Treasures of Angkor

Abuse your Illusions – 2003

Selected Writings - Voltaire – Everyman edition 1995 introduction.

Anti Capitalism – A Guide to the Movement – various authors - 2001

Ewan McGregor & Charley Boorman: Long Way Around – 2004

Susan Tickner: Goodbye, Mummy Darling - 2003.

Trevor Ling: Karl Marx and Religion - In Europe and India - 1980

Richard Dawkins: The God Delusion - 2006

Mark Curtis: Web of Deceit – 2003

Joseph Heller: Catch 22 – 1961

Martin Rees: Our Cosmic Habitat – 2002

Jean-Jacques Rousseau: A Discourse on Inequality – Penguin Classics.

Brian V Peck: Walking on the Moon 2004

The Observer Book of Scandal; 2007

Rabbit proof Fence -a Movie about the Aboriginal people.

The Dish - a Movie about the Moon Landing in 1969, if it happened?

Borat – a Movie about a pretend journalist travelling across the USA – 2006

The Quiet American - a Movie with Michael Caine

Wolfe Creek - a Movie about a serial killer in Big OZ

Walk the Line - a Movie (biopic) about Johnny Cash.

Michael Moore's – Fahrenheit 9/11

The Trap: What happened to our dreams of Freedom BBC 2 TV?

Tasmania's Forests – a Global Treasure – 2004.

Monty Python's: The Life of Brian

Ray Mears BBC 2 TV programme

Billy Connolly's - Worlds Tour of Australia.

The Tribe BBC 2 - Bruce Parry an amazing man…several programmes.

BBC 2 - India with Sanjeev Bhaskar 30th July 2007

BBC2 - The Lost World of the Raj 29th June 2007

BBC World TV.

Channel 5 TV (British)

The Great Warming Swindle Channel 4 British TV

BBC I TV - Victoria's Empire

More 4 News: 25th July 2007.

BBC Radio 2

BBC Radio 4

BBC World Service

Alex Jones – Various Documentary's… one of the few great USA dissidents.

WORLD CITIZEN #3